ABOUT THIS PUBLICATION

FOR SERVICE ASSISTANCE

Customer Service
1.704.898.0770

North Carolina General Statues is published by The Muliti-Media Group of Greater Charlotte in Charlotte, North Carolina. Copyright 2015 by the Multi-Media Group of Greater Charlotte. This book or parts thereof may not be reproduced in any form, stored in a retrieval system, or transmitted in any form by any means—electronic, mechanical, photocopy, recording or otherwise—without prior written permission of the publisher, except as provided by United States of America copyright law.

The records required by U.S. Code 2257(a) through (c) and the pertinent regulations 28 C.F.R. Cli. 1, Part 75 with respect to this publication and all materials associated with such records are maintained by The Multi-Media Group of Greater Charlotte, Publisher and available for review by Attorney General.

www.visionbooks.org

Copyright © 2015 by MMGGC
All rights reserved!

TID: 5107906
ISBN (10) digit: 150324444X
ISBN (13) digit: 978-1503244443

123-4-56789-01239-Paperback
123-4-56789-01239-Hardback

First Edition

090520140547

Printed in the United States of America

2015 EDITION

North Carolina Criminal Law And Procedure-Pamphlet # 84

Printed In conjunction with the Administration of the Courts

North Carolina Criminal Law and Procedure
Pamphlet Reference Guide

Chapters	Pamphlet
Chapter 1 Civil Procedure	1
Chapter 1 Civil Procedure (Continue)	2
Chapter 1A Rules of Civil Procedure	2
Chapter 1B Contribution.	2
Chapter 1C Enforcement of Judgments.	2
Chapter 1D Punitive Damages.	2
Chapter 1E Eastern Band of Cherokee Indians.	2
Chapter 1F North Carolina Uniform Interstate Depositions and Discovery Act.	2
Chapter 2 - Clerk of Superior Court [Repealed and Transferred.]	3
Chapter 3 - Commissioners of Affidavits and Deeds [Repealed.]	3
Chapter 4 - Common Law	3
Chapter 5 - Contempt [Repealed.]	3
Chapter 5A - Contempt	3
Chapter 6 - Liability for Court Costs	3
Chapter 7 - Courts [Repealed and Transferred.]	3
Chapter 7A – Judicial Department	3
Chapter 7A – Continuation (Judicial Department)	4
Chapter 7A – Continuation (Judicial Department)	5
Chapter 7B - Juvenile Code	5
Chapter 8 - Evidence	6
Chapter 8A - Interpreters for Deaf Persons [Recodified.]	6
Chapter 8B - Interpreters for Deaf Persons	6
Chapter 8C - Evidence Code	6
Chapter 9 - Jurors	6
Chapter 10 - Notaries [Repealed.]	6
Chapter 10A - Notaries [Recodified.]	6
Chapter 10B - Notaries	6
Chapter 11 - Oaths	6
Chapter 12 - Statutory Construction	6
Chapter 13 - Citizenship Restored	6
Chapter 14 - Criminal Law	7
Chapter 14 –Criminal Law (Continuation)	8
Chapter 15 - Criminal Procedure	9
Chapter 15A - Criminal Procedure Act (Continuation)	10
Chapter 15A - Criminal Procedure Act (Continuation)	11
Chapter 15B - Victims Compensation	11
Chapter 15C - Address Confidentiality Program	11
Chapter 16 - Gaming Contracts and Futures	11
Chapter 17 - Habeas Corpus	11

Chapter 17A - Law-Enforcement Officers [Recodified.]	11
Chapter 17B - North Carolina Criminal Justice Education and Training System [Recodified.] Chapter 17C - North Carolina Criminal Justice Education and Training Standards Commission	11
Chapter 17D - North Carolina Justice Academy	11
Chapter 17E - North Carolina Sheriffs' Education and Training Standards Commission	11
Chapter 18 - Regulation of Intoxicating Liquors [Repealed.]	12
Chapter 18A - Regulation of Intoxicating Liquors [Repealed.]	12
Chapter 18B - Regulation of Alcoholic Beverages	12
Chapter 18C - North Carolina State Lottery	12
Chapter 19 - Offenses against Public Morals	12
Chapter 19A - Protection of Animals	12
Chapter 20 - Motor Vehicles	13
Chapter 20 - Motor Vehicles (Continuation)	14
Chapter 20 - Motor Vehicles (Continuation)	15
Chapter 20 - Motor Vehicles (Continuation)	16
Chapter 21 - Bills of Lading	17
Chapter 22 - Contracts Requiring Writing	17
Chapter 22A - Signatures	17
Chapter 22B - Contracts Against Public Policy	17
Chapter 22C - Payments to Subcontractors	17
Chapter 23 - Debtor and Creditor	17
Chapter 24 – Interest	17
Chapter 25 – Uniform Commercial Code	18
Chapter 25 – Uniform Commercial Code (Continuation)	19
Chapter 25A – Retail Installment Sales Act	20
Chapter 25B - Credit	20
Chapter 25C - Sales of Artwork	20
Chapter 26 - Suretyship	20
Chapter 27 - Warehouse Receipts [Repealed.]	20
Chapter 28 - Administration [Repealed.]	20
Chapter 28A - Administration of Decedents' Estates	20
Chapter 28B - Estates of Absentees in Military Service	20
Chapter 28C - Estates of Missing Persons	20
Chapter 29 - Intestate Succession	21
Chapter 30 - Surviving Spouses	21
Chapter 31 - Wills	21
Chapter 31A - Acts Barring Property Rights	21
Chapter 31B - Renunciation of Property and Renunciation of Fiduciary Powers Act	21
Chapter 31C - Uniform Disposition of Community Property Rights at Death Act	21
Chapter 32 - Fiduciaries	21
Chapter 32A - Powers of Attorney	21
Chapter 33 - Guardian and Ward [Repealed and Recodified.]	21

Chapter 33A - North Carolina Uniform Transfers to Minors Act	21
Chapter 33B - North Carolina Uniform Custodial Trust Act	21
Chapter 34 - Veterans' Guardianship Act	22
Chapter 35 - Sterilization Procedures	22
Chapter 35A - Incompetency and Guardianship	22
Chapter 36 - Trusts and Trustees [Repealed.]	22
Chapter 36A - Trusts and Trustees	22
Chapter 36B - Uniform Management of Institutional Funds Act [Repealed.]	22
Chapter 36C - North Carolina Uniform Trust Code	22
Chapter 36D - North Carolina Community Third Party Trusts, Pooled Trusts	23
Chapter 36E - Uniform Prudent Management of Institutional Funds Act	23
Chapter 37 - Allocation of Principal and Income [Repealed.]	23
Chapter 37A - Uniform Principal and Income Act	23
Chapter 38 - Boundaries	23
Chapter 38A - Landowner Liability	23
Chapter 39 - Conveyances	23
Chapter 39A - Transfer Fee Covenants Prohibited	23
Chapter 40 - Eminent Domain [Repealed.]	23
Chapter 40A - Eminent Domain	23
Chapter 41 - Estates	23
Chapter 41A - State Fair Housing Act	23
Chapter 42 - Landlord and Tenant	23
Chapter 42A - Vacation Rental Act	23
Chapter 43 - Land Registration	23
Chapter 44 - Liens	24
Chapter 44A - Statutory Liens and Charges	24
Chapter 45 - Mortgages and Deeds of Trust	24
Chapter 45A - Good Funds Settlement Act	24
Chapter 46 - Partition	24
Chapter 47 - Probate and Registration	25
Chapter 47A - Unit Ownership	25
Chapter 47B - Real Property Marketable Title Act	25
Chapter 47C - North Carolina Condominium Act	25
Chapter 47D - Notice of Settlement Act [Expired.]	25
Chapter 47E - Residential Property Disclosure Act	25
Chapter 47F - North Carolina Planned Community Act	25
Chapter 47G - Option to Purchase Contracts	25
Chapter 47H - Contracts for Deed	25
Chapter 48 - Adoptions	26
Chapter 48A - Minors	26
Chapter 49 - Bastardy	26
Chapter 49A - Rights of Children	26
Chapter 50 - Divorce and Alimony	26
Chapter 50A - Uniform Child-Custody Jurisdiction and	

Enforcement Act	26
Chapter 50B - Domestic Violence	26
Chapter 50C - Civil No-Contact Orders	26
Chapter 51 - Marriage	26
Chapter 52 - Powers and Liabilities of Married Persons	27
Chapter 52A - Uniform Reciprocal Enforcement of Support Act [Repealed.]	27
Chapter 52B - Uniform Premarital Agreement Act	27
Chapter 52C - Uniform Interstate Family Support Act	27
Chapter 53 - Banks	27
Chapter 53A - Business Development Corporations and North Carolina Capital Resource Corporations	28
Chapter 53B - Financial Privacy Act	28
Chapter 54 - Cooperative Organizations	28
Chapter 54A - Capital Stock Savings and Loan Associations [Repealed.]	28
Chapter 54B - Savings and Loan Associations	29
Chapter 54C - Savings Banks	29
Chapter 55 - North Carolina Business Corporation Act	30
Chapter 55A - North Carolina Nonprofit Corporation Act	31
Chapter 55B - Professional Corporation Act	31
Chapter 55C - Foreign Trade Zones	31
Chapter 55D - Filings, Names, and Registered Agents for Corporations, Nonprofit Corporations, and Partnerships	31
Chapter 56 - Electric, Telegraph and Power Companies [Repealed.]	31
Chapter 57 - Hospital, Medical and Dental Service Corporations [Recodified.]	31
Chapter 57A - Health Maintenance Organization Act [Recodified.]	31
Chapter 57B - Health Maintenance Organization Act [Recodified.]	31
Chapter 57C - North Carolina Limited Liability Company Act.	31
Chapter 58 - Insurance.	32
Chapter 58 - Insurance (Continuation)	33
Chapter 58 - Insurance (Continuation)	34
Chapter 58 - Insurance (Continuation)	35
Chapter 58 - Insurance (Continuation)	36
Chapter 58 - Insurance (Continuation)	37
Chapter 58 - Insurance (Continuation)	38
Chapter 58A - North Carolina Health Insurance Trust Commission [Recodified.]	38
Chapter 59 - Partnership.	39
Chapter 59B - Uniform Unincorporated Nonprofit Association Act.	39
Chapter 60 - Railroads and Other Carriers [Repealed and Transferred.]	39
Chapter 61 - Religious Societies	39
Chapter 62 - Public Utilities	39

Chapter 62 - Public Utilities (Continuation)	40
Chapter 62A - Public Safety Telephone Service And Wireless Telephone Service	40
Chapter 63 - Aeronautics	40
Chapter 63A - North Carolina Global TransPark Authority	40
Chapter 64 - Aliens	40
Chapter 65 – Cemeteries	40
Chapter 66 - Commerce and Business	41
Chapter 67 - Dogs	41
Chapter 68 - Fences and Stock Law	41
Chapter 69 - Fire Protection	41
Chapter 70 - Indian Antiquities, Archaeological Resources and Unmarked Human Skeletal Remains Protection	42
Chapter 71 - Indians [Repealed.]	42
Chapter 71A - Indians	42
Chapter 72 - Inns, Hotels and Restaurants	42
Chapter 73 - Mills	42
Chapter 74 - Mines and Quarries	42
Chapter 74A - Company Police [Repealed.]	42
Chapter 74B - Private Protective Services Act [Repealed.]	42
Chapter 74C - Private Protective Services	42
Chapter 74D - Alarm Systems	42
Chapter 74E - Company Police Act	42
Chapter 74F - Locksmith Licensing Act	42
Chapter 74G - Campus Police Act	42
Chapter 75 - Monopolies, Trusts and Consumer Protection	42
Chapter 75A - Boating and Water Safety	43
Chapter 75B - Discrimination in Business	43
Chapter 75C - Motion Picture Fair Competition Act	43
Chapter 75D - Racketeer Influenced and Corrupt Organizations	43
Chapter 75E - Unlawful Activities in Connection With Certain Corporate Transactions	43
Chapter 76 - Navigation	43
Chapter 76A - Navigation and Pilotage Commissions	43
Chapter 77 - Rivers, Creeks, and Coastal Waters	43
Chapter 78 - Securities Law [Repealed.]	43
Chapter 78A - North Carolina Securities Act	43
Chapter 78B - Tender Offer Disclosure Act [Repealed.]	43
Chapter 78C - Investment Advisers	43
Chapter 78D - Commodities Act	43
Chapter 79 - Strays [Repealed.]	43
Chapter 80 - Trademarks, Brands, etc.	44
Chapter 81 - Weights and Measures [Recodified.]	44
Chapter 81A - Weights and Measures Act of 1975.	44
Chapter 82 - Wrecks [Repealed.]	44
Chapter 83 - Architects [Recodified.]	44

Chapter 83A - Architects	44
Chapter 84 - Attorneys-at-Law	44
Chapter 84A - Foreign Legal Consultants	44
Chapter 85 - Auctions and Auctioneers [Repealed.]	44
Chapter 85A - Bail Bondsmen and Runners [Recodified.]	44
Chapter 85B - Auctions and Auctioneers	44
Chapter 85C - Bail Bondsmen and Runners [Recodified.]	44
Chapter 86 - Barbers [Recodified.]	44
Chapter 86A - Barbers	44
Chapter 87 - Contractors	44
Chapter 88 - Cosmetic Art [Repealed.]	44
Chapter 88A - Electrolysis Practice Act	44
Chapter 88B - Cosmetic Art	45
Chapter 89 - Engineering and Land Surveying [Recodified.]	45
Chapter 89A - Landscape Architects	45
Chapter 89B - Foresters	45
Chapter 89C - Engineering and Land Surveying	45
Chapter 89D - Landscape Contractors	45
Chapter 89E - Geologists Licensing Act	45
Chapter 89F - North Carolina Soil Scientist Licensing Act	45
Chapter 89G - Irrigation Contractors	45
Chapter 90 - Medicine and Allied Occupations	45
Chapter 90 - Medicine and Allied Occupations (Continuation)	46
Chapter 90 - Medicine and Allicd Occupations (Continuation)	47
Chapter 90 - Medicine and Allied Occupations (Continuation)	48
Chapter 90A - Sanitarians and Water and Wastewater Treatment Facility Operators	48
Chapter 90B - Social Worker Certification and Licensure Act	48
Chapter 90C - North Carolina Recreational Therapy Licensure Act	48
Chapter 90D - Interpreters and Transliterators	48
Chapter 91 - Pawnbrokers [Repealed.]	48
Chapter 91A - Pawnbrokers Modernization Act of 1989	48
Chapter 92 - Photographers [Deleted.]	48
Chapter 93 - Certified Public Accountants	48
Chapter 93A - Real Estate License Law	49
Chapter 93B - Occupational Licensing Boards	49
Chapter 93C - Watchmakers [Repealed.]	49
Chapter 93D - North Carolina State Hearing Aid Dealers and Fitters Board.	49
Chapter 93E - North Carolina Appraisers Act	49
Chapter 94 - Apprenticeship	49
Chapter 95 - Department of Labor and Labor Regulations	49
Chapter 95 - Department of Labor and Labor Regulations (Continuation)	50
Chapter 96 - Employment Security	50
Chapter 97 - Workers' Compensation Act	50
Chapter 97 - Workers' Compensation Act (Continuation)	51

Chapter 98 - Burnt and Lost Records	51
Chapter 99 - Libel and Slander	51
Chapter 99A - Civil Remedies for Criminal Actions	51
Chapter 99B - Products Liability	51
Chapter 99C - Actions Relating to Winter Sports Safety and Accidents	51
Chapter 99D - Civil Rights	51
Chapter 99E - Special Liability Provisions	51
Chapter 100 - Monuments, Memorials and Parks	51
Chapter 101 - Names of Persons	51
Chapter 102 - Official Survey Base	51
Chapter 103 - Sundays, Holidays and Special Days	51
Chapter 104 - United States Lands	51
Chapter 104A - Degrees of Kinship	51
Chapter 104B - Hurricanes or Other Acts of Nature	51
Chapter 104C - Atomic Energy, Radioactivity and Ionizing Radiation [Repealed and Recodified.]	51
Chapter 104D - Southern States Energy Compact	51
Chapter 104E - North Carolina Radiation Protection Act	51
Chapter 104F - Southeast Interstate Low-Level Radioactive Waste Management Compact [Repealed]	51
Chapter 104G - North Carolina Low-Level Radioactive Waste Management Authority Act of 1987 [Repealed]	51
Chapter 105 - Taxation	51
Chapter 105 - Taxation (Continuation)	52
Chapter 105 - Taxation (Continuation)	53
Chapter 105 - Taxation (Continuation)	54
Chapter 105A - Setoff Debt Collection Act	55
Chapter 105B - Defaulted Student Loan Recovery Act	55
Chapter 106 - Agriculture	55
Chapter 106 - Agriculture (Continue)	56
Chapter 106 - Agriculture (Continue)	57
Chapter 107 - Agricultural Development Districts [Repealed.]	57
Chapter 108 - Social Services [Repealed and Recodified.]	57
Chapter 108A - Social Services	57
Chapter 108B - Community Action Programs	58
Chapter 108C Medicaid and Health Choice Provider Requirements.	58
Chapter 108D Medicaid Managed Care for Behavioral Health Services.	58
Chapter 109 - Bonds [Recodified.]	58
Chapter 110 - Child Welfare	58
Chapter 111 - Aid to the Blind	58
Chapter 112 - Confederate Homes and Pensions [Repealed.]	58
Chapter 113 - Conservation and Development	58
Chapter 113 - Conservation and Development (Continuation)	59

Chapter 113A - Pollution Control and Environment	59
Chapter 113A - Pollution Control and Environment (Continuation)	60
Chapter 113B - North Carolina Energy Policy Act of 1975	60
Chapter 114 - Department of Justice	60
Chapter 115 - Elementary and Secondary Education [Repealed.]	60
Chapter 115A - Community Colleges, Technical Institutes, and Industrial Education Centers [Repealed.]	60
Chapter 115B - Tuition and Fee Waivers	60
Chapter 115C - Elementary and Secondary Education	60
Chapter 115C - Elementary and Secondary Education (Continuation)	61
Chapter 115C - Elementary and Secondary Education (Continuation)	62
Chapter 115C - Elementary and Secondary Education (Continuation)	63
Chapter 115D - Community Colleges	63
Chapter 115E - Private Educational Facilities Finance Act [Recodified]	63
Chapter 116 - Higher Education	63
Chapter 116 - Higher Education (Continuation)	63
Chapter 116A - Escheats and Abandoned Property [Repealed.]	64
Chapter 116B - Escheats and Abandoned Property	64
Chapter 116C - Continuum of Education Programs	64
Chapter 116D - Higher Education Bonds	64
Chapter 116E - Education Longitudinal Data System	64
Chapter 117 - Electrification	64
Chapter 118 - Firemen's and Rescue Squad Workers' Relief and Pension Funds [Recodified.]	64
Chapter 118A - Firemen's Death Benefit Act [Repealed.]	64
Chapter 118B - Members of a Rescue Squad Death Benefit Act [Repealed.]	64
Chapter 119 - Gasoline and Oil Inspection and Regulation	64
Chapter 120 - General Assembly	65
Chapter 120 - General Assembly (Continuation)	66
Chapter 120 - General Assembly (Continuation)	67
Chapter 120C - Lobbying	67
Chapter 121 - Archives and History	67
Chapter 122 - Hospitals for the Mentally Disordered [Repealed.]	67
Chapter 122A - North Carolina Housing Finance Agency	67
Chapter 122B - North Carolina Agricultural Facilities Finance Act [Repealed.]	67
Chapter 122C - Mental Health, Developmental Disabilities, and Substance Abuse Act of 1985	67
Chapter 122C - Mental Health, Developmental Disabilities, and Substance Abuse Act of 1985 (Continuation)	68

Chapter 122D - North Carolina Agricultural Finance Act	68
Chapter 122E - North Carolina Housing Trust and Oil Overcharge Act	68
Chapter 123 - Impeachment	69
Chapter 123A - Industrial Development [Repealed.]	69
Chapter 124 - Internal Improvements	69
Chapter 125 - Libraries	69
Chapter 126 - State Personnel System	69
Chapter 127 - Militia [Repealed.]	69
Chapter 127A - Militia	69
Chapter 127B - Military Affairs	69
Chapter 127C - Advisory Commission on Military Affairs	69
Chapter 128 - Offices and Public Officers	69
Chapter 128 - Offices and Public Officers (Continuation)	70
Chapter 129 - Public Buildings and Grounds	70
Chapter 130 - Public Health [Repealed.]	70
Chapter 130A - Public Health	70
Chapter 130A - Public Health (Continuation)	71
Chapter 130A - Public Health (Continuation)	72
Chapter 130B - Hazardous Waste Management Commission [Repealed.]	72
Chapter 131 - Public Hospitals [Repealed.]	72
Chapter 131A - Health Care Facilities Finance Act	72
Chapter 131B - Licensing of Ambulatory Surgical Facilities [Repealed.]	72
Chapter 131C - Charitable Solicitation Licensure Act [Repealed.]	72
Chapter 131D - Inspection and Licensing of Facilities	72
Chapter 131E - Health Care Facilities and Services	72
Chapter 131E - Health Care Facilities and Services (Continuation)	73
Chapter 131F - Solicitation of Contributions	73
Chapter 132 - Public Records	73
Chapter 133 - Public Works	74
Chapter 134 - Youth Development [Recodified.]	74
Chapter 134A - Youth Services [Repealed.]	74
Chapter 135 - Retirement System for Teachers and State Employees; Social Security; Health Insurance Program for Children	74
Chapter 135 - Retirement System for Teachers and State Employees; Social Security; Health Insurance Program for Children	75
Chapter 136 - Transportation	75
Chapter 136 - Transportation (Continuation)	76
Chapter 137 - Rural Rehabilitation [Repealed.]	76
Chapter 138 - Salaries, Fees and Allowances	76
Chapter 138A - State Government Ethics Act	76

Chapter 139 - Soil and Water Conservation Districts	76
Chapter 140 - State Art Museum; Symphony and Art Societies	76
Chapter 140A - State Awards System	76
Chapter 141 - State Boundaries	76
Chapter 142 - State Debt	76
Chapter 143 - State Departments, Institutions, and Commissions	77
Chapter 143 - State Departments, Institutions, and Commissions (Continuation)	78
Chapter 143 - State Departments, Institutions, and Commissions (Continuation)	79
Chapter 143 - State Departments, Institutions, and Commissions (Continuation)	80
Chapter 143A - State Government Reorganization	80
Chapter 143B - Executive Organization Act of 1973	80
Chapter 143B - Executive Organization Act of 1973 (Continuation)	81
Chapter 143B - Executive Organization Act of 1973 (Continuation)	82
Chapter 143C - State Budget Act	83
Chapter 143D - The State Governmental Accountability and Internal Control Act	83
Chapter 144 - State Flag, Official Governmental Flags, Motto, and Colors	83
Chapter 145 - State Symbols and Other Official Adoptions.	83
Chapter 146 - State Lands	83
Chapter 147 - State Officers	83
Chapter 148 - State Prison System	84
Chapter 149 - State Song and Toast	84
Chapter 150 - Uniform Revocation of Licenses [Repealed.]	84
Chapter 150A - Administrative Procedure Act [Recodified.]	84
Chapter 150B - Administrative Procedure Act	84
Chapter 151 - Constables [Repealed.]	84
Chapter 152 - Coroners	84
Chapter 152A - County Medical Examiner [Repealed.]	84
Chapter 153 - Counties and County Commissioners [Repealed.]	84
Chapter 153A - Counties	84
Chapter 153A - Counties (Continue)	85
Chapter 153B - Mountain Resources Planning Act	85
Chapter 153C - Uwharrie Regional Resources Act	85
Chapter 154 - County Surveyor [Repealed.]	85
Chapter 155 - County Treasurer [Repealed.]	85
Chapter 156 - Drainage	85

Chapter 156 – Drainage (Continuation)	86
Chapter 157 - Housing Authorities and Projects	86
Chapter 157A - Historic Properties Commissions [Transferred.]	86
Chapter 158 - Local Development	86
Chapter 159 - Local Government Finance	86
Chapter 159 - Local Government Finance (Continuation)	87
Chapter 159A - Pollution Abatement and Industrial Facilities Financing Act [Unconstitutional.]	87
Chapter 159B - Joint Municipal Electric Power and Energy Act	87
Chapter 159C - Industrial and Pollution Control Facilities Financing Act	87
Chapter 159D - The North Carolina Capital Facilities Financing Act	87
Chapter 159E - Registered Public Obligations Act	87
Chapter 159F - North Carolina Energy Development Authority [Repealed.]	87
Chapter 159G - Water Infrastructure	87
Chapter 159H - [Reserved.]	87
Chapter 159I - Solid Waste Management Loan Program and Local Government Special Obligation Bonds	87
Chapter 160 - Municipal Corporations [Repealed And Transferred.]	87
Chapter 160A - Cities and Towns	88
Chapter 160A - Cities and Towns (Continuation)	89
Chapter 160B - Consolidated City-County Act	89
Chapter 160C - Baseball Park Districts [Repealed.]	90
Chapter 161 - Register of Deeds	90
Chapter 162 - Sheriff	90
Chapter 162A - Water and Sewer Systems	90
Chapter 162B Continuity of Local Government in Emergency.	90
Chapter 163 Elections and Election Laws.	90
Chapter 163 Elections and Election Laws. (Continuation)	91
Chapter 164 Concerning the General Statutes of North Carolina.	92
Chapter 165 Veterans.	92
Chapter 166 Civil Preparedness Agencies [Repealed.]	92
Chapter 166A North Carolina Emergency Management Act.	92
Chapter 167 State Civil Air Patrol [Repealed.]	92
Chapter 168 Persons with Disabilities.	92
Chapter 168A Persons With Disabilities Protection Act.	92

Chapter 148.

State Prison System.

Article 1.

Organization and Management.

§ 148-1. Repealed by Session Laws 1973, c. 1262, s. 10.

§ 148-2. Prison moneys and earnings.

(a) Persons authorized to collect or receive the moneys and earnings of the State prison system shall enter into bonds payable to the State of North Carolina in penal sums and with security approved by the Division of Adult Correction of the Department of Public Safety, conditioned upon the faithful performance by these persons of their duties in collecting, receiving, and paying over prison moneys and earnings to the State Treasurer. Only corporate security with sureties licensed to do business in North Carolina shall be accepted.

(b) Repealed by Session Laws 2007-280, s. 2, effective August 1, 2007.

(c) Notwithstanding G.S. 147-77, Article 6A of Chapter 147 of the General Statutes, or any other provision of law, the Division of Adult Correction of the Department of Public Safety may deposit revenue from prison canteens in local banks. The profits from prison canteens shall be deposited with the State Treasurer on a monthly basis in a fund denominated as the Correction Inmate Welfare Fund. Once the operating budget for the Correction Inmate Welfare Fund has been met, an amount equal to the funds allocated to each prison unit on a per inmate per year basis shall be credited to the Crime Victims Compensation Fund established in G.S 15B-23 as soon as practicable after the total amount paid to each unit per inmate per year has been determined. (1901, c. 472, s. 7; Rev., s. 5389; C.S., s. 7704; 1923, c. 156; 1925, c. 163; 1933, c. 172, s. 18; 1957, c. 349, s. 2; 1967, c. 996, s. 14; 1973, c. 1262, s. 10; 1985 (Reg. Sess., 1986), c. 1014, s. 203; 1991 (Reg. Sess., 1992), c. 902, s. 4; 1993 (Reg. Sess., 1994), c. 769, s. 21.5(a); 2007-280, s. 2; 2011-145, s. 19.1(h).)

§ 148-3. Prison property.

(a) The Division of Adult Correction of the Department of Public Safety shall subject to the provisions of G.S. 143-341, have control and custody of all unexpended surplus highway funds previously allocated for prison purposes and all property of every kind and description now used by or considered a part of units of the State prison system, except vehicles used on a rental basis. The property coming within the provisions of this section shall be identified and agreed upon by the executive heads of the highway and prison systems, or by their duly authorized representatives. The Governor shall have final authority to decide whether or not particular property shall be transferred to the Division of Adult Correction of the Department of Public Safety in event the executive heads of the two systems are unable to agree.

(b) Property, both real and personal, deemed by the Division of Adult Correction of the Department of Public Safety to be necessary or convenient in the operation of the State prison system may, subject to the provisions of G.S. 143-341, be acquired by gift, devise, purchase, or lease. The Division of Adult Correction of the Department of Public Safety may, subject to the provisions of G.S. 143-341, dispose of any prison property, either real or personal, or any interest or estate therein. (1901, c. 472, ss. 2, 6; Rev., s. 5392; C.S., s. 7705; 1925, c. 163; 1933, c. 172, s. 18; 1943, c. 409; 1957, c. 349, s. 3; 1967, c. 996, s. 13; 2011-145, s. 19.1(h); 2012-83, s. 61.)

§ 148-4. Control and custody of prisoners; authorizing prisoner to leave place of confinement.

The Secretary of Public Safety shall have control and custody of all prisoners serving sentence in the State prison system, and such prisoners shall be subject to all the rules and regulations legally adopted for the government thereof. Any sentence to imprisonment in any unit of the State prison system, or to jail to be assigned to work under the Division of Adult Correction of the Department of Public Safety, shall be construed as a commitment, for such terms of imprisonment as the court may direct, to the custody of the Secretary of Public Safety or his authorized representative, who shall designate the places of confinement within the State prison system where the sentences of all such persons shall be served. The authorized agents of the Secretary shall have all the authority of peace officers for the purpose of transferring prisoners from place to place in the State as their duties might require and for apprehending, arresting, and returning to prison escaped prisoners, and may be commissioned by the Governor, either generally or specially, as special officers for returning escaped prisoners or other fugitives from justice from outside the State, when such persons have been extradited or voluntarily surrendered. Employees of departments, institutions, agencies, and political subdivisions of the State hiring prisoners to perform work outside prison confines may be designated as the authorized agents of the Secretary of Public Safety for the purpose of maintaining control and custody of prisoners who may be placed under the supervision and control of such employees, including guarding and transferring such prisoners from place to place in the State as their duties might require, and apprehending and arresting escaped prisoners and returning them to prison. The governing authorities of the State prison system are authorized to determine by rules and regulations the manner of designating these agents and placing prisoners under their supervision and control, which rules and regulations shall be established in the same manner as other rules and regulations for the government of the State prison system.

The Secretary of Public Safety may extend the limits of the place of confinement of a prisoner, as to whom there is reasonable cause to believe he will honor his trust, by authorizing him, under prescribed conditions, to leave the confines of that place unaccompanied by a custodial agent for a prescribed period of time to

(1)   Contact prospective employers; or

(2)   Secure a suitable residence for use when released on parole or upon discharge; or

(3)   Obtain medical services not otherwise available; or

(4)   Participate in a training program in the community; or

(5)   Visit or attend the funeral of a spouse, child (including stepchild, adopted child or child as to whom the prisoner, though not a natural parent, has acted in the place of a parent), parent (including a person though not a natural parent, has acted in the place of a parent), brother, or sister; or

(6)   Participate in community-based programs of rehabilitation, including, but not limited to the existing community volunteer and home-leave programs, pre-release and after-care programs as may be provided for and administered by the Secretary of Public Safety and other programs determined by the Secretary

of Public Safety to be consistent with the prisoner's rehabilitation and return to society; or

(7)   Be on maternity leave, for a period of time not to exceed 60 days. The county departments of social services are expected to cooperate with officials at the North Carolina Correctional Center for Women to coordinate prenatal care, financial services, and placement of the child; or

(8)   Receive palliative care, only in the case of a terminally ill inmate or a permanently and totally disabled inmate that the Secretary finds no longer poses a significant public safety risk, and only after consultation with any victims of the inmate or the victims' families. For purposes of this subdivision, the term "terminally ill" describes an inmate who, as determined by a licensed physician, has an incurable condition caused by illness or disease that was unknown at the time of sentencing and was not diagnosed upon entry to prison, that will likely produce death within six months, and that is so debilitating that it is highly unlikely that the inmate poses a significant public safety risk. For purposes of this subdivision, the term "permanently and totally disabled" describes an inmate who, as determined by a licensed physician, suffers from permanent and irreversible physical incapacitation as a result of an existing physical or medical condition that was unknown at the time of sentencing and was not diagnosed upon entry to prison, and that is so incapacitating that it is highly unlikely that the inmate poses a significant public safety risk. The Department's medical director shall notify the Secretary immediately when an inmate has been classified as terminally ill and shall provide regular reports on inmates classified as permanently and totally disabled. The Secretary shall act expeditiously in determining whether to extend the limits of confinement under this subdivision upon receiving notice that an inmate has been classified as terminally ill or permanently and totally disabled and, in the case of a terminally ill inmate, the Secretary shall make a good faith effort to reach a determination within 30 days of receiving notice of the inmate's terminal condition.

The willful failure of a prisoner to remain within the extended limits of his confinement, or to return within the time prescribed to the place of confinement designated by the Secretary of Public Safety, shall be deemed an escape from the custody of the Secretary of Public Safety punishable as provided in G.S. 148-45. (1901, c. 472, s. 4; Rev., s. 5390; C.S., s. 7706; 1925, c. 163; 1933, c. 172, ss. 5, 18; 1935, c. 257, s. 2; 1943, c. 409; 1955, c. 238, s. 2; 1957, c. 349, s. 10; 1959, c. 109; 1965, c. 1042; 1967, c. 996, ss. 13, 15; 1973, c. 902; c. 1262, s. 10; 1977, c. 704, s. 5; 1985, c. 483; 2001-424, s. 25.9(a); 2005-276, s. 17.13; 2011-145, s. 19.1(h), (i); 2012-83, s. 61.)

§ 148-4.1. Release of inmates.

(a) Whenever the Secretary of Public Safety determines from data compiled by the Division of Adult Correction of the Department of Public Safety that it is necessary to reduce the prison population to a more manageable level or to meet the State's obligations under law, he shall direct the Post-Release Supervision and Parole Commission to release on parole over a reasonable period of time a number of prisoners sufficient to that purpose. From the time the Secretary directs the Post-Release Supervision and Parole Commission until the prison population has been reduced to a more manageable level, the Secretary may not accept any inmates ordered transferred from local confinement facilities to the State prison system under G.S. 148-32.1(b). Further, the Secretary may return any inmate housed in the State prison system under an order entered pursuant to G.S. 148-32.1(b) to the local confinement facility from which the inmate was transferred. In order to meet the requirements of this section, the Parole Commission shall not parole any person convicted under Article 7A of Chapter 14 of a sex offense, under G.S. 14-39, 14-41, or 14-43.3, under G.S. 90-95(h) of a drug trafficking offense, or under G.S. 14-17, or any other violent felon as defined in subsection (a1) of this section. The Parole Commission may continue to consider the suitability for release of such persons in accordance with the criteria set forth in Articles 85 and 85A of Chapter 15A.

(a1) Notwithstanding any other provision of this section, the Division of Adult Correction of the Department of Public Safety shall at all times secure the necessary prison space to house any violent felon or habitual felon for the full active sentence imposed by the court. For purposes of this subsection, the term "violent felon" means any person convicted of the following felony offenses: first or second degree murder, voluntary manslaughter, first or second degree rape, first or second degree sexual offense, any sexual offense involving a minor, robbery, kidnapping, or assault, or attempting, soliciting, or conspiring to commit any of those offenses.

(b) Except as provided in subsection (c), only inmates who are otherwise eligible for parole pursuant to Article 85 of Chapter 15A or pursuant to Article 3B of this Chapter may be released under this section.

(c) Persons eligible for parole under Article 85A of Chapter 15A shall be eligible for early parole under this section nine months prior to the discharge date otherwise applicable, and six months prior to the date of automatic 90-day parole authorized by G.S. 15A-1380.2.

(c1)   through (g). Repealed by 1995 Session Laws, c. 324, s. 19.9(e).

(g1)   Expired July 1, 1996.

(h)   A person sentenced under Article 81B of Chapter 15A of the General Statutes shall not be released pursuant to this section.

(i)   This section does not apply to inmates released pursuant to G.S. 148-64.1. (1983, c. 557, s. 1; 1985 (Reg. Sess., 1986), c. 1014, s. 197(a); 1987, c. 7, ss. 1, 3, 4; c. 879, s. 1.2; 1989, c. 1, s. 1; 1990, Ex. Sess., c. 1, ss. 1-3.3; 1989 (Reg. Sess., 1990), c. 933, ss. 10-13; 1991, c. 187, s. 2; c. 217, ss. 6, 7; c. 437, ss. 1-9; 1991 (Reg. Sess., 1992), c. 1036, ss. 5-7; 1993, c. 91, ss. 1-9; c. 538, s. 31; 1994, Ex. Sess., c. 14, s. 64; c. 15, ss. 1-4; c. 24, s. 14(b), (e); 1995, c. 324, s. 19.9(a)-(e); 2008-199, s. 1; 2011-145, s. 19.1(h), (i).)

§ 148-5. Secretary to manage prison property.

The Secretary of Public Safety shall manage and have charge of all the property and effects of the State prison system, and conduct all its affairs subject to the provisions of this Chapter and the rules and regulations legally adopted for the government thereof. (1933, c. 172, s. 4; 1955, c. 238, s. 3; 1967, c. 996, s. 15; 1973, c. 1262, s. 10; 2011-145, s. 19.1(i).)

§ 148-5.1. Confining inmates away from victims.

If a victim or immediate family member of a victim requests that, for the safety of the victim or family member, an inmate be confined outside the county where the victim or family member resides or is employed, the Department shall make a reasonable effort to house the inmate in a facility in another county. If the inmate is not so housed in another county, the Department shall notify the victim or family member in writing. (2001-433, s. 10; 2001-487, s. 120.)

§ 148-6. Custody, employment and hiring out of convicts.

The Division of Adult Correction of the Department of Public Safety shall provide for receiving, and keeping in custody until discharged by law, all such convicts as may be now confined in the prison and such as may be hereafter sentenced to imprisonment therein by the several courts of this State. The Division shall have full power and authority to provide for employment of such convicts, either in the prison or on farms leased or owned by the State of North Carolina, or elsewhere, or otherwise; and may contract for the hire or employment of any able-bodied convicts upon such terms as may be just and fair, but such convicts so hired, or employed, shall remain under the actual management, control and care of the Division. (1895, c. 194, s. 5; 1897, c. 270; 1901, c. 472, ss. 5, 6; Rev., s. 5391; C.S., s. 7707; 1925, c. 163; 1933, c. 172, s. 18; 1957, c. 349, s. 10; 1967, c. 996, s. 13; 2007-398, s. 2; 2011-145, s. 19.1(h); 2012-83, s. 61.)

§ 148-7: Repealed by Session Laws 1995, c. 233, s. 1.

§ 148-8. Transferred to § 66-58(b)(15) by Session Laws 1975, c. 730, s. 2.

§ 148-8.1. Transferred to § 66-58(b)(16) by Session Laws 1975, c. 730, s. 3.

§ 148-9. Repealed by Session Laws 1973, c. 476, s. 138.

§ 148-10. Department of Environment and Natural Resources to supervise sanitary and health conditions of prisoners.

The Department of Environment and Natural Resources shall have general supervision over the sanitary and health conditions of the central prison, over the prison camps, or other places of confinement of prisoners under the jurisdiction of the Division of Adult Correction of the Department of Public Safety, and shall make periodic examinations of the same and report to the Division of Adult Correction of the Department of Public Safety the conditions found there with respect to the sanitary and hygienic care of such prisoners. (1917, c. 286, s. 8; 1919, c. 80, s. 4; C.S., s. 7714; 1925, c. 163; 1933, c. 172, s. 22; 1943, c. 409; 1957, c. 349, s. 10; 1967, c. 996, s. 13; 1973, c. 476, s. 128; 1989, c. 727, s. 219(37); 1997-443, s. 11A.111; 2011-145, s. 19.1(h); 2012-83, s. 61.)

§ 148-10.1. Employment of clinical chaplains for inmates.

The Division of Adult Correction of the Department of Public Safety is authorized and directed to employ clinical chaplains to provide moral, spiritual and social counselling and ministerial services to inmates in the custody of the Secretary of Public Safety. The Division of Adult Correction of the Department of Public Safety shall seek to employ a diversity of qualified persons having differing faiths which are to the extent practicable reflective of the professed religious composition of the inmate population. (1977, c. 950, s. 1; 2011-145, s. 19.1(h), (i).)

§ 148-10.2. Policy: Certain inmates not to contact family members of victims.

(a) It shall be the policy of the Division of Adult Correction of the Department of Public Safety to prohibit death row inmates from contacting the surviving family members of the victims without the written consent of the family members being contacted. For purposes of this subsection, the term "contact" includes arranging for a third party to forward communications from the inmate to the surviving family members of the victim.

(b) At the request of the victim or a family member of the victim, the Division of Adult Correction of the Department of Public Safety shall prohibit an inmate convicted of an offense listed in G.S. 15A-830(a)(7) from contacting the requesting party. For purposes of this subsection, the term "contact" includes arranging for a third party to forward communications from the inmate to the victim or family member.

(c) The Division of Adult Correction of the Department of Public Safety shall develop and impose sanctions against any inmate who violates the provisions of this section. (1999-358, s. 1; 2001-433, s. 9; 2001-487, s. 120; 2011-145, s. 19.1(h).)

§ 148-10.3. Electronic monitoring costs.

Personnel, equipment, and other costs of providing electronic monitoring of pretrial or sentenced offenders shall be reimbursed to the Division of Adult Correction of the Department of Public Safety by the State or local agency requesting the service in an amount not exceeding the actual costs. (2002-126, s. 17.10(a); 2011-145, s. 19.1(h).)

§ 148-10.4. Statewide Misdemeanant Confinement Fund.

(a) Definitions. - The following definitions apply in this section:

(1) Division. - Division of Adult Correction of the Department of Public Safety.

(2) Fund. - The Statewide Misdemeanant Confinement Fund established by this section.

(3) Program. - Statewide Misdemeanant Confinement Program established under G.S. 148-32.1(b3).

(4) Sheriffs' Association. - North Carolina Sheriffs' Association, Inc.

(b) Intent and Purpose. - It is the intent of the General Assembly that the funds in the Fund established by this section be used to reimburse local governments for expenses incurred for housing misdemeanants under the Program, and other related expenses; and to cover administrative costs incurred by the Sheriffs' Association for services provided by it regarding the housing of these misdemeanants.

(c) Statewide Misdemeanant Confinement Fund established. - There is created within the Division of Adult Correction a special nonreverting fund called the Statewide Misdemeanant Confinement Fund.

(d) Fund Uses. - Moneys in the Fund may be used for the following:

(1) Reimbursements by the Sheriffs' Association to counties for the costs of housing misdemeanants under the Program, including the care, supervision, and transportation of those misdemeanants.

(2) Reimbursements to the Division of Adult Correction for the cost of housing misdemeanants transferred to the Division pursuant to G.S. 148-32.1(b3), including the care, supervision, and transportation of those misdemeanants.

(3) To pay the Sheriffs' Association for administrative and operating expenses pursuant to subsection (e) of this section.

(4) To pay the Division of Adult Correction for administrative and operating expenses pursuant to subsection (e) of this section.

(e) Operating and Administrative Expenses. - Five percent (5%) of the monthly receipts collected and credited to the Statewide Misdemeanant Confinement Fund, not to exceed the sum of one million dollars ($1,000,000) annually, shall be transferred on a monthly basis to the Sheriffs' Association to be used to support the Program and for administrative and operating expenses of the Association and its staff. One percent (1%) of the monthly receipts collected and credited to the Statewide Misdemeanant Confinement Fund shall be transferred on a monthly basis to the General Fund to be allocated to the Division of Adult Correction for its administrative and operating expenses for the Program. (2011-145, s. 19.1(h), (i); 2011-192, s. 7(h); 2013-360, s. 16C.6(a).)

Article 2.

Prison Regulations.

§ 148-11. Authority to adopt rules; authority to designate uniforms.

(a) The Secretary shall adopt rules for the government of the State prison system. The Secretary shall have the rules that pertain to enforcing discipline read to every prisoner when received in the State prison system and a printed copy of these rules made available to the prisoners.

(b) The Secretary of Public Safety has sole authority to designate the uniforms worn by inmates confined in the Section of Prisons of the Division of Adult Correction. (1873-4, c. 158, s. 15; Code, s. 3444; Rev., s. 5401; C.S., s. 7721; 1925, c. 163; 1933, c. 172, s. 18; 1955, c. 238, s. 4; 1957, c. 349, s. 4; 1967, c. 996, ss. 14, 15; 1973, c. 1262, s. 10; 1983, c. 147, s. 1; 1987, c. 827, s. 1; 1991, c. 418, s. 15; c. 477, ss. 6, 8; 1995, c. 507, s. 27.8(u); 1999-109, s. 2; 2011-145, s. 19.1(i), (j).)

§ 148-12. Diagnostic and classification programs.

(a) The Division of Adult Correction of the Department of Public Safety shall, as soon as practicable, establish diagnostic centers to make social, medical, and psychological studies of persons committed to the Division. Full diagnostic studies shall be made before initial classification in cases where such studies have not been made.

(b)   Repealed by Session Laws 1977, c. 711, s. 33, effective July 1, 1978.

(c)   Any prisoner confined in the State prison system while under a sentence of imprisonment imposed upon conviction of a felony shall be classified and treated as a convicted felon even if, before beginning service of the felony sentence, such prisoner has time remaining to be served in the State prison system on a sentence or sentences imposed upon conviction of a misdemeanor or misdemeanors. (1917, c. 278, s. 2; 1919, c. 191, s. 2; C.S., s. 7750; 1925, c. 163; 1933, c. 172, s. 18; 1955, c. 238, s. 5; 1959, c. 50; 1967, c. 996, s. 2; 1973, c. 1446, s. 27; 1977, c. 711, s. 33; 1977, 2nd Sess., c. 1147, s. 32; 2011-145, s. 19.1(h).)

§ 148-13. Regulations as to custody grades, privileges, gain time credit, etc.

(a)   The Secretary of Public Safety may issue regulations regarding the grades of custody in which State prisoners are kept, the privileges and restrictions applicable to each custody grade, and the amount of cash, clothing, etc., to be awarded to State prisoners after their discharge or parole. The amount of cash awarded to a prisoner upon discharge or parole after being incarcerated for two years or longer shall be at least forty-five dollars ($45.00).

(a1)   The Secretary of Public Safety shall adopt rules to specify the rates at, and circumstances under, which earned time authorized by G.S. 15A-1340.13(d) and G.S. 15A-1340.20(d) may be earned or forfeited by persons serving activated sentences of imprisonment for felony or misdemeanor convictions.

(b)   With respect to prisoners who are serving prison or jail terms for impaired driving offenses under G.S. 20-138.1, the Secretary of Public Safety may, in his discretion, issue regulations regarding deductions of time from the terms of such prisoners for good behavior, meritorious conduct, work or study, participation in rehabilitation programs, and the like.

(c),   (d) Repealed by Session Laws 1993, c. 538, s. 32, effective January 1, 1995.

(e) The Secretary's regulations concerning earned time credits authorized by this section shall be distributed to and followed by local jail administrators with regard to sentenced jail prisoners.

(f) The provisions of this section do not apply to persons sentenced to a term of special probation under G.S. 15A-1344(e) or G.S. 15A-1351(a). (1933, c. 172, s. 23; 1935, c. 414, s. 15; 1937, c. 88, s. 1; 1943, c. 409; 1955, c. 238, s. 6; 1979, c. 760, s. 4; 1979, 2nd Sess., c. 1316, ss. 43-47; 1981, c. 63, s. 1; c. 179, s. 14; c. 662, ss. 8, 9; 1983, c. 560, s. 3; 1985, c. 310, ss. 1-4; 1987 (Reg. Sess., 1988), c. 1086, s. 120(a); 1991, c. 187, s. 3; 1993, c. 538, s. 32; 1994, Ex. Sess., c. 24, s. 14(b); 2011-145, s. 19.1(i).)

§§ 148-14 through 148-17. Repealed by Session Laws 1943, c. 409.

§ 148-18. Wages, allowances and loans.

(a) Prisoners employed by Correction Enterprises shall be compensated as set forth in Article 14 of this Chapter. Prisoners participating in work assignments established by the Section of Prisons of the Division of Adult Correction shall be compensated at rates fixed by the Division of Adult Correction of the Department of Public Safety's rules and regulations; provided, that no prisoner so paid shall receive more than one dollar ($1.00) per day, unless the Secretary determines that the work assignment requires special skills or training. Upon approval of the Secretary, inmates working in job assignments requiring special skills or training may be paid up to three dollars ($3.00) per day. The Correction Enterprises Fund shall be the source of wages and allowances provided to inmates who are employed by the Division of Adult Correction of the Department of Public Safety in work assignments established by the Section of Prisons of the Division of Adult Correction.

(b) A prisoner shall be required to contribute to the support of any of his dependents residing in North Carolina who may be receiving public assistance during the period of commitment if funds available to the prisoner are adequate for such purpose. The dependency status and need shall be determined by the department of social services in the county of North Carolina in which such dependents reside.

(c) Repealed by Session Laws 1995, c. 233, s. 2. (1935, c. 414, s. 19; 1967, c. 996, s. 3; 1969, c. 982; 1973, c. 1262, s. 10; 1975, c. 506, s. 3; c. 716,

s. 7; 1991 (Reg. Sess., 1992), c. 902, s. 5; 1993, c. 321, s. 175; 1995, c. 233, s. 2; 2007-280, s. 3; 2011-145, s. 19.1(h), (j).)

§ 148-18.1. Confiscation of unauthorized articles.

Any item of personal property which a prisoner in any correctional facility is prohibited from possessing by State law or which is not authorized by rules adopted by the Secretary of Public Safety shall, when found in the possession of a prisoner, be confiscated and destroyed or otherwise disposed of as the Secretary may direct. Any unauthorized funds confiscated under this section or funds from the sale of confiscated property shall be deposited to Inmate Welfare Fund maintained by the Division of Adult Correction of the Department of Public Safety. (1983, c. 289, s. 1; 2011-145, s. 19.1(h), (i).)

§ 148-19. Health services.

(a) The general policies, rules and regulations of the Division of Adult Correction of the Department of Public Safety shall prescribe standards for health services to prisoners, which shall include preventive, diagnostic, and therapeutic measures on both an outpatient and a hospital basis, for all types of patients. A prisoner may be taken, when necessary, to a medical facility outside the State prison system. The Division of Adult Correction of the Department of Public Safety shall seek the cooperation of public and private agencies, institutions, officials and individuals in the development of adequate health services to prisoners.

(b) Upon request of the Secretary of Public Safety, the Secretary of Health and Human Services may detail personnel employed by the Department of Health and Human Services to the Division of Adult Correction of the Department of Public Safety for the purpose of supervising and furnishing medical, psychiatric, psychological, dental, and other technical and scientific services to the Division of Adult Correction of the Department of Public Safety. The compensation, allowances, and expenses of the personnel detailed under this section may be paid from applicable appropriations to the Department of Health and Human Services, and reimbursed from applicable appropriations to the Division of Adult Correction of the Department of Public Safety. The Secretary of Public Safety may make similar arrangements with any other agency of State government able and willing to aid the Division of Adult

Correction of the Department of Public Safety to meet the needs of prisoners for health services.

(c) Each prisoner committed to the Division of Adult Correction of the Department of Public Safety shall receive a physical and mental examination by a health care professional authorized by the North Carolina Medical Board to perform such examinations as soon as practicable after admission and before being assigned to work. The prisoner's work and other assignments shall be made with due regard for the prisoner's physical and mental condition.

(d) The Commission for Mental Health, Developmental Disabilities, and Substance Abuse Services shall adopt standards for the delivery of mental health and mental retardation services to inmates in the custody of the Division of Adult Correction of the Department of Public Safety. The Commission for Mental Health, Developmental Disabilities, and Substance Abuse Services shall give the Secretary of Public Safety an opportunity to review and comment on proposed standards prior to promulgation of such standards; however, final authority to determine such standards remains with the Commission. The Secretary of the Department of Health and Human Services shall designate an agency or agencies within the Department of Health and Human Services to monitor the implementation by the Division of Adult Correction of the Department of Public Safety of these standards and of substance abuse standards adopted by the Division of Adult Correction of the Department of Public Safety. (1917, c. 286, s. 22; C.S., s. 7727; 1925, c. 163; 1933, c. 172, s. 18; 1957, c. 349, s. 10; 1967, c. 996, s. 4; 1973, c. 476, s. 133; c. 1262, s. 10; 1977, c. 332; c. 679, s. 7; 1981, c. 51, s. 6; c. 707, ss. 1, 2; 1985, c. 589, s. 55.1; 1991, c. 405, s. 1; 1995, c. 94, s. 36; 1997-443, s. 11A.118(a); 2011-145, s. 19.1(h), (i); 2011-266, s. 1.17(b); 2012-83, s. 61; 2013-360, s. 12A.12.)

§ 148-19.1. Exemption from licensure and certificate of need.

(a) Inpatient chemical dependency or substance abuse facilities that provide services exclusively to inmates of the Division of Adult Correction of the Department of Public Safety shall be exempt from licensure by the Department of Health and Human Services under Chapter 122C of the General Statutes. If an inpatient chemical dependency or substance abuse facility provides services both to inmates of the Division of Adult Correction of the Department of Public Safety and to members of the general public, the portion of the facility that serves inmates shall be exempt from licensure.

(b) Any person who contracts to provide inpatient chemical dependency or substance abuse services to inmates of the Division of Adult Correction of the Department of Public Safety may construct and operate a new chemical dependency or substance abuse facility for that purpose without first obtaining a certificate of need from the Department of Health and Human Services pursuant to Article 9 of Chapter 131E of the General Statutes. However, a new facility or addition developed for that purpose without a certificate of need shall not be licensed pursuant to Chapter 122C of the General Statutes and shall not admit anyone other than inmates unless the owner or operator first obtains a certificate of need. (2001-424, s. 25.19(a); 2011-145, s. 19.1(h).)

§ 148-19.2. Mandatory HIV testing.

Each person sentenced to imprisonment and committed to the custody of the Division of Adult Correction of the Department of Public Safety shall be tested to determine whether the person is HIV positive.

Each inmate who has not previously tested positive for HIV shall also be tested:

(1) Not less than once every four years from the date of that inmate's initial testing.

(2) Prior to the inmate's release from the custody of the Division of Adult Correction, except that testing is not mandatory prior to the release of an inmate who has been tested within one year of the inmate's release date.

In each case, the results of the test shall be reported to the inmate. If an inmate tests positive for HIV, that inmate shall be referred to public health officials for counseling. (2013-360, s. 16C.15(a).)

§ 148-20. Corporal punishment of prisoners prohibited.

It is unlawful for the Secretary of Public Safety or any other person having the care, custody, or control of any prisoner in this State to make or enforce any rule or regulation providing for the whipping, flogging, or administration of any similar corporal punishment of any prisoner, or to give any specific order for or cause to be administered or personally to administer or inflict any such corporal punishment. (1917, c. 286, s. 7; C.S., s. 7728; 1925, c. 163; 1933, c. 172, s. 18; 1955, c. 238, s. 9; 1963, c. 1174, s. 1; 1967, c. 996, s. 15; 1973, c. 1262, s. 10; 2011-145, s. 19.1(i).)

§ 148-21. Repealed by Session Laws 1963, c. 1174, s. 5.

§ 148-22. Treatment programs.

(a) The general policies, rules and regulations of the Division of Adult Correction of the Department of Public Safety shall provide for humane treatment of prisoners and for programs to effect their correction and return to the community as promptly as practicable. Visits and correspondence between prisoners and approved friends shall be authorized under reasonable conditions, and family members shall be permitted and encouraged to maintain close contact with the prisoners unless such contacts prove to be hurtful. Casework, counseling, and psychotherapy services provided to prisoners may be extended to include members of the prisoner's family if practicable and necessary to achieve the purposes of such programs. Education, library, recreation, and vocational training programs shall be developed so as to coordinate with corresponding services and opportunities which will be available to the prisoner when he is released. Programs may be established for the treatment and training of mentally retarded prisoners and other special groups. These programs may be operated in segregated sections of facilities housing other prisoners or in separate facilities.

(b) The Division of Adult Correction of the Department of Public Safety may cooperate with and seek the cooperation of public and private agencies, institutions, officials, and individuals in the development and conduct of programs designed to give persons committed to the Division opportunities for physical, mental and moral improvement. The Division may enter into agreements with other agencies of federal, State or local government and with private agencies to promote the most effective use of available resources.

Specifically the Secretary of Public Safety may enter into contracts or agreements with appropriate public or private agencies offering needed services including health, mental health, mental retardation, substance abuse, rehabilitative or training services for such inmates of the Division of Adult Correction of the Department of Public Safety as the Secretary may deem eligible. These agencies shall be reimbursed from applicable appropriations to the Division of Adult Correction of the Department of Public Safety for services rendered at a rate not to exceed that which such agencies normally receive for serving their regular clients.

The Secretary may contract for the housing of work-release inmates at county jails and local confinement facilities. Inmates may be placed in the care of such agencies but shall remain the responsibility of the Division and shall be subject to the complete supervision of the Division. The Division may reimburse such agencies for the support of such inmates at a rate not in excess of the average daily cost of inmate care in the corrections unit to which the inmate would otherwise be assigned. (1917, c. 286, s. 15; C.S., s. 7732; 1925, c. 163; 1933, c. 172, s. 18; 1955, c. 238, s. 9; 1967, c. 996, s. 5; 1975, c. 679, ss. 1, 2; 1977, c. 297; 1983, c. 376; 1985, c. 589, s. 55; 2011-145, s. 19.1(h), (i).)

§ 148-22.1. Educational facilities and programs for selected inmates.

(a) The Division of Adult Correction of the Department of Public Safety is authorized to take advantage of aid available from any source in establishing facilities and developing programs to provide inmates of the State prison system with such academic and vocational and technical education as seems most likely to facilitate the rehabilitation of these inmates and their return to free society with attitudes, knowledge, and skills that will improve their prospects of becoming law-abiding and self-supporting citizens. The State Department of Public Instruction is authorized to cooperate with the Division of Adult Correction of the Department of Public Safety in planning academic and vocational and technical education of prison system inmates, but the State Department of Public Instruction is not authorized to expend any funds in this connection.

(b) In expending funds that may be made available for facilities and programs to provide inmates of the State prison system with academic and vocational and technical education, the Division of Adult Correction of the Department of Public Safety shall give priority to meeting the needs of inmates who are less than 21 years of age when received in the prison system with a sentence or sentences under which they will be held for not less than six months nor more than five years before becoming eligible to be considered for a parole or unconditional release. These inmates shall be given appropriate tests to determine their educational needs and aptitudes. When the necessary arrangements can be made, they shall receive such instruction as may be deemed practical and advisable for them.

(c) The Secretary of Public Safety, in consultation with the Office of Human Resources, shall set the salary supplement paid to teachers, instructional support personnel, and school-based administrators who are Division of Prison employees and are licensed by the State Board of Education. The salary supplement shall be at least five percent (5%), but not more than the percentage supplement they would receive if they were employed in the local school administrative unit where the job site is located. These salary supplements shall not be paid to central office staff. Nothing in this subsection shall be construed to include "merit pay" under the term "salary supplement". (1959, c. 431; 1967, c. 996, s. 13; 1985, c. 226, s. 1; 1993, c. 180, s. 8; 2005-276, s. 29.19(c); 2011-145, s. 19.1(h), (i); 2012-83, s. 61; 2013-382, s. 9.1(c).)

§ 148-22.2. Procedure when surgical operations on inmates are necessary.

The medical staff of any penal institution of the State of North Carolina is hereby authorized to perform or cause to be performed by competent and skillful surgeons surgical operations upon any inmate when such operation is necessary for the improvement of the physical condition of the inmate. The decision to perform an operation shall be made by the chief medical officer of the institution, with the approval of the superintendent of the institution, and with the advice of the medical staff of the institution. No operation shall be performed without the consent of the inmate; or, if the inmate is a minor, without the consent of a responsible member of the inmate's family, a guardian, or one having legal custody of the minor; or, if the inmate be non compos mentis, then the consent of a responsible member of the inmate's family or of a guardian shall be obtained. Any surgical operations on inmates of State penal institutions shall also be subject to the provisions of Article 1A of Chapter 90 of the General Statutes, G.S. 90-21.13, and G.S. 90-21.16.

If the operation on the inmate is determined by the chief medical officer to be an emergency situation in which immediate action is necessary to preserve the life or health of the inmate, and the inmate, if sui juris, is unconscious or otherwise incapacitated so as to be incapable of giving consent or in the case of a minor or inmate non compos mentis, the consent of a responsible member of the inmate's family, guardian, or one having legal custody of the inmate cannot be obtained within the time necessitated by the nature of the emergency situation, then the decision to proceed with the operation shall be made by the chief medical officer and the superintendent of the institution with the advice of the medical staff of the institution.

In all cases falling under this section, the chief medical officer of the institution and the medical staff of the institution shall keep a careful and complete record of the measures taken to obtain the permission for the operation and a complete medical record signed by the medical superintendent or director, the surgeon performing the operation and all surgical consultants of the operation performed. (1919, c. 281, ss. 1, 2; C.S., ss. 7221, 7222; 1947, c. 537, s. 24; 1951, c. 775; 1957, c. 1357, s. 1; 1981, c. 307, ss. 2, 3; 2003-13, s. 8; 2004-203, s. 53(a).)

§ 148-23. Prison employees not to use intoxicants, narcotic drugs or profanity.

No one addicted to the use of alcoholic beverages, or narcotic drugs, shall be employed as superintendent, warden, guard, or in any other position connected with the Division of Adult Correction of the Department of Public Safety, where such position requires the incumbent to have any charge or direction of the prisoners; and anyone holding such position, or anyone who may be employed in any other capacity in the State prison system, who shall come under the influence of alcoholic beverages during hours of employment, or reports for duty under the effect of intoxicants, or narcotic drugs, or who shall become intoxicated, or uses narcotic drugs, under circumstances that bring discredit on the Division of Adult Correction of the Department of Public Safety, shall be subject to immediate dismissal from employment by any of the institutions and shall not be eligible for reinstatement to such position or be employed in any other position in any of the institutions. Any superintendent, warden, guard, supervisor, or other person holding any position in the Division of Adult Correction of the Department of Public Safety who curses a prisoner under his charge shall be subject to immediate dismissal from employment and shall not be eligible for reinstatement. (1917, c. 286, s. 16; 1919, c. 80, s. 8; C.S., s. 7733; 1925, c. 163; 1933, c. 172, s. 18; 1957, c. 349, s. 10; 1967, c. 996, s. 13; 1969, c. 382; 1981, c. 412, s. 4(4); c. 747, s. 66; 2011-145, s. 19.1(h); 2012-83, s. 61.)

§ 148-23.1. Tobacco products prohibited on State correctional facilities premises.

(a) The General Assembly finds that in order to protect the health, welfare, and comfort of inmates in the custody of the Division of Adult Correction of the

Department of Public Safety and to reduce the costs of inmate health care, it is necessary to prohibit inmates from using tobacco products on the premises of State correctional facilities and to ensure that employees and visitors do not use tobacco products on the premises of those facilities.

(b) No person may use tobacco products on the premises of a State correctional facility, except for authorized religious purposes. Notwithstanding any other provision of law, inmates in the custody of the Division of Adult Correction of the Department of Public Safety and persons facilitating religious observances may use and possess tobacco products for religious purposes consistent with the policies of the Division.

(b1) Except as provided in subsection (b) of this section, no person may possess tobacco products on the premises of a State correctional facility. Notwithstanding the provisions of this subsection, an employee or visitor may possess tobacco products within the confines of a motor vehicle located in a designated parking area of a correctional facility's premises if the tobacco product remains in the vehicle and the vehicle is locked when the employee or visitor has exited the vehicle.

(c) The Division of Adult Correction of the Department of Public Safety may adopt rules to implement the provisions of this section. Inmates in violation of this section are subject to disciplinary measures to be determined by the Division, including the potential loss of sentence credits earned prior to that violation. Employees in violation of this section are subject to disciplinary action by the Division. Visitors in violation of this section are subject to removal from the facility and loss of visitation privileges.

(d) As used in this section, the following terms mean:

(1) State correctional facility. - All buildings and grounds of a State correctional institution operated by the Division of Adult Correction of the Department of Public Safety.

(2) Tobacco products. - Cigars, cigarettes, snuff, loose tobacco, or similar goods made with any part of the tobacco plant that are prepared or used for smoking, chewing, dipping, or other personal use. (2005-372, s. 2; 2009-560, s. 1; 2011-145, s. 19.1(h).)

§ 148-23.2. Mobile phones prohibited on State correctional facilities premises.

Except as authorized by Division of Adult Correction of the Department of Public Safety policy, no person shall possess a mobile telephone or other wireless communications device on the premises of a State correctional facility. Notwithstanding the provisions of this section, an employee or visitor may possess a mobile telephone or other wireless communications device within the confines of a motor vehicle located in a designated parking area of a correctional facility's premises if the mobile telephone or other wireless communications device remains in the vehicle and the vehicle is locked when the employee or visitor has exited the vehicle. (2009-560, s. 2; 2011-145, s. 19.1(h).)

§ 148-24. Religious services.

The general policies, rules and regulations of the Division of Adult Correction of the Department of Public Safety shall provide for religious services to be held in all units of the State prison system on Sunday and at such other times as may be deemed appropriate. Attendance of prisoners at religious services shall be voluntary. The Secretary of Public Safety shall if possible secure the visits of some minister at the prison hospitals to administer to the spiritual wants of the sick. (1873-4, c. 158, s. 18; 1883, c. 349; Code, s. 3446; Rev., s. 5405; 1915, c. 125, ss. 1, 2; 1917, c. 286, s. 15; C.S., s. 7735; 1925, c. 163; c. 275, s. 6; 1933, c. 172, s. 18; 1955, c. 238, s. 9; 1967, c. 996, s. 6; 1973, c. 1262, s. 10; 2011-145, s. 19.1(h), (i).)

§ 148-25. Secretary to investigate death of convicts.

The Secretary of Public Safety, upon information of the death of a convict other than by natural causes, shall investigate the cause thereof and report the result of such investigation to the Governor, and for this purpose the Secretary may administer oaths and send for persons and papers. (1885, c. 379, s. 2; Rev., s. 5409; C.S., s. 7746; 1925, c. 163; 1933, c. 172, s. 18; 1955, c. 238, s. 9; 1967, c. 996, s. 15; 1973, c. 1262, s. 10; 2011-145, s. 19.1(i).)

Article 3.

Labor of Prisoners.

§ 148-26. State policy on employment of prisoners.

(a)   It is declared to be the public policy of the State of North Carolina that all able-bodied prison inmates shall be required to perform diligently all work assignments provided for them. The failure of any inmate to perform such a work assignment may result in disciplinary action. Work assignments and employment shall be for the public benefit to reduce the cost of maintaining the inmate population while enabling inmates to acquire or retain skills and work habits needed to secure honest employment after their release.

In exercising his power to enter into contracts to supply inmate labor as provided by this section, the Secretary of Public Safety shall not assign any inmate to work under any such contract who is eligible for work release as provided in this Article, study release as provided by G.S. 148-4(4), or who is eligible for a program of vocational rehabilitation services through the State Vocational Rehabilitation Agency, unless suitable work release employment or educational opportunity cannot be found for the inmate, and the inmate is not eligible for a program of vocational rehabilitation services through the State Vocational Rehabilitation Agency, and shall not agree to supply inmate labor for any project or service unless it meets all of the following criteria:

(1)   The project or service involves a type of work by which inmates can develop a skill to better equip themselves to return to society;

(2)   The project or service is of benefit to the citizens of North Carolina or units of State or local government thereof, regardless of whether the project or service is performed on public or private property;

(3)   Repealed by Session Laws 1977, c. 824, s. 2.

(4)   Wages shall be paid in an amount not exceeding one dollar ($1.00) per day per inmate by the local or State contracting agency.

(b)   As many minimum custody prisoners as are available and fit for road work, who cannot appropriately be placed on work release, study release, or other full-time programs, and as many medium custody prisoners as are available, fit for road work and can be adequately guarded during such work without reducing security levels at prison units, shall be employed in the maintenance and construction of public roads of the State. The number and location of prisoners to be kept available for work on the public roads shall be agreed upon by the governing authorities of the Department of Transportation and the Division of Adult Correction of the Department of Public Safety far enough in advance of each budget to permit proper provisions to be made in the request for appropriations submitted by the Department of Transportation. Any dispute between the Departments will be resolved by the Governor. Prisoners so employed shall be compensated, at rates fixed by the Division of Adult Correction of the Department of Public Safety's rules and regulations for work performed; provided, that no prisoner working on the public roads under the provisions of this section shall be paid more than one dollar ($1.00) per day from funds provided by the Department of Transportation to the Division of Adult Correction of the Department of Public Safety for this purpose. The Division of Adult Correction of the Department of Public Safety and the Department of Transportation shall develop a program to be implemented no later than July 1, 1982, to the extent money is herein appropriated, which shall include:

(1)   The use of portable toilets for inmate road crews.

(c)   As many of the male prisoners available and fit for forestry work shall be employed in the development and improvement of state-owned forests as can be used for this purpose by the agencies controlling these forests.

(d)   The remainder of the able-bodied inmates of the State prison system shall be employed so far as practicable in prison industries and agriculture, giving preference to the production of food supplies and other articles needed by state-supported institutions or activities.

(e)   The Division of Adult Correction of the Department of Public Safety may make such contracts with departments, institutions, agencies, and political subdivisions of the State for the hire of prisoners to perform other appropriate work as will help to make the prisons as nearly self-supporting as is consistent with the purposes of their creation. The Division of Adult Correction of the Department of Public Safety may contract with any person or any group of persons for the hire of prisoners for forestry work, soil erosion control, water conservation, hurricane damage prevention, or any similar work certified by the Secretary of Environment and Natural Resources as beneficial in the conservation of the natural resources of this State. All contracts for the employment of prisoners shall provide that they shall be fed, clothed, quartered, guarded, and otherwise cared for by the Division of Adult Correction of the

Department of Public Safety. Such work may include but is not limited to work with State or local government agencies in cleaning, construction, landscaping and maintenance of roads, parks, nature trails, bikeways, cemeteries, landfills or other government-owned or operated facilities.

(e1)   The Division of Adult Correction of the Department of Public Safety may establish work assignments for inmates or allow inmates to volunteer in service projects that benefit units of State or local government or 501(c)(3) entities that serve the citizens of this State. The work assignments may include the use of inmate labor and the use of Division of Adult Correction of the Department of Public Safety resources in the production of finished goods. Any products made pursuant to this section shall not be subject to the provisions of Article 3A of Chapter 143 of the General Statutes and may be donated to the government unit or 501(c)(3) organization at no cost.

(f)   Adult inmates of the State prison system shall be prohibited from working at or being on the premises of any schools or institutions operated or administered by the Youth Development Section of the Division of Juvenile Justice of the Department of Public Safety unless a complete sight and sound barrier is erected and maintained during the course of the labor performed by the adult inmates.

(g)   The Division of Adult Correction of the Department of Public Safety shall establish rules, standards, and procedures for establishing inmate labor services contracts with any county or municipality expressing interest in contracting for inmate labor. (1933, c. 172, ss. 1, 14; 1957, c. 349, s. 5; 1967, c. 996, s. 13; 1971, c. 193; 1973, c. 1262, s. 86; 1975, c. 278; c. 506, ss. 1, 2; c. 682, s. 2; c. 716, s. 7; 1977, c. 771, s. 4; c. 802, s. 25.36; c. 824, ss. 1-3; 1981, c. 516; 1981 (Reg. Sess., 1982), c. 1400; 1989, c. 727, s. 218(156); 1997-443, s. 11A.123; 1999-237, s. 18.21; 2001-95, s. 8; 2007-398, s. 1; 2011-145, s. 19.1(h), (i), (l); 2012-83, ss. 59, 61.)

§ 148-26.1. Definitions.

The following definitions apply:

(1)   to (3) Repealed by Session Laws 1983, c. 709, s. 1, effective July 1, 1983.

(4) to (7) Repealed by Session Laws 1985, c. 226, s. 2, effective May 23, 1985.

(8) "State public work project" or "State public work": A useful service other than the construction of buildings performed on any land, or any structure thereon, belonging to any principal department of State government as defined in subdivision (6) above, including, but not limited to, State parks, campuses, playgrounds, highways, roads, lakes, forests and waterways.

(9) Repealed by Session Laws 1985, c. 226, s. 2, effective May 23, 1985. (1975, c. 682, s. 3; 1983, c. 709, s. 1; 1985, c. 226, s. 2.)

§§ 148-26.2 through 148-26.4. Repealed by Session Laws 1983, c. 709, s. 1, effective July 1, 1983.

§ 148-26.5. Pay and time allowances for work.

The provisions of G.S. 148-18 and 148-13 shall be applicable to inmate work on local or State public work projects contracted for by the Secretary of Public Safety as provided by G.S. 148-26 through 148-26.4. Travel, cost of inmate wages and custodial supervision expenses incurred by the Division of Adult Correction of the Department of Public Safety and arising out of a local or State public work project shall be reimbursed on a cost basis to the Division of Adult Correction of the Department of Public Safety by the local or State contracting agency. (1975, c. 682, s. 3; 2011-145, s. 19.1(h), (i).)

§ 148-27: Repealed by Session Laws 2007-398, s. 3, effective August 21, 2007.

§ 148-28. Sentencing prisoners to Central Prison; youthful offenders.

When a sentenced offender is to be taken to the Central Prison at Raleigh, a sheriff or other appropriate officer of the county shall cause such prisoner to be delivered with the proper commitment papers to the warden of the Central

Prison. A person under 16 years of age convicted of a felony shall not be imprisoned in the Central Prison at Raleigh unless:

(1)   The person was convicted of a capital felony; or

(2)   He has previously been imprisoned in a county jail or under the authority of the Division of Adult Correction of the Department of Public Safety upon conviction of a felony.

This provision shall not limit the authority of the Secretary of Public Safety from transferring a person under 16 years of age to Central Prison when in the Secretary's determination this person would not benefit from confinement in separate facilities for youthful offenders or when it has been determined that his presence would be detrimental to the implementation of programs designed for the benefit of other youthful offenders. Nor shall this provision limit the authority of the judges of the superior courts of this State or the Secretary of Public Safety from committing or transferring a person under 16 years of age to Central Prison for medical or psychiatric treatment. (1933, c. 172, s. 7; 1971, c. 691; 1973, c. 1262, s. 10; 1977, c. 711, s. 27; 1977, 2nd Sess., c. 1147, s. 32; 2011-145, s. 19.1(h), (i).)

§ 148-29. Transportation of convicts to prison; reimbursement to counties; sheriff's expense affidavit.

(a)   The sheriff having in charge any prisoner to be taken to the State prison system shall send the prisoner to the custody of the Division of Adult Correction of the Department of Public Safety after sentencing and the disposal of all pending charges against the prisoner, if no appeal has been taken. Beginning on the day after the Section of Prisons of the Division of Adult Correction has been notified by the sheriff that a prisoner is ready for transfer and the Division has informed the sheriff that bedspace is not available for that prisoner, and continuing through the day the prisoner is received by the Section of Prisons of the Division of Adult Correction, the Division of Adult Correction of the Department of Public Safety shall pay the county:

(1)   A standard sum set by the General Assembly in its appropriations acts for the cost of providing food, clothing, personal items, supervision, and necessary ordinary medical services to the prisoner awaiting transfer to the State prison system; and

(2) Extraordinary medical costs, as defined in G.S. 148-32.1(a), incurred by prisoners awaiting transfer to the State prison system.

If the Section of Prisons of the Division of Adult Correction determines that bedspace is not available for a prisoner after the sheriff has notified the Division that the prisoner is ready for transfer, reimbursement under this subsection shall be made beginning on the day after the sheriff gave the notification.

(b) The sheriff having in charge any parolee or post-release supervisee to be taken to the State prison system shall send the prisoner to the custody of the Division of Adult Correction of the Department of Public Safety after preliminary hearing held under G.S. 15A-1368.6(b) or G.S. 15A-1376(b). Beginning on the day after the Section of Prisons of the Division of Adult Correction has been notified by the sheriff that a prisoner is ready for transfer and the Division has informed the sheriff that bedspace is not available for that prisoner, and continuing through the day the prisoner is received by the Section of Prisons of the Division of Adult Correction, the Division of Adult Correction of the Department of Public Safety shall pay the county:

(1) A standard sum set by the General Assembly in its appropriations acts for the cost of providing food, clothing, personal items, supervision, and necessary ordinary medical services to the parolee or post-release supervisee awaiting transfer to the State prison system; and

(2) Extraordinary medical costs, as defined in G.S. 148-32.1(a), incurred by parolees or post-release supervisees awaiting transfer to the State prison system.

If the Section of Prisons of the Division of Adult Correction determines that bedspace is not available for a prisoner after the sheriff has notified the Division that the prisoner is ready for transfer, reimbursement under this subsection shall be made beginning on the day after the sheriff gave the notification.

(c) The sheriff shall file with the board of commissioners of his county a copy of his affidavit as to necessary guard, together with a copy of his itemized account of expenses, both certified to by him as true copies of those on file in his office. (1869-70, c. 180, s. 3; 1870-1, c. 124, s. 3; 1874-5, c. 107, s. 3; Code, ss. 3432, 3437, 3438; Rev., ss. 5398, 5399, 5400; C. S., ss. 7718, 7719, 7720; 1925, c. 163; 1933, c. 172, s. 18; 1957, c. 349, s. 10; 1967, c. 996, s. 13; 1977, c. 711, s. 28; 1977, 2nd Sess., c. 1147, s. 32; 1993, c. 257, s. 18; 1996,

2nd Ex. Sess., c. 18, s. 20.2(a); 1997-443, s. 19(a); 1999-237, s. 18.10(b); 2011-145, s. 19.1(h), (j).)

§ 148-30. Repealed by Session Laws 1977, c. 711, s. 33.

§ 148-31. Maintenance of Central Prison; warden; powers and duties.

The Central Prison shall be maintained in such a manner as to conform to all the requirements of Article XI of the State Constitution, relating to a State's prison. A suitable person shall be appointed warden of the Central Prison, and he shall succeed to and be vested with all the rights, duties, and powers heretofore vested by law in the superintendent of the State's prison or the warden thereof with respect to capital punishment, or any matter of discipline of the inmates of the prison not otherwise provided for in this Article. (1933, c. 172, s. 14.)

§ 148-32. Repealed by Session Laws 1977, c. 450, s. 2.

§ 148-32.1. Local confinement, costs, alternate facilities, parole, work release.

(a) Repealed by Session Laws 2009-451, s. 19.22A, effective July 1, 2009.

(b) In the event that the custodian of the local confinement facility certifies in writing to the clerk of the superior court in the county in which the local confinement facility is located that the local confinement facility is filled to capacity, or that the facility cannot reasonably accommodate any more prisoners due to segregation requirements for particular prisoners, or that the custodian anticipates, in light of local experiences, an influx of temporary prisoners at that time, or if the local confinement facility does not meet the minimum standards published pursuant to G.S. 153A-221, any judge of the district court in the district court district as defined in G.S. 7A-133 where the facility is located, or any superior court judge who has jurisdiction pursuant to G.S. 7A-47.1 or G.S. 7A-48 in a district or set of districts as defined in G.S. 7A-41.1 where the facility is located may order that a prisoner not housed pursuant to the Statewide Misdemeanant Confinement Program established in subsection (b2) of this section be transferred to any other qualified local confinement facility within that district or within another such district where space is available, including a satellite jail unit operated pursuant to G.S. 153A-230.3 if the prisoner is a non-violent misdemeanant, which local facility shall accept the transferred prisoner.

If no other local confinement facility is available and the reason for the requested transfer is that the local confinement facility that would be required to house the prisoner cannot reasonably accommodate any more prisoners due to segregation requirements for particular prisoners or the local facility does not meet the minimum standards published pursuant to G.S. 153A-221, then the judge may order that a prisoner not housed pursuant to the Statewide Misdemeanant Confinement Program established in subsection (b2) of this section be transferred to a facility operated by the Division of Adult Correction of the Department of Public Safety as designated by the Division of Adult Correction. In no event, however, shall a prisoner whose term of imprisonment is less than 30 days be assigned or ordered transferred to a facility operated by the Division of Adult Correction.

(b1)   It is the intent of the General Assembly to authorize the Division of Adult Correction to enter into voluntary agreements with counties to provide housing for misdemeanants serving periods of confinement of more than 90 days and up to 180 days, except for those serving a sentence for an impaired driving offense. It is further the intent of the General Assembly that the Division of Adult Correction, in conjunction with the North Carolina Sheriffs' Association, Inc., establish a program for housing misdemeanants serving periods of confinement of more than 90 days and up to 180 days, except for those serving sentences for an impaired driving offense. It is also the intent of the General Assembly that the Division of Adult Correction contract with the North Carolina Sheriffs' Association, Inc., to provide a service that identifies space in local confinement facilities that is available for housing these misdemeanants.

The General Assembly intends that the cost of housing and caring for these misdemeanants, including, but not limited to, care, supervision, transportation, medical, and any other related costs, be covered by State funds and not be imposed as a local cost. Therefore, the General Assembly intends that the funds in the Statewide Misdemeanant Confinement Fund established in G.S. 148-10.4 be used to provide funding to cover the costs of managing a system for providing that housing of misdemeanants in local confinement facilities as well as reimbursing the counties for housing and related expenses for those misdemeanants.

(b2) The Statewide Misdemeanant Confinement Program is established. The Program shall provide for the housing of misdemeanants from all counties serving sentences imposed for a period of more than 90 days and up to 180 days, except for those serving sentences for an impaired driving offense under G.S. 20-138.1. Those misdemeanants shall be confined in local confinement facilities except as provided in subsections (b3) and (b4) of this section. The Program shall address methods for the placement and transportation of inmates and reimbursement to counties for the housing of those inmates. Any county that voluntarily agrees to house misdemeanants from that county or from other counties pursuant to the Program may enter into a written agreement with the Division of Adult Correction to do so.

This Program shall only operate as long as sufficient State funds are available through the Statewide Misdemeanant Confinement Fund established in G.S. 148-10.4(c).

(b3) The custodian of a local confinement facility may request a judicial order to transfer a misdemeanant housed pursuant to the Statewide Misdemeanant Confinement Program to a facility operated by the Division of Adult Correction by certifying in writing to the clerk of the superior court in the county in which the local confinement facility is located that:

(1) The misdemeanant poses a security risk because the misdemeanant:

a. Poses a serious escape risk;

b. Exhibits violently aggressive behavior that cannot be contained and warrants a higher level of supervision;

c. Needs to be protected from other inmates, and the county jail facility cannot provide such protection;

d. Is a female or a person 18 years of age or younger, and the county jail facility does not have adequate housing for such prisoners;

e. Is in custody at a time when a fire or other catastrophic event has caused the county jail facility to cease or curtail operations; or

f. Otherwise poses an imminent danger to the staff of the county jail facility or to other prisoners in the facility.

(2) The misdemeanant requires medical or mental health treatment that the county decides can best be provided by the Division of Adult Correction.

(3) The local confinement facility that would be required to house the prisoner (i) cannot reasonably accommodate any more prisoners due to segregation requirements for particular prisoners, or the local facility does not meet the minimum standards published pursuant to G.S. 153A-221, and (ii) no other local confinement facility is available.

Upon receiving such request and certification in writing, any superior or district court judge for the district in which the local confinement facility is located may, after ascertaining that the request meets the criteria set forth in subdivision (1), (2), or (3) of this subsection, order the misdemeanant transferred to a unit of the State prison system designated by the Secretary of Public Safety or the Secretary's authorized representative. The Division of Adult Correction shall be reimbursed from the Statewide Misdemeanant Confinement Fund for the costs of housing the misdemeanant, including the care, supervision, and transportation of the misdemeanant.

(b4) A misdemeanant housed under the Statewide Misdemeanant Confinement Program established pursuant to subsection (b2) of this section may be transferred to a facility operated by the Division of Adult Correction if the North Carolina Sheriffs' Association, Inc., determines that the local confinement facilities available for housing misdemeanants under the Program are filled to capacity. The Division of Adult Correction shall be reimbursed from the Statewide Misdemeanant Confinement Fund for the costs of housing the misdemeanant, including the care, supervision, and transportation of the misdemeanant.

(c) When a prisoner sentenced for a conviction of impaired driving under G.S. 20-138.1 is assigned to a local confinement facility pursuant to this section, the clerk of the superior court in the county in which the sentence was imposed shall immediately forward a copy of the commitment order to the Post-Release Supervision and Parole Commission so that the prisoner will be eligible for parole pursuant to G.S. 15A-1371.

(d) When a prisoner serving a sentence of 30 days or more in a local confinement facility is placed on work release pursuant to a recommendation of the sentencing court, the custodian of the facility shall forward the prisoner's work-release earnings to the Division of Adult Correction, which shall disburse the earnings as determined under G.S. 148-33.1(f). When a prisoner serving a sentence of 30 days or more in a local confinement facility is placed on work release pursuant to an order of the sentencing court, the custodian of the facility shall forward the prisoner's work-release earnings to the clerk of the court that sentenced the prisoner or to the Division of Adult Correction, as provided in the prisoner's commitment order. The clerk or the Division, as appropriate, shall disburse the earnings as provided in the prisoner's commitment order. Upon agreement between the Division of Adult Correction and the custodian of the local confinement facility, however, the clerk may disburse to the local confinement facility the amount of the earnings to be paid for the cost of the prisoner's keep, and that amount shall be set off against the reimbursement to be paid by the Department to the local confinement facility pursuant to G.S. 148-32.1(a).

(e)   Upon entry of a prisoner serving a sentence of imprisonment for impaired driving under G.S. 20-138.1 into a local confinement facility pursuant to this section, the custodian of the local confinement facility shall forward to the Post-Release Supervision and Parole Commission information pertaining to the prisoner so as to make him eligible for parole consideration pursuant to G.S. 15A-1371. Such information shall include date of incarceration, jail credit, and such other information as may be required by the Post-Release Supervision and Parole Commission. The Post-Release Supervision and Parole Commission shall approve a form upon which the custodian shall furnish this information, which form will be provided to the custodian by the Division of Adult Correction. (1977, c. 450, s. 3; c. 925, s. 2; 1981, c. 859, s. 25; 1985, c. 226, s. 3(1), (2); 1985 (Reg. Sess., 1986), c. 1014, ss. 199, 201(e); 1987, c. 7, ss. 2, 6; 1987 (Reg. Sess., 1988), c. 1037, s. 120; c. 1100, s. 17.4(a); 1989, c. 1, s. 2; c. 761, s. 3; 1991, c. 217, s. 6; 1993, c. 538, s. 33; 1994, Ex. Sess., c. 14, s. 65; c. 24, s. 14(b); 1995, c. 324, s. 19.9(f); 1997-456, s. 23; 2004-199, s. 48; 2004-203, s. 54; 2009-451, s. 19.22A; 2011-145, s. 19.1(h), (i); 2011-192, s. 7(a), (d), (e), (g).)

§ 148-32.2. Community work crew fee.

The Division of Adult Correction of the Department of Public Safety may charge a fee to any unit of local government to which it provides, upon request, a community work crew. The amount of the fee shall be no more than the cost to the Division to provide the crew to the unit of local government, not to exceed a daily rate of one hundred fifty dollars ($150.00) per work crew. (2009-451, s. 19.24; 2011-145, s. 19.1(h).)

§ 148-33. Prison labor furnished other State agencies.

The Division of Adult Correction of the Department of Public Safety may furnish to any of the other State departments, State institutions, or agencies, upon such conditions as may be agreed upon from time to time between the Division and the governing authorities of such Department, institution or agency, prison labor for carrying on any work where it is practical and desirable to use prison labor in the furtherance of the purposes of any State department, institution or agency, and such other employment as is now provided by law for inmates of the State's prison under the provisions of G.S. 148-6: Provided that such prisoners shall at all times be under the custody of and controlled by the duly authorized agent of such Division. Provided, further, that notwithstanding any provisions of law contained in this Article or in this Chapter, no prisoner or group of prisoners may be assigned to work in any building utilized by any State department, agency, or institution unless a duly designated custodial agent of the Secretary of Public Safety is assigned to the building to maintain supervision and control of the prisoner or prisoners working there. (1933, c. 172, s. 30; 1957, c. 349, s. 10; 1961, c. 966; 1967, c. 996, ss. 13, 15; 1973, c. 1262, s. 10; 2007-398, s. 4; 2011-145, s. 19.1(h), (i); 2012-83, s. 61.)

§ 148-33.1. Sentencing, quartering, and control of prisoners with work-release privileges.

(a)   Whenever a person is sentenced to imprisonment for a term to be served in the State prison system or a local confinement facility, the Secretary of Public Safety may authorize the Director of Prisons or the custodian of the local confinement facility to grant work-release privileges to any inmate who is eligible for work release and who has not been granted work-release privileges by order of the sentencing court. The Secretary of Public Safety shall authorize immediate work-release privileges for any person serving a sentence not exceeding five years in the State prison system and for whom the presiding judge shall have recommended work-release privileges when (i) it is verified that appropriate employment for the person is available in an area where, in the judgment of the Secretary, the Division of Adult Correction of the Department of Public Safety has facilities to which the person may suitably be assigned, and (ii) custodial and correctional considerations would not be adverse to releasing the person without supervision into the free community.

(b)   Repealed by Session Laws 1981, c. 541, s. 2.

(c) The Division of Adult Correction of the Department of Public Safety shall from time to time, as the need becomes evident, designate and adapt facilities in the State prison system for quartering prisoners with work-release privileges. No State or county prisoner shall be granted work-release privileges by the Director of Prisons or the custodian of a local confinement facility until suitable facilities for quartering him have been provided in the area where the prisoner has employment or the offer of employment.

(d) The Secretary of Public Safety is authorized and directed to establish a work-release plan under which an eligible prisoner may be released from actual custody during the time necessary to proceed to the place of his employment, perform his work, and return to quarters designated by the prison authorities. If the prisoner shall violate any of the conditions prescribed by prison rules and regulations for the administration of the work-release plan, then such prisoner may be withdrawn from work-release privileges, and the prisoner may be transferred to the general prison population to serve out the remainder of his sentence. Rules and regulations for the administration of the work-release plan shall be established in the same manner as other rules and regulations for the government of the State prison system.

(e) The State Department of Labor shall exercise the same supervision over conditions of employment for persons working in the free community while serving sentences imposed under this section as the Department does over conditions of employment for free persons.

(f) A prisoner who is convicted of a felony and who is granted work-release privileges shall give his work-release earnings, less standard payroll deductions required by law, to the Division of Adult Correction of the Department of Public Safety. A prisoner who is convicted of a misdemeanor, is committed to a local confinement facility, and is granted work-release privileges by order of the sentencing court shall give his work-release earnings, less standard payroll deductions required by law, to the custodian of the local confinement facility. Other misdemeanants granted work-release privileges shall give their work-release earnings, less standard payroll deductions required by law, to the Division of Adult Correction of the Department of Public Safety. The Division of Adult Correction of the Department of Public Safety or the sentencing court, as appropriate, shall determine the amount to be deducted from a prisoner's work-release earnings to pay for the cost of the prisoner's keep and to accumulate a reasonable sum to be paid the prisoner when he is paroled or discharged from prison. The Division or sentencing court shall also determine the amount to be disbursed by the Division or clerk of court, as appropriate, for each of the following:

(1)   To pay travel and other expenses of the prisoner made necessary by his employment;

(2)   To provide a reasonable allowance to the prisoner for his incidental personal expenses;

(3)   To make payments for the support of the prisoner's dependents in accordance with an order of a court of competent jurisdiction, or in the absence of a court order, in accordance with a determination of dependency status and need made by the local department of social services in the county of North Carolina in which such dependents reside;

(3a)   To make restitution or reparation as provided in G.S. 148-33.2.

(4)   To comply with an order from any court of competent jurisdiction regarding the payment of an obligation of the prisoner in connection with any judgment rendered by the court.

(5)   To comply with a written request by the prisoner to withhold an amount, when the request has been granted by the Division or the sentencing court, as appropriate.

Any balance of his earnings remaining at the time the prisoner is released from prison shall be paid to him. The Social Services Commission is authorized to promulgate uniform rules and regulations governing the duties of county social services departments under this section.

(g)   No prisoner employed in the free community under the provisions of this section shall be deemed to be an agent, employee, or involuntary servant of the State prison system while working in the free community or going to or from such employment.

(h)   Any prisoner employed under the provisions of this section shall not be entitled to any benefits under Chapter 96 of the General Statutes entitled "Employment Security" during the term of the sentence.

(i)   No recommendation for work release shall be made at the time of sentencing in any case in which the presiding judge shall suspend the imposition of sentence and place a convicted person on probation; however, if probation be subsequently revoked and the active sentence of imprisonment executed, the court may at that time recommend work release. Neither a recommendation for work release by the court or the decision of the Secretary of Public Safety to place a person on work release shall give rise to any vested statutory right to an individual to be placed on or continued on work release.

(j) The provisions of subsections (f), (g), and (h) of this section shall also apply to prisoners employed in private prison enterprises conducted pursuant to G.S. 148-70. (1957, c. 540; 1959, c. 126; 1961, c. 420; 1963, c. 469, ss. 1, 2; 1967, c. 684; c. 996, s. 13; 1969, c. 982; 1973, c. 476, s. 138; c. 1262, s. 10; 1975, c. 22, ss. 1-3; c. 679, s. 3; 1977, c. 450, ss. 4, 5; c. 614, s. 6; c. 623, ss. 1, 2; c. 711, s. 29; 1977, 2nd Sess., c. 1147, s. 32; 1981, c. 541, ss. 1-3; 1985, c. 474, s. 3; 1985 (Reg. Sess., 1986), c. 1014, s. 201(f)-(i); 1991 (Reg. Sess., 1992), c. 902, s. 6; 2011-145, s. 19.1(h), (i); 2012-83, s. 61.)

§ 148-33.2. Restitution by prisoners with work-release privileges.

(a) Repealed by Session Laws 1985, c. 474, s. 4.

(b) As a rehabilitative measure, the Secretary of Public Safety is authorized to require any prisoner granted work-release privileges to make restitution or reparation to an aggrieved party from any earnings gained by the defendant while on work release when the sentencing court recommends that restitution or reparation be paid by the defendant out of any earnings gained by the defendant if he is granted work-release privileges and out of other resources of the defendant, including all real and personal property owned by the defendant and the income derived from such property. The Secretary shall not be bound by such recommendation, but if they elect not to implement the recommendation, they shall state in writing the reasons therefor, and shall forward the same to the sentencing court.

(c) When an active sentence is imposed, the court shall consider whether, as a rehabilitative measure, it should recommend to the Secretary of Public Safety that restitution or reparation be made by the defendant out of any earnings gained by the defendant if he is granted work-release privileges and out of other resources of the defendant, including all real and personal property owned by the defendant, and income derived from such property. If the court determines that restitution or reparation should not be recommended, it shall so indicate on the commitment. If, however, the court determines that restitution or reparation should be recommended, the court shall make its recommendation a part of the order committing the defendant to custody. The recommendation shall be in accordance with the applicable provisions of G.S. 15A-1343(d) and Article 81C of Chapter 15A of the General Statutes. If the offense is one in which there is evidence of physical, mental or sexual abuse of a minor, the court may order the defendant to pay from work release earnings the cost of rehabilitative treatment for the minor. The Administrative Office of the Courts shall prepare and distribute forms which provide ample space to make restitution or reparation recommendations incident to commitments, which forms shall be conveniently structured to enable the sentencing court to make its recommendation.

(d) The Secretary of Public Safety shall establish rules and regulations to implement this section, which shall include adequate notice to the prisoner that the payment of restitution or reparation from any earnings gained by the prisoner while on work release is being considered as a condition of any work-release privileges granted the prisoner, and opportunity for the prisoner to be heard. Such rules and regulations shall also provide additional methods whereby facts may be obtained to supplement the recommendation of the sentencing court. (1977, c. 614, s. 7; 1977, 2nd Sess., c. 1147, s. 33; 1981, c. 541, ss. 4-9; 1985, c. 474, s. 4; 1987, c. 397, ss. 2, 3; c. 598, s. 5; 1998-212, s. 19.4(g); 2011-145, s. 19.1(i).)

§§ 148-34 through 148-35. Repealed by Session Laws 1957, c. 349, s. 11.

§ 148-36. Secretary of Public Safety to control classification and operation of prison facilities.

All facilities established or acquired by the Division of Adult Correction of the Department of Public Safety shall be under the administrative control and direction of the Secretary of Public Safety, and operated under rules and regulations proposed by the Secretary and adopted by the Division of Adult Correction of the Department of Public Safety as provided in G.S. 148-11. Subject to such rules and regulations, the Secretary shall classify the facilities of the State prison system and develop a variety of programs so as to permit proper segregation and treatment of prisoners according to the nature of the offenses committed, the character and mental condition of the prisoners, and such other factors as should be considered in providing an individualized system of discipline, care, and correctional treatment of persons committed to the Division. The Secretary of Public Safety, or his authorized representative, shall designate the places of confinement where sentences to imprisonment in the State's prison system shall be served. The Secretary or his representative may designate any available facility appropriate for the individual in view of custodial and correctional considerations. (1931, c. 145, s. 28; c. 277, s. 8; 1933, c. 46, ss. 3, 4; c. 172, ss. 4, 17; 1943, c. 409; 1955, c. 238, s. 7; 1957, c. 349, s. 10; 1967, c. 996, s. 7; 1973, c. 1262, s. 10; 2011-145, s. 19.1(h), (i); 2012-83, s. 61.)

§ 148-37. Additional facilities authorized; contractual arrangements.

(a) Subject to the provisions of G.S. 143-341, the Division of Adult Correction of the Department of Public Safety may establish additional facilities for use by the Division, such facilities to be either of a permanent type of construction or of a temporary or movable type as the Division may find most advantageous to the particular needs, to the end that the prisoners under its supervision may be so distributed throughout the State as to facilitate individualization of treatment designed to prepare them for lawful living in the community where they are most likely to reside after their release from prison. For this purpose, the Division may purchase or lease sites and suitable lands adjacent thereto and erect necessary buildings thereon, or purchase or lease existing facilities, all within the limits of allotments as approved by the Department of Administration.

(b) The Secretary of Public Safety may contract with the proper official of the United States or of any county or city of this State for the confinement of federal prisoners after they have been sentenced, county, or city prisoners in facilities of the State prison system or for the confinement of State prisoners in any county or any city facility located in North Carolina, or any facility of the United States Bureau of Prisons, when to do so would most economically and effectively promote the purposes served by the Division of Adult Correction of the Department of Public Safety. Except as otherwise provided, any contract made under the authority of this subsection shall be for a period of not more than two years, and shall be renewable from time to time for a period not to exceed two years. Contracts made under the authority of this subsection for the confinement of State prisoners in local or district confinement facilities may be for a period of not more than 10 years and renewable from time to time for a period not to exceed 10 years, and shall be subject to the approval of the Council of State and the Department of Administration after consultation with the

Joint Legislative Commission on Governmental Operations. Contracts for receiving federal, county and city prisoners shall provide for reimbursing the State in full for all costs involved. The financial provisions shall have the approval of the Department of Administration before the contract is executed. Payments received under such contracts shall be deposited in the State treasury for the use of the Division of Adult Correction of the Department of Public Safety. Such payments are hereby appropriated to the Division of Adult Correction of the Department of Public Safety as a supplementary fund to compensate for the additional care and maintenance of such prisoners as are received under such contracts.

(b1)   Recodified as G.S. 148-37.2 by Session Laws 2001-84, s. 1, effective May 17, 2001.

(c)   In addition to the authority contained in subsections (a) and (b) of this section, and in addition to the contracts ratified by subsection (f) of this section, the Secretary of Public Safety may enter into contracts with any public entity or any private nonprofit or for-profit firms for the confinement and care of State prisoners in any out-of-state correctional facility when to do so would most economically and effectively promote the purposes served by the Division of Adult Correction of the Department of Public Safety. Contracts entered into under the authority of this subsection shall be for a period not to exceed two years and shall be renewable from time to time for a period not to exceed two years. Prisoners may be sent to out-of-state correctional facilities only when there are no available facilities in this State within the State prison system to appropriately house those prisoners. Any contract made under the authority of this subsection shall be approved by the Department of Administration before the contract is executed. Before expending more than the amount specifically appropriated by the General Assembly for the out-of-state housing of inmates, the Division shall obtain the approval of the Joint Legislative Commission on Governmental Operations and shall report such expenditures to the Chairs of the Senate and House Appropriations Committees, the Chairs of the Senate and House Appropriations Subcommittees on Justice and Public Safety, and the Chairs of the Joint Legislative Oversight Committee on Justice and Public Safety.

(d)   Prisoners confined in out-of-state correctional facilities pursuant to subsection (c) of this section shall remain subject to the rules adopted for the conduct of persons committed to the State prison system. The rules regarding good time and gain time, discipline, classification, extension of the limits of confinement, transfers, housing arrangements, and eligibility for parole shall apply to inmates housed in those out-of-state correctional facilities. The operators of those out-of-state correctional facilities may promulgate any other rules as may be necessary for the operation of those facilities with the written approval of the Secretary of Public Safety. Custodial officials employed by an out-of-state correctional facility are agents of the Secretary of Public Safety and may use those procedures for use of force authorized by the Secretary of Public Safety not inconsistent with the laws of the State of situs of the facility to defend themselves, to enforce the observance of discipline in compliance with correctional facility rules, to secure the person of a prisoner, and to prevent escape. Prisoners confined to out-of-state correctional facilities may be required to perform reasonable work assignments within those facilities. Private firms under subsection (c) of this section shall employ inmate disciplinary and grievance policies of the Division of Adult Correction of the Department of Public Safety.

(e)   Repealed by Session Laws 1995, c. 324, s. 19.10.

(f)   Any contracts entered into by the Division of Adult Correction of the Department of Public Safety with public contractors prior to March 25, 1994, for the out-of-state housing of inmates are ratified.

(g)   The Secretary of Public Safety may contract with private for-profit or nonprofit firms for the provision and operation of four or more confinement facilities totaling up to 2,000 beds in the State to house State prisoners when to do so would most economically and effectively promote the purposes served by the Division of Adult Correction of the Department of Public Safety. This 2,000-bed limitation shall not apply to the 500 beds in private substance abuse treatment centers authorized by the General Assembly prior to July 1, 1995. Whenever the Division of Adult Correction of the Department of Public Safety determines that new prison facilities are required in addition to existing and planned facilities, the Division may contract for any remaining beds authorized by this section before constructing State-operated facilities.

Contracts entered under the authority of this subsection shall be for a period not to exceed 10 years, shall be renewable from time to time for a period not to exceed 10 years. The Secretary of Public Safety shall enter contracts under this subsection only if funds are appropriated for this purpose by the General Assembly. Contracts entered under the authority of this subsection may be subject to any requirements for the location of the confinement facilities set forth by the General Assembly in appropriating those funds.

Once the Division has made a determination to contract for additional private prison beds, it shall issue a request for proposals within 30 days of the decision. The request for proposals shall require bids to be submitted within two months, and the Division shall award contracts at the earliest practicable date after the submission of bids. The Secretary of Public Safety, in consultation with the Chairs of the Joint Legislative Oversight Committee on Justice and Public Safety and the Chairs of the House and Senate Appropriations Subcommittees on Justice and Public Safety, shall make recommendations to the State Purchasing Officer on the final award decision. The State Purchasing Officer shall make the final award decision, and the contract shall then be subject to the approval of the Council of State after consultation with the Joint Legislative Commission on Governmental Operations.

Contracts made under the authority of this subsection may provide the State with an option to purchase the confinement facility or may provide for the purchase of the confinement facility by the State. Contracts made under the authority of this subsection shall state that plans and specifications for private confinement facilities shall be furnished to and reviewed by the Office of State Construction. The Office of State Construction shall inspect and review each project during construction to ensure that the project is suitable for habitation and to determine whether the project would be suitable for future acquisition by the State. All contracts for the housing of State prisoners in private confinement facilities shall require a minimum of ten million dollars ($10,000,000) of occurrence-based liability insurance and shall hold the State harmless and provide reimbursement for all liability arising out of actions caused by operations and employees of the private confinement facility.

Prisoners housed in private confinement facilities pursuant to this subsection shall remain subject to the rules adopted for the conduct of persons committed to the State prison system. The Secretary of Public Safety may review and approve the design and construction of private confinement facilities before housing State prisoners in these facilities. The rules regarding good time, gain time, and earned credits, discipline, classification, extension of the limits of confinement, transfers, housing arrangements, and eligibility for parole shall apply to inmates housed in private confinement facilities pursuant to this subsection. The operators of private confinement facilities may adopt any other rules as may be necessary for the operation of those facilities with the written approval of the Secretary of Public Safety. Custodial officials employed by a private confinement facility are agents of the Secretary of Public Safety and may use those procedures for use of force authorized by the Secretary of Public Safety to defend themselves, to enforce the observance of discipline in compliance with confinement facility rules, to secure the person of a prisoner, and to prevent escape. Private firms under this subsection shall employ inmate disciplinary and grievance policies of the Division of Adult Correction of the Department of Public Safety.

(h)   Private confinement facilities under this section shall be designed, built, and operated in accordance with applicable State laws, court orders, fire safety codes, and local regulations.

(i)   The Division of Adult Correction of the Department of Public Safety shall make a written report no later than March 1 of every odd-numbered year, beginning in 1997, on the substance of all outstanding contracts for the housing of State prisoners entered into under the authority of this section. The report shall be submitted to the Council of State, the Department of Administration, the Joint Legislative Commission on Governmental Operations, and the Joint Legislative Oversight Committee on Justice and Public Safety. In addition to the report, the Division of Adult Correction of the Department of Public Safety shall provide information on contracts for the housing of State prisoners as requested by these groups. (1933, c. 172, s. 19; 1957, c. 349, s. 10; 1967, c. 996, s. 8; 1973, c. 1262, s. 10; 1975, c. 879, s. 46; 1977, 2nd Sess., c. 1147, s. 34; 1994, Ex. Sess., c. 24, s. 16(a), (b); 1995, c. 324, s. 19.10(a), (b); c. 507, s. 19; 1996, 2nd Ex. Sess., c. 18, s. 20.18; 1997-443, ss. 21.4(c)-(e); 1999-237, s. 18.20(a); 2001-84, s. 1; 2001-138, s. 2; 2011-145, s. 19.1(h), (i); 2011-291, ss. 2.56-2.58; 2012-83, s. 61.)

§ 148-37.1.   Prohibition on private prisons housing out-of-state inmates.

(a)   Except as otherwise provided in this section or authorized by North Carolina law, no municipality, county, or private entity may authorize, construct, own, or operate any type of correctional facility for the confinement of inmates serving sentences for violation of the laws of a jurisdiction other than North Carolina.

(b)   The provisions of this section shall not apply to facilities owned or operated by the federal government and used exclusively for the confinement of inmates serving sentences for violation of federal law, but only to the extent that such facilities are not subject to restriction by the states under the provisions of the United States Constitution. (2000-67, s. 16.3(a).)

§ 148-37.2. Lease-purchase of prison facilities.

(a)   Authorization. - The Secretary of Public Safety may, as provided in this section, enter contracts with private for-profit or nonprofit firms for the construction of close security correctional facilities described in subsection (a1) of this section to be operated by the Division pursuant to a lease that contains a schedule for purchase of the facilities over a period of up to 20 years.

The State, with the prior approval of the Council of State and the State Treasurer as provided in this section, is authorized to execute and deliver one or more lease-purchase agreements with a special nonprofit corporation providing for the lease-purchase by the State of the Projects from the special nonprofit corporation in connection with and under an arrangement whereby certificates of participation are sold and delivered by the special nonprofit corporation in order to provide funds to pay the purchase price of the Projects. The Projects will be constructed by selected contractors designated to the special nonprofit corporation by the State Property Office of the Department of Administration in consultation with the Division of Adult Correction of the Department of Public Safety. The Projects will be sold to the special nonprofit corporation, with the purchase price paid by the special nonprofit corporation from the proceeds of the certificates of participation. The State may lease the real property upon which the Projects will be located, if owned by the State, to the selected contractors constructing the Projects and to the special nonprofit corporation for nominal consideration.

(a1)   Facilities Authorized. - The following facilities are authorized under this section:

(1)   2001 Facilities. - Three close security correctional facilities totaling up to 3,000 cells.

(2)   2003 Facilities. - Three close security correctional facilities substantially identical to the facilities described in subdivision (1) of this subsection and totaling up to 3,000 cells. If the State and the special nonprofit corporation are able to negotiate a contract for one or more of these facilities with the construction contractor that constructed the facilities described in subdivision (1) of this subsection on terms that are reasonable and desirable to the State as determined by the State Treasurer, the Secretary of Administration, and the Council of State, then a request for proposals under subsection (c) of this section is not required. The remaining provisions of this section continue to apply.

(b) Definitions. - The following definitions apply in this section:

(1) Certificates of participation. - Certificates or other instruments delivered by a special nonprofit corporation as provided in this section evidencing the assignment of proportionate and undivided interests in the rights to receive lease payments to be made by the State pursuant to a lease-purchase agreement.

(2) Construction contract agreement. - Either of the following:

a. A contract between the Division of Adult Correction of the Department of Public Safety and the selected contractors for construction of the Projects, under which the selected contractors will be responsible for arranging for and obtaining their own construction financing, which will consist solely of private funds.

b. A contract between the special nonprofit corporation and the selected contractors for construction of the Projects, but only if the contract has provisions sufficient to carry out the requirements of the last paragraph of subsection (c) of this section. The Secretary of Public Safety shall determine the sufficiency of the contract and shall approve the contract only if it is sufficient.

(3) Lease-purchase agreement. - A lease-purchase agreement entered into pursuant to this section, under which the State will lease the Projects from the special nonprofit corporation, with option to purchase.

(4) Projects. - Facilities described in subsection (a1) of this section to be constructed by selected contractors, sold to the special nonprofit corporation, and leased to the State pursuant to this section.

(5) Purchase agreement. - A contract under which the special nonprofit corporation will purchase the Projects from the selected contractors.

(6) Selected contractors. - One or more private firms selected to construct the Projects.

(7) Special nonprofit corporation. - A nonprofit corporation created under Chapter 55A of the General Statutes and designated by the State Treasurer for entering into the transactions contemplated by this act.

(c) Request for Proposals. - The Secretary of Public Safety may issue a request for proposals to private firms for the private firms to construct the Projects in accordance with plans and specifications developed by the Division of Adult Correction of the Department of Public Safety and reviewed by the Office of State Construction.

The Secretary of Public Safety shall make recommendations to the State Property Office of the Department of Administration on the final award decision. The Division of Adult Correction of the Department of Public Safety and the State Property Office of the Department of Administration shall consult with the Joint Legislative Commission on Governmental Operations before making the final award decision. The Department of Administration shall make the final award decision, which shall then be subject to the approval of the Council of State. If the contract for construction of the 2003 facilities is entered into with the construction contractor who constructed the 2001 facilities as provided by subdivision (a1)(2) of this section, the general terms and conditions of the construction contract for the 2003 facilities shall be substantially similar to the terms and conditions of the construction contracts for the construction of the 2001 facilities, including, without limitation, terms and conditions regarding the activities, performance, and construction standards required of the contractor, the arrangements for selection and retention of subcontractors by the contractor, and the responsibility of the contractor for the performance by the selected subcontractors. The construction contract for the 2003 facilities may, however, contain any changes from the construction contracts for the 2001 facilities that may be necessary or desirable to reflect the financing arrangements for the 2003 facilities, including provisions for the periodic payment of construction costs based upon construction progress.

The Division of Adult Correction of the Department of Public Safety will enter into a construction contract agreement with the selected contractors for the construction of the Projects or, alternatively, the construction contract may be entered into with the selected contractor by the special nonprofit corporation, with the approval of the Division of Adult Correction of the Department of Public Safety. The special nonprofit corporation will enter into a purchase agreement with the selected contractors for the sale of the Projects to the special nonprofit corporation. With respect to the 2003 facilities, the purchase agreement may provide for the periodic payment by the special nonprofit corporation to the selected contractor of portions of the purchase price during the construction of the 2003 facilities on the basis of construction progress, rather than a payment of the entire purchase price upon delivery of the 2003 facilities. The Division of Adult Correction of the Department of Public Safety shall furnish plans and specifications for review by the State Construction Office. Construction contract agreements entered into under this section shall provide that the Division of Adult Correction of the Department of Public Safety and the Office of State Construction shall inspect and review each facility during construction to ensure and determine jointly that the facility is suitable for use as a correctional facility and for future acquisition by the State. The Division of Adult Correction of the Department of Public Safety may contract with a design consortium for construction administration services.

(d) Approval of Lease-Purchase Agreement. - A lease-purchase agreement may not be entered into pursuant to this section unless the following conditions are met before the lease-purchase agreement is entered into: (i) the Council of State, by resolution, approves the execution and delivery of the lease-purchase agreement, and (ii) the State Treasurer approves the lease-purchase agreement and all other documentation related to it, including any leasehold deed of trust or trust agreement in connection with it. The resolution of the Council of State may include any matters the Council of State determines. In determining whether to approve the lease-purchase agreement, the State Treasurer may consider any factors as the State Treasurer considers relevant in order to find and determine that all of the following conditions are met:

(1) The principal amount to be financed under the lease-purchase agreement is adequate and not excessive for the purpose of paying the cost of the Projects.

(2) The increase, if any, in State revenues necessary to pay the sums to become due under the lease-purchase agreement is not excessive.

(3) The lease-purchase agreement can be entered into on terms desirable to the State.

(4) The sale of certificates of participation will not have an adverse effect on any scheduled or proposed sale of obligations of the State or any State agency or of any unit of local government in the State.

(e) Terms and Conditions. - The following provisions apply to a lease-purchase agreement entered into under this section:

(1) In order to secure the performance by the State of its obligations under the lease-purchase agreement, the lease-purchase agreement may require the eviction of the State from the occupancy of one or more of the Projects in the

event that the State breaches its obligations and agreements under the lease-purchase agreement.

(2)   No deficiency judgment may be rendered against the State or any agency, department, or commission of the State in any action for breach of any obligation contained in the lease-purchase agreement or any other related documentation, and the taxing power of the State or any agency, department, or commission of the State is not and may not be pledged to secure any moneys due under the lease-purchase agreement.

(3)   The lease-purchase agreement shall not contain a nonsubstitution clause that restricts the right of the State to replace or provide a substitute for the Projects.

(4)   The lease-purchase agreement may include provisions requesting the Governor to submit in the Governor's budget proposal, or any amendments or supplements to it, appropriations necessary to make the payments required under the lease-purchase agreement.

(5)   The lease-purchase agreement may contain any provisions for protecting and enforcing the rights and remedies of the special nonprofit corporation that are reasonable and proper and not in violation of law, including covenants setting forth the duties of the State with respect to the Projects, which may include provisions relating to insuring, operating, and maintaining the Projects and the custody, safeguarding, investment, and application of moneys.

(6)   The lease-purchase agreement may designate the lease payments to be paid by the State under it to be "principal components" and "interest components." Any interest component of the lease payments may be calculated based upon a fixed or variable interest rate or rates as determined by the State Treasurer.

(7)   The lease-purchase agreement may be entered into by the State, and certificates of participation may be delivered by the special nonprofit corporation, at any time, including at times prior to the delivery of the completed Projects to the special nonprofit corporation, and the related delivery of occupancy of the Projects to the State by the special nonprofit corporation. The lease-purchase agreement may require the State to make prepayments of lease payments at a time prior to when the State accepts occupancy of the Projects. The lease-purchase agreement and related financing arrangements may provide for the funding of interest during construction from the proceeds of

certificates of participation. The costs incurred in connection with the preparation of the lease-purchase agreement and related documents and the delivery of the certificates of participation may be paid from the proceeds of the certificates of participation.

(8) The State is authorized to agree in the lease-purchase agreement to indemnify the special corporation and its directors and agents for any liabilities that arise to the special corporation or directors or agents on account of their participation in the activities contemplated by this act.

(f) Faith and Credit Not Pledged. - The payment of amounts payable by the State under the lease-purchase agreement and other related documentation during any fiscal biennium or fiscal year is limited to funds appropriated for that purpose by the General Assembly in its discretion. No provision of this section and no lease-purchase agreement creates any pledge of the faith and credit of the State or any agency, department, or commission of the State within the meaning of any constitutional debt limitation.

(g) Certificates of Participation. - The State may cooperate as necessary to effectuate the delivery by the special nonprofit corporation of tax-exempt certificates of participation, including participating in the preparation of offering documents, the filing of required tax forms and agreeing to comply with restrictions on the use of the Projects as required in order for the interest component of the lease payments to be tax-exempt. Disclosures and compliance with other federal law requirements by the special nonprofit corporation shall be under the direction of the State Treasurer. Certificates of participation may be sold at the direction of the State Treasurer in the manner, either at public or private sale, and for any price or prices that the State Treasurer determines to be in the best interest of the State and to effect the purposes of this section. Interest payable with respect to certificates of participation shall accrue at the rate or rates determined by the State Treasurer with the approval of the special nonprofit corporation.

Certificates of participation may be delivered pursuant to a trust agreement with a corporate trustee approved by the State Treasurer. The corporate trustee may be any trust company or bank having the powers of a trust company within or without the State. A trust agreement may (i) provide for security and pledges and assignments with respect to the security as may be permitted under this section and further provide for the enforcement of any lien or security interest created pursuant to this section, and (ii) contain any provisions for protecting and enforcing the rights and remedies of the owners of any certificates of participation that are reasonable and proper and not in violation of law as determined by the State Treasurer. The State Treasurer shall designate the professionals providing legal or financial services relating to the lease-purchase agreement and the delivery of certificates of participation, including the provider of any credit facility and the underwriter or placement agent for any certificates of participation.

(h)   Tax Exemption. - The lease-purchase agreement and any certificates of participation relating to it shall at all times be free from taxation by the State or any political subdivision or any of their agencies, excepting estate, inheritance, or gift taxes, income taxes on the gain from the transfer of the lease-purchase agreement and certificates of participation, and franchise taxes. The interest component of the lease payments made by the State under the lease-purchase agreement, including the interest payable with respect to any certificates of participation, is not subject to taxation as income.

(i)   Licensing Requirements. - The private for-profit or nonprofit firms authorized to respond to requests for proposals authorized by this section, or entitled to be a selected contractor pursuant to this section, need not be a licensed general contractor within the meaning of G.S. 87-1 so that providing a response to the request or entering a construction contract agreement or purchase agreement is not general contracting within the meaning of G.S. 87-1. This subsection does not remove the actual construction of any prison facility from the provisions of G.S. 87-1.

(j)   Minority Business Participation. - G.S. 143-128.2 applies to the Projects authorized in this section.

(k)   Upon completion of the construction of a facility authorized by this section and the commencement of the State's leasehold interest pursuant to the terms of a valid lease-purchase agreement:

(1)   The facility shall not be subject to county or municipal building codes and requirements and shall not be subject to inspection by any county or municipal authorities under G.S. 143-135.1.

(2)   The Department of Administration may exercise all powers and perform all duties set forth in G.S. 143-341 regarding the facility.

(3)   The Commissioner of Insurance shall conduct the inspections, reviews, and examinations of the facility set forth in G.S. 58-31-40 and shall conduct

electrical inspections of the facility pursuant to G.S. 143-143.2. (1999-237, s. 18.20(a); 2001-84, s. 1; 2001-202, s. 1; 2003-284, s. 47.1; 2005-98, s. 1; 2011-145, s. 19.1(h), (i).)

§ 148-37.3. Authority of private correctional officers employed pursuant to a contract with the Federal Bureau of Prisons.

(a)   Correctional officers and security supervisors employed at private correctional facilities pursuant to a contract between their employer and the Federal Bureau of Prisons may, in the course of their employment as correctional officers or security supervisors, use necessary force and make arrests consistent with the laws applicable to the Division of Adult Correction of the Department of Public Safety, which force shall not exceed that authorized to Division of Adult Correction of the Department of Public Safety officers, provided that the employment policies of such private corporations meet the same minimum standards and practices followed by the Division of Adult Correction of the Department of Public Safety in employing its correctional personnel, and if:

(1)   Those correctional officers and security supervisors have been certified as correctional officers as provided under Chapter 17C of the General Statutes; or

(2)   Those correctional officers and security supervisors employed by the private corporation at the facility have completed a training curriculum that meets or exceeds the standards required by the North Carolina Criminal Justice Education and Training Standards Commission for correctional personnel.

(b)   Any private corporation described in subsection (a) of this section shall without limit defend, indemnify, and hold harmless the State, its officers, employees, and agents from any claims arising out of the operation of the private correctional facility, or the granting of the powers authorized under this section, including any attorneys' fees or other legal costs incurred by the State, its officers, employees, or agents as a result of such claims.

(c)   Any private corporation described in subsection (a) of this section shall reimburse the State and any county or other law enforcement agency for the full cost of any additional expenses incurred by the State or the county or other law enforcement agency in connection with the pursuit and apprehension of an escaped inmate from the facility.

In the event of an escape from the facility, any private corporation described in subsection (a) of this section shall immediately notify the sheriff in the county in which the facility is located, who shall cause an immediate entry into the State Bureau of Investigation Division of Criminal Information network. The sheriff of the county in which the facility is located shall be the lead law enforcement officer in connection with the pursuit and apprehension of an escaped inmate from the facility.

(d)   Any private corporation described in subsection (a) of this section must maintain in force liability insurance to satisfy any final judgment rendered against the private corporation or the State, its officers, employees, and agents that arises out of the operation of the correctional facility or the indemnification requirements in subsection (b) of this section. The minimum amount of liability insurance that will be required under this section is ten million dollars ($10,000,000) per occurrence, and twenty-five million dollars ($25,000,000) aggregate per occurrence.

(e)   Repealed by Session Laws 2007-162, s. 1, effective July 1, 2007.

(f)   The authority set forth in this section to use necessary force and make arrests shall be in addition to any existing authority set forth in the statutory or common law of the State, but shall not exceed the authority to use necessary force and make arrests set out in subsection (a) of this section.

(g)   A private corporation described in subsection (a) of this section shall bear the reasonable costs of services provided by the State, its officers, employees, and agents for the corporation. The amount of the costs shall be determined by the member of the Council of State or Cabinet member of the agency or department that provided the services.

(h)   This section is effective August 18, 2001 and applies to private correctional facilities and the employees of those correctional facilities constructed and contracted to be operated by August 18, 2001. (2001-378, ss. 1-7; 2003-351, s. 1; 2007-162, s. 1; 2011-145, s. 19.1(h); 2012-83, s. 61.)

§§ 148-38 through 148-39. Repealed by Session Laws 1957, c. 349, s. 11.

§ 148-40. Recapture of escaped prisoners.

The rules and regulations for the government of the State prison system may provide for the recapture of convicts that may escape, or any convicts that may have escaped from the State's prison or prison camps, or county road camps of this State, and the Division of Adult Correction of the Department of Public Safety may pay to any person recapturing an escaped convict such reward or expense of recapture as the regulations may provide. Any citizen of North Carolina shall have authority to apprehend any convict who may escape before the expiration of his term of imprisonment whether he be guilty of a felony or misdemeanor, and retain him in custody and deliver him to the Division of Adult Correction of the Department of Public Safety. (1933, c. 172, s. 21; 1955, c. 238, s. 8; 1957, c. 349, s. 10; 1967, c. 996, s. 13; 2011-145, s. 19.1(h); 2012-83, s. 61.)

§ 148-41. Recapture of escaping prisoners; reward.

The Secretary of Public Safety shall use every means possible to recapture, regardless of expense, any prisoners escaping from or leaving without permission any of the State prisons, camps, or farms. When any person who has been confined or placed to work escapes from the State prison system, the Secretary shall immediately notify the Governor, and accompany the notice with a full description of the escaped prisoner, together with such information as will aid in the recapture. The Governor may offer such rewards as he may deem desirable and necessary for the recapture and return to the State prison system of any person who may escape or who heretofore has escaped therefrom. Such reward earned shall be paid by warrant of the Division of Adult Correction of the Department of Public Safety and accounted for as a part of the expense of maintaining the State's prisons. (1873-4, c. 158, s. 13; Code, s. 3442; Rev., s. 5407; 1917, c. 236; c. 286, s. 13; C. S., ss. 7742, 7743; 1925, c. 163; 1933, c. 172, s. 18; 1935, c. 414, s. 16; 1943, c. 409; 1955, c. 238, s. 9; c. 279, s. 3; 1957, c. 349, s. 10; 1967, c. 996, ss. 13, 15; 1973, c. 1262, s. 10; 2011-145, s. 19.1(h), (i); 2012-83, s. 61.)

§ 148-42. Repealed by Session Laws 1977, c. 711, s. 33.

§ 148-43. Repealed by Session Laws 1963, c. 1174, s. 5.

§ 148-44. Separation as to sex.

The Department shall provide quarters for female prisoners separate from those for male prisoners. (1933, c. 172, s. 25; 1947, c. 262, s. 2; 1957, c. 349, s. 10; 1963, c. 1174, s. 2; 1985, c. 226, s. 3(3).)

§ 148-45. Escaping or attempting escape from State prison system; failure of conditionally and temporarily released prisoners and certain youthful offenders to return to custody of Division of Adult Correction of the Department of Public Safety.

(a) Any person in the custody of the Division of Adult Correction of the Department of Public Safety in any of the classifications hereinafter set forth who shall escape from the State prison system, shall for the first such offense, except as provided in subsection (g) of this section, be guilty of a Class 1 misdemeanor:

(1) A prisoner serving a sentence imposed upon conviction of a misdemeanor;

(2) A person who has been charged with a misdemeanor and who has been committed to the custody of the Division of Adult Correction of the Department of Public Safety under the provisions of G.S. 162-39;

(3) Repealed by Session Laws 1985, c. 226, s. 4.

(4) A person who shall have been convicted of a misdemeanor and who shall have been committed to the Division of Adult Correction of the Department of Public Safety for presentence diagnostic study under the provisions of G.S. 15A-1332(c).

(b) Any person in the custody of the Division of Adult Correction of the Department of Public Safety, in any of the classifications hereinafter set forth, who shall escape from the State prison system, shall, except as provided in subsection (g) of this section, be punished as a Class H felon.

(1) A prisoner serving a sentence imposed upon conviction of a felony;

(2) A person who has been charged with a felony and who has been committed to the custody of the Division of Adult Correction of the Department of Public Safety under the provisions of G.S. 162-39;

(3) Repealed by Session Laws 1985, c. 226, s. 5.

(4) A person who shall have been convicted of a felony and who shall have been committed to the Division of Adult Correction of the Department of Public Safety for presentence diagnostic study under the provisions of G.S. 15A-1332(c); or

(5) Any person previously convicted of escaping or attempting to escape from the State prison system.

(c) Repealed by Session Laws 1979, c. 760, s. 5.

(d) Any person who aids or assists other persons to escape or attempt to escape from the State prison system shall be guilty of a Class 1 misdemeanor.

(e) Repealed by Session Laws 1983, c. 465, s. 5.

(f) Any person convicted of an escape or attempt to escape classified as a felony by this section shall be immediately classified and treated as a convicted felon even if such person has time remaining to be served in the State prison system on a sentence or sentences imposed upon conviction of a misdemeanor or misdemeanors.

(g) (1) Any person convicted and in the custody of the Division of Adult Correction of the Department of Public Safety and ordered or otherwise assigned to work under the work-release program, G.S. 148-33.1, or any convicted person in the custody of the Division of Adult Correction of the Department of Public Safety and temporarily allowed to leave a place of confinement by the Secretary of Public Safety or his designee or other authority of law, who shall fail to return to the custody of the Division of Adult Correction of the Department of Public Safety, shall be guilty of the crime of escape and subject to the applicable provisions of this section and shall be deemed an escapee. For the purpose of this subsection, escape is defined to include, but is not restricted to, willful failure to return to an appointed place and at an appointed time as ordered.

(2) If a person, who would otherwise be guilty of a first violation of G.S. 148-45(g)(1), voluntarily returns to his place of confinement within 24 hours of the time at which he was ordered to return, such person shall not be charged with an escape as provided in this section but shall be subject to such administrative action as may be deemed appropriate for an escapee by the Division of Adult

Correction of the Department of Public Safety; said escapee shall not be allowed to be placed on work release for a four-month period or for the balance of his term if less than four months; provided, however, that if such person commits a subsequent violation of this section then such person shall be charged with that offense and, if convicted, punished under the provisions of this section. (1933, c. 172, s. 26; 1955, c. 279, s. 2; 1963, c. 681; 1965, c. 283; 1967, c. 996, s. 13; 1973, c. 1120; c. 1262, s. 10; 1975, cc. 170, 241, 705; c. 770, ss. 1, 2; 1977, c. 732, ss. 3, 4; c. 745; 1979, c. 760, s. 5; 1979, 2nd Sess., c. 1316, s. 47; 1981, c. 63, s. 1; c. 179, s. 14; 1983, c. 465, ss. 1-5; 1985, c. 226, ss. 3(4)-6; 1993, c. 539, ss. 1058, 1321, 1322; 1994, Ex. Sess., c. 24, s. 14(c); 1997-443, s. 19.25(t); 2011-145, s. 19.1(h), (i); 2012-83, s. 61.)

§ 148-46. Degree of protection against violence allowed.

(a) When any prisoner, or several combined shall offer violence to any officer, overseer, or guard, or to any fellow prisoner, or attempt to do any injury to the prison building, or to any workshop, or other equipment, or shall attempt to escape, or shall resist, or disobey any lawful command, the officer, overseer, or guard shall use any means necessary to defend himself, or to enforce the observance of discipline, or to secure the person of the offender, and to prevent an escape.

(b) A misdemeanor prisoner classified and treated as a convicted felon as the result of a consecutive felony sentence or sentences, or a convicted felon placed in the custody of the Secretary of Public Safety pending the outcome of an appeal, or a defendant charged with a felony or felonies and placed in the custody of the Secretary of Public Safety pending trial, shall be considered as a convicted felon in the custody of the Secretary of Public Safety against whom any means reasonably necessary, including deadly force, may be used to prevent an escape. (1933, c. 172, s. 27; 1975, c. 230; 2011-145, s. 19.1(i).)

§ 148-46.1. Inflicting or assisting in infliction of self injury to prisoner resulting in incapacity to perform assigned duties.

Any person serving a sentence or sentences within the State prison system who, during the term of such imprisonment, willfully and intentionally inflicts upon himself any injury resulting in a permanent or temporary incapacity to perform work or duties assigned to him by the Division of Adult Correction of the Department of Public Safety, or any prisoner who aids or abets any other prisoner in the commission of such offense, shall be punished as a Class H felon. (1959, c. 1197; 1967, c. 996, s. 13; 1979, c. 760, s. 5; 1979, 2nd Sess., c. 1316, s. 47; 1981, c. 63, s. 1; c. 179, s. 14; 1993, c. 539, s. 1323; 1994, Ex. Sess., c. 24, s. 14(c); 1997-443, s. 19.25(v); 2011-145, s. 19.1(h); 2012-83, s. 61.)

§ 148-46.2. Procedure when consent is refused by prisoner.

When the Secretary of Public Safety finds as a fact that the injury to any prisoner was willfully and intentionally self-inflicted and that an operation or treatment is necessary for the preservation or restoration of the health of the prisoner and that the prisoner is competent to act for himself or herself; and that attempts have been made to obtain consent for the proposed operation or treatment but such consent was refused, and the findings have been reduced to writing and entered into the prisoner's records as a permanent part thereof, then the chief medical officer of the prison hospital or prison institution shall be authorized to give or withhold, on behalf of the prisoner, consent to the operation or treatment.

In all cases coming under the provisions of this section, the medical staff of the hospital or institution shall keep a careful and complete medical record of the treatment and surgical procedures undertaken. The record shall be signed by the chief medical officer of the hospital or institution and the surgeon performing any surgery. Any treatment of self-inflicted injuries shall also be subject to the provisions of G.S. 90-21.13 and G.S. 90-21.16. (1959, c. 1196; 1967, c. 996, s. 15; 1969, c. 982; 1973, c. 1262, s. 10; 1981, c. 307, ss. 4-7, 9; 2004-203, s. 53(b); 2011-145, s. 19.1(i).)

§ 148-47. Disposition of child born of female prisoner.

Any child born of a female prisoner while she is in custody shall as soon as practicable be surrendered to the director of social services of the county wherein the child was born upon a proper order of the domestic relations court or juvenile court of said county affecting the custody of said child. When it appears to be for the best interest of the child, the court may place custody beyond the geographical bounds of Wake County: Provided, however, that all subsequent proceedings and orders affecting custody of said child shall be within the jurisdiction of the proper court of the county where the infant is residing at the time such proceeding is commenced or such order is sought: Provided, further, that nothing in this section shall affect the right of the mother to consent to the adoption of her child nor shall the right of the mother to place her child with the legal father or other suitable relative be affected by the provisions of this section. (1933, c. 172, s. 28; 1955, c. 1027; 1961, c. 186; 1969, c. 982.)

§ 148-48. Parole powers of Parole Commission unaffected.

Nothing in this Chapter shall be construed to limit or restrict the power of the Parole Commission to parole prisoners under such conditions as it may impose or prevent the reimprisonment of such prisoners upon violation of the conditions of such parole, as now provided by law. (1933, c. 172, s. 29; 1955, c. 867, s. 8; 1973, c. 1262, s. 10.)

§ 148-49. Prison indebtedness not assumed by Board of Transportation.

The Board of Transportation shall not assume or pay off any part of the deficit of the State prison existing on March 22, 1933. (1933, c. 172, s. 33; 1973, c. 507, s. 5.)

Article 3A.

Facilities and Programs for Youthful Offenders.

§§ 148-49.1 through 148-49.9: Repealed by Session Laws 1977, c. 732, s. 1.

Article 3B.

Facilities and Programs for Youthful Offenders.

§§ 148-49.10 through 148-49.16: Repealed by Session Laws 1993, c. 538, s. 34.

Article 4.

Paroles.

§§ 148-50 through 148-51: Repealed by Session Laws 1955, c. 867, s. 13.

§ 148-51.1. Repealed by Session Laws 1985, c. 226, s. 9, effective May 23, 1985.

§ 148-52. Repealed by Session Laws 1973, c. 1262, s. 10.

§ 148-52.1. Prohibited political activities of member of Post-Release Supervision and Parole Commission.

No member of the Post-Release Supervision and Parole Commission shall be permitted to use his position to influence elections or the political action of any person, serve as a member of the campaign committee of any political party, interfere with or participate in the preparation for any election or the conduct thereof at the polling place, or be in any manner concerned in the demanding, soliciting or receiving of any assessments, subscriptions or contributions, whether voluntary or involuntary, to any political party. Any Post-Release Supervision and Parole Commission member who shall violate any of the provisions of this section shall be subject to dismissal from office. (1953, c. 17, s. 4; 1973, c. 1262, s. 10; 1981, c. 260; 1993, c. 538, s. 44; 1994, Ex. Sess., c. 24, s. 14(b).)

§ 148-53. Investigators and investigations of cases of prisoners.

For the purpose of investigating the cases of prisoners, the Division of Adult Correction of the Department of Public Safety is hereby authorized and empowered to appoint an adequate staff of competent investigators, particularly qualified for such work, with such reasonable clerical assistance as may be required, who shall, under the rules and regulations duly adopted by the Post-Release Supervision and Parole Commission, investigate all cases designated by it, investigate cases of prisoners eligible for post-release supervision, and otherwise aid the Commission in passing upon the question of the parole and post-release supervision of prisoners, to the end that every prisoner in the custodial care of the State may receive full, fair, and just consideration. (1935, c. 414, s. 3; 1955, c. 867, s. 2; 1973, c. 1262, s. 10; 1977, c. 704, s. 3; c. 711, s. 30; 1977, 2nd Sess., c. 1147, s. 32; 1993, c. 538, s. 45; 1994, Ex. Sess., c. 24, s. 14(b); 2011-145, s. 19.1(h).)

§ 148-54. Parole and post-release supervision supervisors provided for; duties.

The Division of Adult Correction of the Department of Public Safety is hereby authorized to appoint a sufficient number of competent parole and post-release supervision supervisors, who shall be particularly qualified for and adapted for the work required of them, and who shall under the direction of the Division of Adult Correction of the Department of Public Safety, and under regulations prescribed by the Division of Adult Correction of the Department of Public Safety after consultation with the Commission, exercise supervision and authority over paroled prisoners and persons on post-release supervision, assist paroled prisoners and persons on post-release supervision, and those who are to be paroled or released for post-release supervision in finding and retaining self-supporting employment, and to promote rehabilitation work with paroled and post-release supervised prisoners, to the end that they may become law-abiding citizens. The supervisors shall also, under the direction of the Division of Adult Correction of the Department of Public Safety, maintain frequent contact with paroled and post-release supervised prisoners and find out whether or not they are observing the conditions of their paroles or post-release supervision, and assist them in every possible way toward compliance with the conditions, and they shall perform such other duties in connection with paroled prisoners as the Division of Adult Correction of the Department of Public Safety may require. The number of supervisors may be increased by the Division of Adult Correction of the Department of Public Safety as and when the number of paroled and post-release supervised prisoners to be supervised requires or justifies such increase. (1935, c. 414, s. 4; 1955, c. 867, s. 11; 1973, c. 1262, s. 10; 1977, c. 704, s. 4; 1993, c. 538, s. 46; 1994, Ex. Sess., c. 24, s. 14(b); 2011-145, s. 19.1(h).)

§ 148-54.1. Repealed by Session Laws 1955, c. 867, s. 13.

§ 148-55. Repealed by Session Laws 1973, c. 1262, s. 10.

§ 148-56. Assistance in supervision of parolees or post-release supervisees and preparation of case histories.

Upon request by the Post-Release Supervision and Parole Commission, the county directors of social services shall assist in the supervision of parolees and shall prepare and submit to the Post-Release Supervision and Parole Commission case histories or other information in connection with any case under consideration for parole or some form of executive clemency. (1935, c. 414, s. 6; 1955, c. 867, s. 9; 1961, c. 186; 1969, c. 982; 1973, c. 1262, s. 10; 1993, c. 538, s. 47; 1994, Ex. Sess., c. 24, s. 14(b).)

§ 148-57. Rules and regulations for parole consideration.

The Post-Release Supervision and Parole Commission is hereby authorized and empowered to set up and establish rules and regulations in accordance with which prisoners eligible for parole consideration may have their cases reviewed and by which such proceedings may be initiated and considered. That the rules and regulations shall include but not be limited to, a plan whereby the Post-Release Supervision and Parole Commission may determine parole eligibility, and, when eligibility is so approved, provide for parole of a prisoner to a plan approved by the Secretary of Public Safety. (1935, c. 414, s. 7; 1955, c. 867, s. 4; 1973, c. 1262, s. 10; 1977, c. 704, s. 2; 1993, c. 538, s. 48; 1994, Ex. Sess., c. 24, s. 14(b); 2011-145, s. 19.1(i).)

§ 148-57.1. Restitution as a condition of parole or post-release supervision.

(a)   Repealed by Session Laws 1985, c. 474, s. 5.

(b)   As a rehabilitative measure, the Post-Release Supervision and Parole Commission is authorized to require a prisoner to whom parole or post-release supervision is granted to make restitution or reparation to an aggrieved party as a condition of parole or post-release supervision when the sentencing court recommends that restitution or reparation to an aggrieved party be made a condition of any parole or post-release supervision granted the defendant. When imposing restitution as a condition and setting up a payment schedule for the restitution, the Post-Release Supervision and Parole Commission shall take into consideration the resources of the defendant, including all real and personal property owned by the defendant and the income derived from such property, his ability to earn, and his obligation to support dependents. The Post-Release Supervision and Parole Commission shall not be bound by such recommendation, but if it elects not to implement the recommendation, it shall state in writing the reasons therefor, and shall forward the same to the sentencing court.

(c) When an active sentence is imposed, the court shall consider whether, as a rehabilitative measure, it should recommend to the Post-Release Supervision and Parole Commission that restitution or reparation by the defendant be made a condition of any parole or post-release supervision granted the defendant. If the court determines that restitution or reparation should not be recommended, it shall so indicate on the commitment. If, however, the court determines that restitution or reparation should be recommended, the court shall make its recommendation a part of the order committing the defendant to custody. The recommendation shall be in accordance with the applicable provisions of Article 81C of Chapter 15A of the General Statutes. The Administrative Office of the Courts shall prepare and distribute forms which provide ample space to make restitution or reparation recommendations incident to commitments, which forms shall be conveniently structured to enable the sentencing court to make its recommendation.

If the offense is one in which there is evidence of physical, mental or sexual abuse of a minor, the court may order, as a condition of parole or post-release supervision, that the defendant pay the cost of any rehabilitative treatment for the minor.

(d) The Post-Release Supervision and Parole Commission shall establish rules and regulations to implement this section, which shall include adequate notice to the prisoner that the payment of restitution or reparation by the prisoner is being considered as a condition of any parole or post-release supervision granted the prisoner, and opportunity for the prisoner to be heard. Such rules and regulations shall also provide additional methods whereby facts may be obtained to supplement the recommendation of the sentencing court. (1977, c. 614, s. 8; 1977, 2nd Sess., c. 1147, s. 36; 1985, c. 474, s. 5; 1987, c. 397, s. 4; c. 598, s. 4; 1993, c. 538, s. 49; 1994, Ex. Sess., c. 24, s. 14(b); 1998-212, s. 19.4(h).)

§§ 148-58 through 148-58.1. Repealed by Session Laws 1977, c. 711, s. 33.

§ 148-59. Duties of clerks of superior courts as to commitments; statements filed with Division of Adult Correction of the Department of Public Safety.

The several clerks of the superior courts shall attach to the commitment of each prisoner sentenced in such courts a statement furnishing such information as the Post-Release Supervision and Parole Commission shall by regulations prescribe, which information shall contain, among other things, the following:

(1) The court in which the prisoner was tried;

(2) The name of the prisoner and of all codefendants;

(3) The date or session when the prisoner was tried;

(4) The offense with which the prisoner was charged and the offense for which convicted;

(5) The judgment of the court and the date of the beginning of the sentence;

(6) The name and address of the presiding judge;

(7) The name and address of the prosecuting solicitor;

(8) The name and address of private prosecuting attorney, if any;

(9) The name and address of the arresting officer;

(10) All available information of the previous criminal record of the prisoner; and

(11) For all Class G or more serious felonies, the names and addresses of the following persons, where the presiding judge makes a finding of such facts:

a. Any victims of the offense for which the prisoner was convicted;

b. The parent or legal guardian of any minor victims of the offense for which the prisoner was convicted; and

c. The next of kin of any homicide victims of the offense for which the prisoner was convicted.

The prison authorities receiving the prisoner for the beginning of the service of sentence shall detach from the commitment the statement furnishing such information and forward it to the Division of Adult Correction of the Department of Public Safety, together with any additional information in the possession of such prison authorities relating to the previous criminal record of such prisoner, and the information thus furnished shall constitute the foundation and file of the prisoner's case. Forms for furnishing the information required by this section shall, upon request, be furnished to the said clerks by the Division of Adult Correction of the Department of Public Safety without charge. (1935, c. 414, s. 9; 1953, c. 17, s. 2; 1955, c. 867, s. 12; 1957, c. 349, s. 10; 1967, c. 996, s. 13; 1973, c. 108, s. 90; c. 1262, s. 10; 1993, c. 538, s. 50; 1994, Ex. Sess., c. 12, s. 2; c. 24, s. 14(b); 2011-145, s. 19.1(h); 2012-83, s. 61.)

§ 148-60. Repealed by Session Laws 1977, c. 711, s. 33.

§ 148-60.1. Allowances for paroled prisoner and prisoner on post-release supervision.

Upon the release of any prisoner upon parole or post-release supervision, the superintendent or warden of the institution shall provide the prisoner with suitable clothing and, if needed, an amount of money sufficient to purchase transportation to the place within the State where the prisoner is to reside. The Post-Release Supervision and Parole Commission may, in its discretion, provide that the prisoner shall upon his release on parole or post-release supervision receive a sum of money of at least forty-five dollars ($45.00). (1953, c. 17, s. 8; 1973, c. 1262, s. 10; 1987 (Reg. Sess., 1988), c. 1086, s. 120(b); 1993, c. 538, s. 51; 1994, Ex. Sess., c. 24, s. 14(b).)

§§ 148-60.2 through 148-62. Repealed by Session Laws 1977, c. 711, s. 33.

§ 148-62.1. Entitlement of indigent parolee and post-release supervisee to counsel, in discretion of Post-Release Supervision and Parole Commission.

Any parolee or post-release supervisee who is an indigent under the terms of G.S. 7A-450(a) may be determined entitled, in the discretion of the Post-

Release Supervision and Parole Commission, to the services of counsel at State expense at a parole revocation hearing at which either:

(1) The parolee or post-release supervisee claims not to have committed the alleged violation of the parole or post-release supervision conditions; or

(2) The parolee or post-release supervisee claims there are substantial reasons which justified or mitigated the violation and make revocation inappropriate, even if the violation is a matter of public record or is uncontested, and that the reasons are complex or otherwise difficult to develop or present; or

(3) The parolee or post-release supervisee is incapable of speaking effectively for himself;

and where the Commission feels, on a case by case basis, that such appointment in accordance with either (1), (2) or (3) above is necessary for fundamental fairness.

If the parolee or post-release supervisee is determined to be indigent and entitled to services of counsel, counsel shall be appointed in accordance with rules adopted by the Office of Indigent Defense Services. (1973, c. 1116, s. 2; 1993, c. 538, s. 52; 1994, Ex. Sess., c. 24, s. 14(b); 2000-144, s. 45.)

§ 148-63. Arrest powers of police officers.

Any officer who is authorized to make arrests of fugitives from justice shall have full authority and power to arrest any parolee whose parole has been revoked or any post-release supervisee who has been revoked. (1935, c. 414, s. 13; 1993, c. 538, s. 53; 1994, Ex. Sess., c. 24, s. 14(b).)

§ 148-64. Cooperation of prison and parole officials and employees.

The officials and employees of the Division of Adult Correction of the Department of Public Safety and the Post-Release Supervision and Parole Commission shall at all times cooperate with and furnish each other such information and assistance as will promote the purposes of this Chapter and the purposes for which these agencies were established. The Commission shall have free access to all prisoners. (1935, c. 414, s. 14; 1955, c. 867, s. 7; 1967, c. 996, ss. 11, 15; 1973, c. 1262, s. 10; 1993, c. 538, s. 54; 1994, Ex. Sess., c. 24, s. 14(b); 2011-145, s. 19.1(h).)

§ 148-64.1. Early conditional release of inmates subject to a removal order; revocation of release.

(a) Eligibility for Early Release. - Notwithstanding any other provision of law, the Post-Release Supervision and Parole Commission may conditionally release an inmate into the custody and control of United States Immigration and Customs Enforcement if all of the following requirements are satisfied:

(1) The Division of Adult Correction of the Department of Public Safety has received a final order of removal for the inmate from United States Immigration and Customs Enforcement.

(2) The inmate was convicted of a nonviolent criminal offense and is incarcerated for that offense. If the inmate was convicted of and is incarcerated for more than one offense, then all of the offenses of which the inmate was convicted and is incarcerated must be nonviolent criminal offenses. As used in this subdivision, the term "nonviolent criminal offense" means a conviction for an impaired driving offense or a felony violation of any of the following:

a. G.S. 14-54.

b. G.S. 14-56.

c. G.S. 14-71.1.

d. G.S. 14-100, where the thing of value is less than one hundred thousand dollars ($100,000).

e. G.S. 90-95(d)(4).

(3) The inmate has served at least half of the minimum sentence imposed by the court or, in the case of an inmate convicted of an impaired driving offense under G.S. 20-138.1, the inmate has met all of the parole eligibility requirements under G.S. 15A-1371, notwithstanding G.S. 20-179(p)(3).

(4) The inmate was not convicted of an impaired driving offense resulting in death or serious bodily injury, as that term is defined in G.S. 14-32.4.

(5) The inmate agrees not to reenter the United States unlawfully.

(b) Release Is Discretionary. - The decision to release an inmate once the requirements of subsection (a) of this section are satisfied is in the sole, unappealable discretion of the Post-Release Supervision and Parole Commission.

(c) Return of Inmates. - In the event that the United States Immigration and Customs Enforcement is unable to or does not deport the inmate, the inmate shall be returned to the custody of the Division of Adult Correction of the Department of Public Safety to serve the remainder of the original sentence.

(d) Unlawful Reentry Constitutes Violation. - An inmate released pursuant to this section who returns unlawfully and willfully to the United States violates the conditions of the inmate's early release.

(e) Arrest Authority. - An inmate who violates the conditions of the inmate's early release is subject to arrest by a law enforcement officer.

(f) Effect of Violation. - Upon notification from any federal or state law enforcement agency that the inmate is in custody, and after notice and opportunity to be heard, the Post-Release Supervision and Parole Commission shall revoke the inmate's release and reimprison the inmate for a period equal to the inmate's maximum sentence minus time already served by the inmate upon a finding that an inmate has violated the conditions of the inmate's early release.

(g) Violators Ineligible for Future Release. - Upon revocation of release under this subsection, the inmate shall not be eligible for any future release under this section or for any other release from confinement, other than post-release supervision, until the remainder of the sentence of imprisonment is served. (2008-199, s. 3; 2011-145, s. 19.1(h).)

§ 148-65. Repealed by Session Laws 1955, c. 867, s. 13.

Article 4A.

Out-of-State Parolee Supervision.

§ 148-65.1: Repealed by Session Laws 2002-166, s. 2, effective October 23, 2003.

§ 148-65.1A: Repealed by Session Laws 2002-166, s. 2, effective October 23, 2003.

§ 148-65.2: Repealed by Session Laws 2002-166, s. 2, effective October 23, 2003.

§ 148-65.3: Repealed by Session Laws 2002-166, s. 2, effective October 23, 2003.

Article 4B.

Interstate Compact for Adult Offender Supervision.

§ 148-65.4. Short title.

This Article may be cited as "The Interstate Compact for Adult Offender Supervision." (2002-166, s. 1; 2008-189, s. 1.)

§ 148-65.5. Governor to execute compact; form of compact.

The Governor of North Carolina is authorized and directed to execute a compact on behalf of the State of North Carolina with any state of the United States legally joining therein in the form substantially as follows:

Preamble.

Whereas: The Interstate Compact for the Supervision of Parolees and Probationers was established in 1937, it is the earliest corrections "compact" established among the states, and has not been amended since its adoption over 62 years ago;

Whereas: This compact is the only vehicle for the controlled movement of adult parolees and probationers across state lines, and it currently has jurisdiction over more than a quarter of a million offenders;

Whereas: The complexities of the compact have become more difficult to administer, and many jurisdictions have expanded supervision expectations to include currently unregulated practices such as victim input, victim notification requirements, and sex offender registration;

Whereas: After hearings, national surveys, and a detailed study by a task force appointed by the National Institute of Corrections, the overwhelming recommendation has been to amend the document to bring about an effective management capacity that addresses public safety concerns and offender accountability;

Whereas: The General Assembly hereby finds, determines, and declares that this act is necessary for the immediate preservation of the public peace, health, and safety. The Governor is hereby authorized and directed to enter into a compact on behalf of the State of North Carolina with any state of the United States and other territorial possessions of the United States legally joining therein in the form substantially as follows;

Whereas: Upon the adoption of this Interstate Compact for Adult Offender Supervision, it is the intention of the General Assembly to repeal the previous Interstate Compact for the Supervision of Parolees and Probationers one year after the effective date of this compact.

Article I.

Purpose.

(a) The compacting states to this Interstate Compact recognize that each state is responsible for the supervision of adult offenders in the community who are authorized pursuant to the bylaws and rules of this compact to travel across state lines both to and from each compacting state in such a manner as to track the location of offenders, transfer supervision authority in an orderly and efficient manner, and when necessary return offenders to the originating jurisdictions. The compacting states also recognize that Congress, by enacting the Crime Control Act, 4 U.S.C. § 112 (1965), has authorized and encouraged compacts for cooperative efforts and mutual assistance in the prevention of crime.

(b) It is the purpose of this compact and the Interstate Commission created hereunder, through means of joint and cooperative action among the compacting states:

(1) To provide the framework for the promotion of public safety and to protect the rights of victims through the control and regulation of the interstate movement of offenders in the community;

(2) To provide for the effective tracking, supervision, and rehabilitation of these offenders by the sending and receiving states; and

(3) To equitably distribute the costs, benefits, and obligations of the compact among the compacting states.

(c) In addition, this compact will:

(1) Create an Interstate Commission which will establish uniform procedures to manage the movement between states of adults placed under community supervision and released to the community under the jurisdiction of courts, paroling authorities, corrections, or other criminal justice agencies, which will promulgate rules to achieve the purpose of this compact;

(2) Ensure an opportunity for input and timely notice to victims and to jurisdictions where defined offenders are authorized to travel or to relocate across state lines;

(3) Establish a system of uniform data collection, access to information on active cases by authorized criminal justice officials, and regular reporting of compact activities to heads of state councils, state executive, judicial, and legislative branches and criminal justice administrators;

(4) Monitor compliance with rules governing interstate movement of offenders and initiate interventions to address and correct noncompliance; and

(5) Coordinate training and education regarding regulations of interstate movement of offenders for officials involved in such activity.

(d)   The compacting states recognize that there is no "right" of any offender to live in another state and that duly accredited officers of a sending state may at all times enter a receiving state and there apprehend and retake any offender under supervision subject to the provision of this compact and bylaws and rules promulgated hereunder. It is the policy of the compacting states that the activities conducted by the Interstate Commission created herein are the formation of the public policies and are therefore public business.

Article II.

Definitions.

(a)   As used in this compact, unless the context clearly requires a different construction:

(1)   "Adult" means both individuals legally classified as adults and juveniles treated as adults by court order, statute, or operation of law.

(2)   "Bylaws" means those bylaws established by the Interstate Commission for its governance, or for directing or controlling the Interstate Commission's actions or conduct.

(3)   "Compact Administrator" means the individual in each compacting state appointed pursuant to the terms of this compact responsible for the administration and management of the state's supervision and transfer of offenders subject to the terms of this compact, the rules adopted by the Interstate Commission, and policies adopted by the state council under this compact.

(4)   "Compacting state" means any state that has enacted the enabling legislation for this compact.

(5)   "Commissioner" means the voting representative of each compacting state appointed pursuant to Article III of this compact.

(6)   "Interstate Commission" means the Interstate Commission for Adult Offender Supervision established by this compact.

(7) "Member" means the commissioner of a compacting state or designee, who shall be a person officially connected with the commissioner.

(8) "Noncompacting state" means any state that has not enacted the enabling legislation for this compact.

(9) "Offender" means an adult placed under, or subject to, supervision as the result of the commission of a criminal offense and released to the community under the jurisdiction of courts, paroling authorities, corrections, or other criminal justice agencies.

(10) "Person" means any individual, corporation, business enterprise, or other legal entity, either public or private.

(11) "Rules" means acts of the Interstate Commission, duly promulgated pursuant to Article VIII of this compact, substantially affecting interested parties in addition to the Interstate Commission, which shall have the force and effect of law in the compacting states.

(12) "State" means a state of the United States, the District of Columbia, and any other territorial possessions of the United States.

(13) "State council" means the resident member of the State Council for Interstate Adult Offender Supervision created by each state under Article III of this compact.

Article III.

The Compact Commission.

(a) The compacting states hereby create the "Interstate Commission for Adult Offender Supervision". The Interstate Commission shall be a body corporate and joint agency of the compacting states. The Interstate Commission shall have all the responsibilities, powers, and duties set forth herein, including the power to sue and be sued, and such additional powers as may be conferred upon it by subsequent action of the respective legislatures of the compacting states in accordance with the terms of this compact.

(b)   The Interstate Commission shall consist of commissioners selected and appointed by resident members of a State Council for Interstate Adult Offender Supervision for each state. In addition to the commissioners who are the voting representatives of each state, the Interstate Commission shall include individuals who are not commissioners but who are members of interested organizations; such noncommissioner members must include a member of the national organizations of governors, legislators, state chief justices, attorneys general, and crime victims. All noncommissioner members of the Interstate Commission shall be ex officio (nonvoting) members. The Interstate Commission may provide in its bylaws for such additional, ex officio, nonvoting members as it deems necessary.

(c)   Each compacting state represented at any meeting of the Interstate Commission is entitled to one vote. A majority of the compacting states shall constitute a quorum for the transaction of business, unless a larger quorum is required by the bylaws of the Interstate Commission.

(d)   The Interstate Commission shall meet at least once each calendar year. The chairperson may call additional meetings and, upon the request of 27 or more compacting states, shall call additional meetings. Public notice shall be given of all meetings, and meetings shall be open to the public.

(e)   The Interstate Commission shall establish an executive committee that shall include commission officers, members, and others as shall be determined by the bylaws. The executive committee oversees the day-to-day activities managed by the executive director and Interstate Commission staff; administers enforcement and compliance with the provisions of the compact, its bylaws, and as directed by the Interstate Commission; and performs other duties as directed by the commission or set forth in the bylaws.

Article IV.

The State Council.

(a)   Each member state shall create a State Council for Interstate Adult Offender Supervision that shall be responsible for the appointment of the commissioner who shall serve on the Interstate Commission from that state. Each state council shall appoint as its commissioner the Compact Administrator from that state to serve on the Interstate Commission in such capacity under or pursuant to applicable law of the member state. While each member state may determine the membership of its own state council, its membership must include at least one representative from the legislative, judicial, and executive branches of government, victims groups, and compact administrators.

(b)   Each compacting state retains the right to determine the qualifications of the Compact Administrator, who shall be appointed by the state council or by the Governor in consultation with the legislature and the judiciary. In addition to appointment of its own commissioner to the National Interstate Commission, each state council shall exercise oversight and advocacy concerning its participation in Interstate Commission activities and other duties as may be determined by each member state including, but not limited to, development of policy operations and procedures of the compact within that state.

Article V.

Powers and Duties of the Interstate Commission.

The Interstate Commission shall have the following powers:

(1)   To adopt a seal and suitable bylaws governing the management and operation of the interstate commission.

(2)   To promulgate rules that shall have the force and effect of statutory law and shall be binding in the compacting states to the extent and in the manner provided in this compact.

(3)   To oversee, supervise, and coordinate the interstate movement of offenders subject to the terms of this compact and any bylaws adopted and rules promulgated by the compact commission.

(4)   To enforce compliance with compact provisions, Interstate Commission rules, and bylaws, using all necessary and proper means, including, but not limited to, the use of judicial process.

(5)   To establish and maintain offices.

(6)   To purchase and maintain insurance and bonds.

(7) To borrow, accept, or contract for services of personnel, including, but not limited to, members and their staffs.

(8) To establish and appoint committees and hire staff when it deems necessary for the carrying out of its functions including, but not limited to, an executive committee as required by Article III which shall have the power to act on behalf of the Interstate Commission in carrying out its powers and duties hereunder.

(9) To elect or appoint such officers, attorneys, employees, agents, or consultants, and to fix their compensation, define their duties, and determine their qualifications; and to establish the Interstate Commission's personnel policies and programs relating to, among other things, conflicts of interest, rates of compensation, and qualifications of personnel.

(10) To accept any and all donations and grants of money, equipment, supplies, materials, and services, and to receive, utilize, and dispose of same.

(11) To lease, purchase, accept contributions or donations of, or otherwise to own, hold, improve, or use any property, real, personal, or mixed.

(12) To sell, convey, mortgage, pledge, lease, exchange, abandon, or otherwise dispose of any property, real, personal, or mixed.

(13) To establish a budget and make expenditures and levy dues as provided in Article X of this compact.

(14) To sue or be sued.

(15) To provide for dispute resolution among compacting states.

(16) To perform such functions as may be necessary or appropriate to achieve the purposes of this compact.

(17) To report annually to the legislatures, governors, judiciary, and state councils of the compacting states concerning the activities of the Interstate Commission during the preceding year. Such reports shall also include any recommendations that may have been adopted by the Interstate Commission.

(18) To coordinate education, training, and public awareness regarding the interstate movement of offenders for officials involved in such activity.

(19) To establish uniform standards for the reporting, collecting, and exchanging of data.

Article VI.

Organization and Operation of the Interstate Commission.

(a) Bylaws. - The Interstate Commission shall, by a majority of the members, within 12 months of the first Interstate Commission meeting, adopt bylaws to govern its conduct as may be necessary or appropriate to carry out the purposes of the compact, including, but not limited to:

(1) Establishing the fiscal year of the Interstate Commission;

(2) Establishing an executive committee and such other committees as may be necessary and providing reasonable standards and procedures:

a. For the establishment of committees, and

b. Governing any general or specific delegation of any authority or function of the Interstate Commission;

(3) Providing reasonable procedures for calling and conducting meetings of the Interstate Commission, and ensuring reasonable notice of each such meeting;

(4) Establishing the titles and responsibilities of the officers of the Interstate Commission;

(5) Providing reasonable standards and procedures for the establishment of the personnel policies and programs of the Interstate Commission. Notwithstanding any civil service or other similar laws of any compacting state, the bylaws shall exclusively govern the personnel policies and programs of the Interstate Commission;

(6) Providing a mechanism for winding up the operations of the Interstate Commission and the equitable return of any surplus funds that may exist upon the termination of the compact after the payment and/or reserving of all of its debts and obligations;

(7) Providing transition rules for "start- up" administration of the compact; and

(8) Establishing standards and procedures for compliance and technical assistance in carrying out the compact.

(b) Officers and Staff. - The Interstate Commission shall, by a majority of the members, elect from among its members a chair and a vice-chair, each of whom shall have such authorities and duties as may be specified in the bylaws. The chair or, in the chair's absence or disability, the vice-chair shall preside at all meetings of the Interstate Commission. The officers so elected shall serve without compensation or remuneration from the Interstate Commission; provided that, subject to the availability of budgeted funds, the officers shall be reimbursed for any actual and necessary costs and expenses incurred by them in the performance of their duties and responsibilities as officers of the Interstate Commission.

The Interstate Commission shall, through its executive committee, appoint or retain an executive director for such period, upon such terms and conditions and for such compensation as the Interstate Commission may deem appropriate. The executive director shall serve as secretary to the Interstate Commission, and hire and supervise such other staff as may be authorized by the Interstate Commission, but shall not be a member.

(c) Corporate Records of the Interstate Commission. - The Interstate Commission shall maintain its corporate books and records in accordance with the bylaws.

(d) Qualified Immunity, Defense, and Indemnification. - The members, officers, executive director, and employees of the Interstate Commission shall be immune from suit and liability, either personally or in their official capacity, for any claim for damage to or loss of property or personal injury or other civil liability caused or arising out of any actual or alleged act, error, or omission that occurred within the scope of Interstate Commission employment, duties, or responsibilities; provided, that nothing in this paragraph shall be construed to protect any such person from suit and/or liability for any damage, loss, injury, or liability caused by the intentional or willful and wanton misconduct of any such person.

The Interstate Commission shall defend the commissioner of a compacting state, or the commissioner's representatives or employees, or the Interstate

Commission's representatives or employees, in any civil action seeking to impose liability, arising out of any actual or alleged act, error, or omission that occurred within the scope of Interstate Commission employment, duties, or responsibilities, or that the defendant had a reasonable basis for believing occurred within the scope of Interstate Commission employment, duties, or responsibilities; provided, that the actual or alleged act, error, or omission did not result from intentional wrongdoing on the part of such person.

The Interstate Commission shall indemnify and hold the commissioner of a compacting state, the appointed designee or employees, or the Interstate Commission's representatives or employees, harmless in the amount of any settlement or judgment obtained against such persons arising out of any actual or alleged act, error, or omission that occurred within the scope of Interstate Commission employment, duties, or responsibilities, or that such persons had a reasonable basis for believing occurred within the scope of Interstate Commission employment, duties, or responsibilities, provided that the actual or alleged act, error, or omission did not result from gross negligence or intentional wrongdoing on the part of such person.

Article VII.

Activities of the Interstate Commission.

(a)   The interstate commission shall meet and take such actions as are consistent with the provisions of this compact.

(b)   Except as otherwise provided in this compact and unless a greater percentage is required by the bylaws, in order to constitute an act of the Interstate Commission, such act shall have been taken at a meeting of the Interstate Commission and shall have received an affirmative vote of a majority of the members present.

(c)   Each member of the Interstate Commission shall have the right and power to cast a vote to which the compacting state is entitled and to participate in the business and affairs of the Interstate Commission. A member shall vote in person on behalf of the state and shall not delegate a vote to another member state. However, a state council shall appoint another authorized representative, in the absence of the commissioner from that state, to cast a vote on behalf of the member state at a specified meeting. The bylaws may provide for members' participation in meetings by telephone or other means of telecommunication or electronic communication. Any voting conducted by telephone or other means of telecommunication or electronic communication shall be subject to the same quorum requirements of meetings where members are present in person.

(d)   The Interstate Commission shall meet at least once during each calendar year. The chairperson of the Interstate Commission may call additional meetings at any time and, upon the request of a majority of the members, shall call additional meetings.

(e)   The Interstate Commission's bylaws shall establish conditions and procedures under which the Interstate Commission shall make its information and official records available to the public for inspection or copying. The Interstate Commission may exempt from disclosure any information or official records to the extent they would adversely affect personal privacy rights or proprietary interests. In promulgating such rules, the Interstate Commission may make available to law enforcement agencies records and information otherwise exempt from disclosure, and may enter into agreements with law enforcement agencies to receive or exchange information or records subject to nondisclosure and confidentiality provisions.

(f)   Public notice shall be given of all meetings, and all meetings shall be open to the public, except as set forth in the rules or as otherwise provided in the compact. The Interstate Commission shall promulgate rules consistent with the principles contained in the "Government in Sunshine Act", U.S.C. § 552(b), as may be amended. The Interstate Commission and any of its committees may close a meeting to the public where it determines by two-thirds vote that an open meeting would be likely to:

(1)   Relate solely to the Interstate Commission's internal personnel practices and procedures;

(2)   Disclose matters specifically exempted from disclosure by statute;

(3)   Disclose trade secrets or commercial or financial information which is privileged or confidential;

(4)   Involve accusing any person of a crime or formally censuring any person;

(5) Disclose information of a personal nature where disclosure would constitute a clearly unwarranted invasion of personal privacy;

(6) Disclose investigatory records compiled for law enforcement purposes;

(7) Disclose information contained in or related to examination, operating, or condition reports prepared by, on behalf of, or for the use of, the Interstate Commission with respect to a regulated entity for the purpose of regulation or supervision of such entity;

(8) Disclose information, the premature disclosure of which would significantly endanger the life of a person or the stability of a regulated entity; and

(9) Specifically relate to the Interstate Commission's issuance of a subpoena, or its participation in a civil action or proceeding.

(g) For every meeting closed pursuant to this provision, the Interstate Commission's chief legal officer shall publicly certify that, in the officer's opinion, the meeting may be closed to the public and shall reference each relevant exemptive provision. The Interstate Commission shall keep minutes which shall fully and clearly describe all matters discussed in any meeting and shall provide a full and accurate summary of any actions taken and the reasons therefor, including a description of each of the views expressed on any item and the record of any recall vote (reflected in the vote of each member on the question). All documents considered in connection with any action shall be identified in such minutes.

(h) The Interstate Commission shall collect standardized data concerning the interstate movement of offenders as directed through its bylaws and rules which shall specify the data to be collected, the means of collection, and data exchange and reporting requirements.

Article VIII.

Rule-making Functions of the Interstate Commission.

(a) The Interstate Commission shall promulgate rules in order to effectively and efficiently achieve the purposes of the compact including transition rules governing administration of the compact during the period in which it is being considered and enacted by the states.

(b) Rule making shall occur pursuant to the criteria set forth in this article and the bylaws and rules adopted pursuant thereto. Such rule making shall substantially conform to the principles of the federal Administrative Procedure Act, 5 U.S.C.S. section 551, et seq., and the Federal Advisory Committee Act, 5 U.S.C. § 1, et seq., as may be amended (hereinafter "APA"). All rules and amendments shall become binding as of the date specified in each rule or amendment.

(c) If a majority of the legislatures of the compacting states rejects a rule, by enactment of a statute or resolution in the same manner used to adopt the compact, then such rule shall have no further force and effect in any compacting state.

(d) When promulgating a rule, the Interstate Commission shall:

(1) Publish the proposed rule stating with particularity the text of the rule that is proposed and the reason for the proposed rule;

(2) Allow persons to submit written data, facts, opinions, and arguments, which information shall be publicly available;

(3) Provide an opportunity for an informal hearing; and

(4) Promulgate a final rule and its effective date, if appropriate, based on the rule-making record. Not later than 60 days after a rule is promulgated, any interested person may file a petition in the United States District Court for the District of Columbia or in the Federal District Court where the Interstate Commission's principle office is located for judicial review of such rule. If the court finds that the Interstate Commission's action is not supported by substantial evidence, (as defined in the APA), in the rule-making record, the court shall hold the rule unlawful and set it aside. Subjects to be addressed within 12 months after the first meeting must, at a minimum, include:

a. Notice to victims and opportunity to be heard;

b. Offender registration and compliance;

c. Violations/returns;

d. Transfer procedures and forms;

e. Eligibility for transfer;

f. Collection of restitution and fees from offenders;

g. Data collection and reporting;

h. The level of supervision to be provided by the receiving state;

i. Transition rules governing the operation of the compact and the Interstate Commission during all or part of the period between the effective date of the compact and the date on which the last eligible state adopts the compact; and

j. Mediation, arbitration, and dispute resolution.

(e) The existing rules governing the operation of the previous compact superceded by this Act shall be null and void 12 months after the first meeting of the Interstate Commission created hereunder.

(f) Upon determination by the Interstate Commission that an emergency exists, it may promulgate an emergency rule which shall become effective immediately upon adoption, provided that the usual rule-making procedures provided hereunder shall be retroactively applied to said rule as soon as reasonably possible, in no event later than 90 days after the effective date of the rule.

Article IX.

Oversight, Enforcement, and Dispute Resolution by the Interstate Commission.

(a) Oversight. - The Interstate Commission shall oversee the interstate movement of adult offenders in the compacting states and shall monitor such activities being administered in noncompacting states that may significantly affect compacting states.

The courts and executive agencies in each compacting state shall enforce this compact and shall take all actions necessary and appropriate to effectuate the compact's purposes and intent. In any judicial or administrative proceeding in a compacting state pertaining to the subject matter of this compact which may affect the powers, responsibilities, or actions of the Interstate Commission, the Interstate Commission shall be entitled to receive all service of process in any such proceeding and shall have standing to intervene in the proceeding for all purposes.

(b) Dispute Resolution. - The compacting states shall report to the Interstate Commission on issues or activities of concern to them and cooperate with and support the Interstate Commission in the discharge of its duties and responsibilities.

The Interstate Commission shall attempt to resolve any disputes or other issues which are subject to the compact and which may arise among compacting states and noncompacting states.

The Interstate Commission shall enact a bylaw or promulgate a rule providing for both mediation and binding dispute resolution for disputes among the compacting states.

(c) Enforcement. - The Interstate Commission, in the reasonable exercise of its discretion, shall enforce the provisions of this compact using any and all means set forth in Article XII, subsection (b) of this compact.

Article X.

Finance.

(a) The Interstate Commission shall pay or provide for the payment of the reasonable expenses of its establishment, organization, and ongoing activities.

(b) The Interstate Commission shall levy on and collect an annual assessment for each compacting state to cover the cost of the internal operations and activities of the Interstate Commission and its staff that must be in a total amount sufficient to cover the Interstate Commission's annual budget as approved each year. The aggregate annual assessment amount shall be allocated based upon a formula to be determined by the Interstate Commission, taking into consideration the population of the state and the volume of interstate movement of offenders in each compacting state and shall promulgate a rule binding upon all compacting states which governs said assessment.

(c) The Interstate Commission shall not incur any obligations of any kind prior to securing the funds adequate to meet the same; nor shall the Interstate Commission pledge the credit of any of the compacting states, except by and with the authority of the compacting state.

(d) The Interstate Commission shall keep accurate accounts of all receipts and disbursements. The receipts and disbursements of the Interstate Commission shall be subject to the audit and accounting procedures established under its bylaws. However, all receipts and disbursements of funds handled by the Interstate Commission shall be audited yearly by a certified or licensed public accountant, and the report of the audit shall be included in and become part of the annual report of the Interstate Commission.

Article XI.

Compacting State, Effective Date, and Amendment.

(a) Any state, as defined in article ii of this compact, is eligible to become a compacting state.

(b) The compact shall become effective and binding upon legislative enactment of the compact into law by no less than 35 of the states. The initial effective date shall be the later of July 1, 2002, or upon enactment into law by the 35th jurisdiction. Therefore, it shall become effective and binding as to any other compacting state, upon enactment of the compact into law by that state. The governors of nonmember states or their designees will be invited to participate in Interstate Commission activities on a nonvoting basis prior to adoption of the compact by all states and territories of the United States.

(c) Amendments to the compact may be proposed by the Interstate Commission for enactment by the compacting states. No amendment shall become effective and binding upon the Interstate Commission and the compacting states unless and until it is enacted into law by unanimous consent of the compacting states.

Article XII.

Withdrawal, Default, Termination, and Judicial Enforcement.

(a)   Withdrawal. - Once effective, the compact shall continue in force and remain binding upon each and every compacting state; provided that a compacting state may withdraw from the compact ("withdrawing state") by enacting a statute specifically repealing the statute which enacted the compact into law.

The effective date of withdrawal is the effective date of the repeal.

The withdrawing state shall immediately notify the Chair of the Interstate Commission in writing upon the introduction of legislation repealing this compact in the withdrawing state. The Interstate Commission shall notify the other compacting states of the withdrawing state's intent to withdraw within 60 days of its receipt thereof.

The withdrawing state is responsible for all assessments, obligations, and liabilities incurred through the effective date of withdrawal, including any obligations, the performance of which extend beyond the effective date of withdrawal.

Reinstatement following withdrawal of any compacting state shall occur upon the withdrawing state's reenacting the compact or upon such later date as determined by the Interstate Commission.

(b)   Default. - If the Interstate Commission determines that any compacting state has at any time defaulted ("defaulting state") in the performance of any of its obligations or responsibilities under this compact, the bylaws, or any duly promulgated rules, the Interstate Commission may impose any or all of the following penalties:

(1)   Fines, fees, and costs in such amounts as are deemed to be reasonable as fixed by the Interstate Commission;

(2)   Remedial training and technical assistance as directed by the Interstate Commission;

(3)   Suspension and termination of membership in the compact. Suspension shall be imposed only after all other reasonable means of securing compliance

under the bylaws and rules have been exhausted. Immediate notice of suspension shall be given by the Interstate Commission to the Governor; the Chief Justice or Chief Judicial Officer of the state; the Majority and Minority Leaders of the defaulting state's legislature; and the state council.

The grounds of default include, but are not limited to, failure of a compacting state to perform such obligations or responsibilities imposed upon it by this compact, Interstate Commission bylaws, or duly promulgated rules. The Interstate Commission shall immediately notify the defaulting state in writing of the penalty imposed by the Interstate Commission on the defaulting state pending a cure of the default. The Interstate Commission shall stipulate the conditions and the time period within which the defaulting state must cure its default. If the defaulting state fails to cure the default within the time period specified by the Interstate Commission, in addition to any other penalties imposed herein, the defaulting state may be terminated from the compact upon an affirmative vote of a majority of the compacting states, and all rights, privileges, and benefits conferred by this compact shall be terminated from the effective date of suspension. Within 60 days of the effective date of termination of a defaulting state, the Interstate Commission shall notify the Governor; the Chief Justice or Chief Judicial Officer of the state; the Majority and Minority Leaders of the defaulting state's legislature; and the state council of such termination.

The defaulting state is responsible for all assessments, obligations, and liabilities incurred through the effective date of termination, including any obligations the performance of which extends beyond the effective date of termination.

The Interstate Commission shall not bear any costs relating to the defaulting state unless otherwise mutually agreed upon between the Interstate Commission and the defaulting state. Reinstatement following termination of any compacting state requires both a reenactment of the compact by the defaulting state and the approval of the Interstate Commission pursuant to the rules.

(c)   Judicial Enforcement. - The Interstate Commission may, by majority vote of the members, initiate legal action in the United States District Court for the District of Columbia or, at the discretion of the Interstate Commission, in the Federal District where the Interstate Commission has its offices to enforce compliance with the provisions of the compact, its duly promulgated rules and bylaws against any compacting state in default. In the event judicial enforcement is necessary, the prevailing party shall be awarded all costs of such litigation including reasonable attorney's fees.

(d)   Dissolution of Compact. - The compact dissolves effective upon the date of the withdrawal or default of the compacting state that reduces membership in the compact to one compacting state.

Upon the dissolution of this compact, the compact becomes null and void and shall be of no further force or effect, and the business and affairs of the Interstate Commission shall be wound up, and any surplus funds shall be distributed in accordance with the bylaws.

Article XIII.

Severability and Construction.

(a)   The provisions of this compact shall be severable, and if any phrase, clause, sentence, or provision is deemed unenforceable, the remaining provision of the compact shall be enforceable.

(b)   The provisions of this compact shall be liberally constructed to effectuate its purposes.

Article XIV.

Binding Effect of Compact and Other Laws.

(a)   Other Laws. - Nothing herein prevents the enforcement of any other law of a compacting state that is not inconsistent with this compact.

All compacting states' laws conflicting with this compact are superseded to the extent of the conflict.

(b)   Binding Effect of the Compact. - All lawful actions of the Interstate Commission, including all rules and bylaws promulgated by the Interstate Commission, are binding upon the compacting states.

All agreements between the Interstate Commission and the compacting states are binding in accordance with their terms.

Upon the request of a party to a conflict over meaning or interpretation of Interstate Commission actions, and upon a majority vote of the compacting states, the Interstate Commission may issue advisory opinions regarding such meaning or interpretation.

In the event any provision of this compact exceeds the constitutional limits imposed on the legislature of any compacting state, the obligations, duties, powers, or jurisdiction sought to be conferred by such provision upon the Interstate Commission shall be ineffective, and such obligations, duties, powers, or jurisdiction shall remain in the compacting state and shall be exercised by the agency thereof to which such obligations, duties, powers, or jurisdiction are delegated by law in effect at the time this compact becomes effective. (2002-166, s. 1; 2008-189, s. 1.)

§ 148-65.6. Implementation of the compact.

(a)   The North Carolina State Council for Interstate Adult Offender Supervision shall be established, consisting of 14 members. North Carolina's Commissioner to the Interstate Compact Commission is a member of the State Council and serves as chair of the State Council. The remaining members of the State Council shall consist of the following:

(1)   One member representing the executive branch, to be appointed by the Governor;

(2)   One member from a victim's assistance group, to be appointed by the Governor;

(3)   One at-large member, to be appointed by the Governor;

(4)   One member of the Senate, to be appointed by the President Pro Tempore of the Senate;

(5)   One member of the House of Representatives, to be appointed by the Speaker of the House of Representatives;

(6)   A superior court judge, to be appointed by the Chief Justice of the Supreme Court;

(6a) A district court judge, to be appointed by the Chief Justice of the Supreme Court;

(7) Four members representing the Section of Community Corrections of the Division of Adult Correction, to be appointed by the Director of the Section of Community Corrections of the Division of Adult Correction;

(8) A district attorney, to be appointed by the Governor; and

(9) A sheriff, to be appointed by the Governor.

(a1) The Governor, in consultation with the legislature and judiciary, shall appoint the Compact Administrator. The Compact Administrator shall be appointed by the State Council as North Carolina's Commissioner to the Interstate Compact Commission.

(b) The State Council shall meet at least twice a year and may also hold special meetings at the call of the chairperson. All terms are for three years.

(c) The State Council may advise the Compact Administrator on participation in the Interstate Commission activities and administration of the compact.

(d) The members of the State Council shall serve without compensation but shall be reimbursed for necessary travel and subsistence expenses in accordance with the policies of the Office of State Budget and Management.

(e) The State Council shall act in an advisory capacity to the Secretary of Public Safety concerning this State's participation in Interstate Commission activities and other duties as may be determined by each member state, including recommendations for policy concerning the operations and procedures of the compact within this State.

(f) The Governor shall by executive order provide for any other matters necessary for implementation of the compact at the time that it becomes effective, and, except as otherwise provided for in this section, the State Council may promulgate rules or regulations necessary to implement and administer the compact. (2002-166, s. 1; 2008-189, s. 1; 2011-145, s. 19.1(i), (k).)

§ 148-65.7. Fees.

(a)   Persons convicted in this State who make a request for transfer to another state pursuant to the compact shall pay a transfer application of two hundred fifty dollars ($250.00) for each transfer application submitted. The transfer application fee shall be paid to the Compact Commissioner upon submission of the transfer application. The Commissioner or the Commissioner's designee may waive the application fee if either the Commissioner or the Commissioner's designee finds that payment of the fee will constitute an undue economic burden on the offender.

All fees collected pursuant to this section shall be deposited in the Interstate Compact Fund and shall be used only to support administration of the Interstate Compact.

The Interstate Compact Fund is established within the Division of Adult Correction of the Department of Public Safety as a nonreverting, interest-bearing special revenue account. Accordingly, revenue in the Fund at the end of a fiscal year does not revert, and interest and other investment income earned by the Fund shall be credited to it. All moneys collected by the Division of Adult Correction of the Department of Public Safety pursuant to this subsection shall be remitted to the State Treasurer to be deposited and held in this Fund. Moneys in the Fund shall be used to supplement funds otherwise available to the Division of Adult Correction of the Department of Public Safety for the administration of the Interstate Compact.

(b)   Persons supervised in this State pursuant to this compact shall pay the supervision fee specified in G.S. 15A-1374(c). The fee shall be paid to the clerk of court in the county in which the person initially receives supervision services in this State. The Commissioner or the Commissioner's designee may waive the fee if either the Commissioner or the Commissioner's designee finds that payment of the fee will constitute an undue economic burden on the offender. (2002-166, s. 1; 2008-189, s. 1; 2011-145, ss. 19.1(h), 31.25.)

§ 148-65.8. Interstate parole and probation hearing procedures.

(a)   Where supervision of an offender is being administered pursuant to the Interstate Compact for Adult Offender Supervision, the appropriate judicial or administrative authorities in this State shall notify the Compact Administrator of the sending state whenever, in their view, consideration should be given to retaking or reincarceration for a parole, probation, or post-release supervision violation. Prior to the giving of any such notification, a hearing shall be held in accordance with this section within a reasonable time, unless such hearing is waived by the offender. Pending any proceeding pursuant to this section, the appropriate officers of this State may take custody of and detain the offender involved for a period not to exceed 15 days prior to the hearing. The offender shall not be entitled to bail pending the hearing.

(b)   Any hearing pursuant to this section may be before the Administrator of the Interstate Compact for Adult Offender Supervision, a deputy of the Administrator, any other person appointed by the Administrator, or any person authorized pursuant to the laws of this State to hear cases of alleged parole, probation, or post-release supervision violation, except that no hearing officer shall be the person making the allegation of violation.

(c)   With respect to any hearing pursuant to this section, the offender:

(1)   Shall have reasonable notice in writing of the nature and content of the allegations to be made, including notice that its purpose is to determine whether there is probable cause to believe that the offender has committed a violation that may lead to a revocation of parole, probation, or post-release supervision.

(2)   Shall be permitted to advise with any persons whose assistance the offender reasonably desires, prior to the hearing.

(3)   Shall have the right to confront and examine any persons who have made allegations against the offender, unless the hearing officer determines that such confrontation would present a substantial present or subsequent danger of harm to such person or persons.

(4)   May admit, deny, or explain the violation alleged and may present proof, including affidavits and other evidence, in support of the offender's contentions.

(c1)   A record of the hearing shall be made and preserved. As soon as practicable following termination of any hearing conducted pursuant to this section or the waiver of such hearing, the appropriate officer or officers of this State shall report to the sending state, furnish a copy of the hearing record, and make recommendations regarding the disposition to be made of the offender by the sending state. If the hearing recommendation is to retake or reincarcerate the offender, the hearing officer or officers may detain the offender until notice is received from the sending state. If the sending state provides notice that it intends to retake or reincarcerate the offender, the offender shall remain in custody for such reasonable period after the hearing or waiver as may be necessary to arrange for the retaking or reincarceration.

(d) In any case of alleged parole or probation violation by a person being supervised in another state pursuant to the Interstate Compact for Adult Offender Supervision, any appropriate judicial or administrative officer or agency in another state may hold a hearing on the alleged violation. Upon receipt of the record of a parole, probation, or post-release supervision violation hearing held in another state pursuant to a statute substantially similar to this section, that record shall have the same standing and effect as though the proceeding of which it is a record was had before the appropriate officer or officers in this State, and any recommendations contained in or accompanying the record shall be fully considered by the appropriate officer or officers of this State in making disposition of the matter. (2002-166, s. 1; 2008-189, s. 1.)

§ 148-65.9. North Carolina sentence to be served in another jurisdiction.

The Post-Release Supervision and Parole Commission, with the concurrence of the Secretary of Public Safety, may direct that the balance of any sentence imposed by the courts of this State shall be served concurrently with a sentence or sentences in another state or federal institution and may effect a transfer of custody of such individual to the other jurisdiction for such purpose. In the event the individual's sentence liability in the other jurisdiction terminates prior to the expiration of the individual's North Carolina sentence, the individual shall be either paroled (if eligible) or returned to the prison department of this State, in the discretion of the Post-Release Supervision and Parole Commission. (2002-166, s. 1; 2011-145, s. 19.1(i).)

Article 5.

Farming Out Convicts.

§ 148-66. Cities and towns and Department of Agriculture and Consumer Services may contract for prison labor.

The corporate authorities of any city or town may contract in writing with the Division of Adult Correction of the Department of Public Safety for the employment of convicts upon the highways or streets of such city or town, and such contracts when so exercised shall be valid and enforceable against such city or town, and the Attorney General may prosecute an action in the Superior Court of Wake County in the name of the State for their enforcement.

The Department of Agriculture and Consumer Services is hereby authorized and empowered to contract, in writing, with the Division of Adult Correction of the Department of Public Safety for the employment and use of convicts under its supervision to be worked on the State test farms and/or State experimental stations. (1881, c. 127, s. 1; Code, s. 3449; Rev., s. 5410; C.S., s. 7758; 1925, c. 163; 1931, c. 145, s. 35; 1933, c. 172, s. 18; 1943, c. 605, s. 1; 1957, c. 349, s. 10; 1967, c. 996, s. 13; 1985, c. 226, s. 10(1); 1997-261, s. 106; 2011-145, s. 19.1(h); 2012-83, s. 61.)

§ 148-67. Hiring to cities and towns and State Department of Agriculture and Consumer Services.

The Division of Adult Correction of the Department of Public Safety shall in their discretion, upon application to them, hire to the corporate authorities of any city or town for the purposes specified in G.S. 148-66, such convicts as are mentally and physically capable of performing the work or labor contemplated and are not at the time of such application hired or otherwise engaged in labor under the direction of the Division; but the convicts so hired for services shall be fed, clothed and quartered while so employed by the Division.

Upon application to it, it shall be the duty of the Division of Adult Correction of the Department of Public Safety, in its discretion, to hire to the Department of Agriculture and Consumer Services for the purposes of working on the State test farms and/or State experimental stations, such convicts as may be mentally and physically capable of performing the work or labor contemplated; but the convicts so hired for services under this paragraph shall be fed, clothed and quartered while so employed by the Division of Adult Correction of the Department of Public Safety. (1881, c. 127, s. 2; Code, s. 3450; Rev., s. 5411; C.S., s. 7759; 1925, c. 163; 1931, c. 145, s. 35; 1933, c. 172, s. 18; 1943, c. 605, s. 2; 1957, c. 349, s. 10; 1967, c. 996, s. 13; 1985, c. 226, s. 10(2); 1997-261, s. 107; 2011-145, s. 19.1(h); 2012-83, s. 61.)

§ 148-68. Payment of contract price; interest; enforcement of contracts.

The corporate authorities of any city or town so hiring convicts shall pay into the treasury of the State for the labor of any convict so hired such sum or sums of money at such time or times as may be agreed upon in the contract of hire; and if any such city or town fails to pay the State money due for such hiring, the same shall bear interest from the time it is due until paid at the rate of six percent (6%) per annum; and an action to recover the same may be instituted by the Attorney General in the name of the State in the courts of Wake County. (1881, c. 127, s. 3; Code, s. 3451; Rev., s. 5412; C.S., s. 7760; 1925, c. 163; 1931, c. 145, s. 35.)

§ 148-69. Agents; levy of taxes; payment of costs and expenses.

The corporate authorities of any city or town so hiring convicts may appoint and remove at will all such necessary agents to superintend the construction or improvement of such highways and streets as they may deem proper, or to pay the costs and expenses incident to such hiring may levy taxes and raise money as in other respects. (1881, c. 127, s. 4; Code, s. 3452; Rev., s. 5413; C. S., s. 7761; 1925, c. 163; 1931, c. 145, s. 35.)

§ 148-70. Management and care of inmates.

The Division of Adult Correction of the Department of Public Safety in all contracts for labor shall provide for feeding and clothing the inmates and shall maintain, control and guard the quarters in which the inmates live during the time of the contracts; and the Division shall provide for the guarding and working of such inmates under its sole supervision and control. The Division may make such contracts for the hire of the inmates confined in the State prison as may in its discretion be proper. (1917, c. 286, s. 2; 1919, c. 80, s. 1; C.S., s. 7762; 1925, c. 163; 1931, c. 145, s. 35; 1933, c. 172, s. 18; 1957, c. 349, s. 10; 1959, c. 170, s. 2; 1967, c. 996, s. 13; 1975, c. 730, s. 1; 1983, c. 717, s. 14; 1985, c. 118; c. 226, s. 11; 1991 (Reg. Sess., 1992), c. 902, s. 2; 2007-280, s. 4; 2011-145, s. 19.1(h); 2012-83, s. 61.)

Article 5A.

Prison Labor for Farm Work.

§§ 148-70.1 through 148-70.7. Repealed by Session Laws 1957, c. 349, s. 11.

Article 6.

Reformatory.

§§ 148-71 through 148-73. Repealed by Session Laws 1947, c. 262, s. 3.

Article 7.

Records, Statistics, Research and Planning.

§ 148-74. Records Section.

Case records and related materials compiled for the use of the Secretary of Public Safety and the Parole Commission shall be maintained in a single central file system designed to minimize duplication and maximize effective use of such records and materials. When an individual is committed to the State prison system after a period on probation, the probation files on that individual shall be made a part of the combined files used by the Division of Adult Correction of the Department of Public Safety and the Parole Commission. The administration of the Records Section shall be under the control and direction of the Secretary of Public Safety. (1925, c. 228, s. 1; 1953, c. 55, ss. 2, 4; 1967, c. 996, s. 12; 1973, c. 1262, s. 10; 1985, c. 226, s. 12; 2011-145, s. 19.1(h), (i).)

§ 148-75. Repealed by Session Laws 1963, c. 1174, s. 5.

§ 148-76. Duties of Records Section.

The Records Section shall maintain the combined case records and receive and collect fingerprints, photographs, and other information to assist in locating, identifying, and keeping records of criminals. The information collected shall be classified, compared, and made available to law-enforcement agencies, courts, correctional agencies, or other officials requiring criminal identification, crime statistics, and other information respecting crimes and criminals. (1925, c. 228, s. 3; 1953, c. 55, s. 4; 1967, c. 996, s. 12.)

§ 148-77: Repealed by Session Laws 2012-168, s. 5(a), effective July 12, 2012.

§ 148-78. Reports.

The Secretary of Public Safety may prepare and release reports on the work of the Division of Adult Correction of the Department of Public Safety, including statistics and other data, accounts of research, and recommendations for legislation. (1925, c. 228, s. 5; 1953, c. 55, s. 4; 1967, c. 996, s. 12; 1973, c. 1262, s. 10; 2011-145, s. 19.1(h), (i).)

§ 148-79. Repealed by Session Laws 1965, c. 1049, s. 2.

§ 148-80. Seal of Records Section; certification of records.

A seal shall be provided to be affixed to any paper, record, copy or form or true copy of any of the same in the files or records of the Records Section, and when so certified under seal by the duly appointed custodian, such record or copy shall be admitted as evidence in any court of the State. (1925, c. 228, s. 7; 1953, c. 55, s. 4; 1967, c. 996, s. 12.)

§ 148-81: Repealed by Session Laws 1965, c. 1049, s. 2.

Article 8.

Compensation to Persons Erroneously Convicted of Felonies.

§ 148-82. Provision for compensation.

(a)   Any person who, having been convicted of a felony and having been imprisoned therefor in a State prison of this State, and who was thereafter or who shall hereafter be granted a pardon of innocence by the Governor upon the grounds that the crime with which the person was charged either was not committed at all or was not committed by that person, may as hereinafter provided present by petition a claim against the State for the pecuniary loss sustained by the person through his or her erroneous conviction and imprisonment, provided the petition is presented within five years of the granting of the pardon.

(b) Any person who, having been convicted of a felony after pleading not guilty or nolo contendere and having been imprisoned therefor in a State prison of this State, and who is determined to be innocent of all charges and against whom the charges are dismissed pursuant to G.S. 15A-1469 may as hereinafter provided present by petition a claim against the State for the pecuniary loss sustained by the person through his or her erroneous conviction and imprisonment, provided the petition is presented within five years of the date that the dismissal of the charges is entered by the three-judge panel under G.S. 15A-1469. (1947, c. 465, s. 1; 1997-388, s. 1; 2010-171, s. 3; 2012-7, s. 11.)

§ 148-83. Form, requisites and contents of petition; nature of hearing.

Such petition shall be addressed to the Industrial Commission, and must include a full statement of the facts upon which the claim is based, verified in the manner provided for verifying complaints in civil actions, and it may be supported by affidavits substantiating such claim. Upon its presentation the Industrial Commission shall fix a time and a place for a hearing, and shall mail notice to the claimant, and shall notify the Attorney General, at least 15 days before the time fixed therefor. (1947, c. 465, s. 2; 1963, c. 1174, s. 4; 1973, c. 1262, s. 10; 1997-388, s. 2.)

§ 148-84. Evidence; action by Industrial Commission; payment and amount of compensation.

(a) At the hearing the claimant may introduce evidence in the form of affidavits or testimony to support the claim, and the Attorney General may introduce counter affidavits or testimony in refutation. If the Industrial Commission finds from the evidence that the claimant received a pardon of innocence for the reason that the crime was not committed at all, received a pardon of innocence for the reason that the crime was not committed by the claimant, or that the claimant was determined to be innocent of all charges by a three-judge panel under G.S. 15A-1469 and also finds that the claimant was imprisoned and has been vindicated in connection with the alleged offense for which he or she was imprisoned, the Industrial Commission shall award to the claimant an amount equal to fifty thousand dollars ($50,000) for each year or the pro rata amount for the portion of each year of the imprisonment actually served, including any time spent awaiting trial. However, (i) in no event shall the compensation, including the compensation provided in subsection (c) of this section, exceed a total amount of seven hundred fifty thousand dollars ($750,000), and (ii) a claimant is not entitled to compensation for any portion of a prison sentence during which the claimant was also serving a concurrent sentence for conviction of a crime other than the one for which the pardon of innocence was granted.

The Director of the Budget shall pay the amount of the award to the claimant out of the Contingency and Emergency Fund, or out of any other available State funds. The Industrial Commission shall give written notice of its decision to all parties concerned. The determination of the Industrial Commission shall be subject to judicial review upon appeal of the claimant or the State according to the provisions and procedures set forth in Article 31 of Chapter 143 of the General Statutes.

(b)   Reserved.

(c)   In addition to the compensation provided under subsection (a) of this section, the Industrial Commission shall determine the extent to which incarceration has deprived a claimant of educational or training opportunities and, based upon those findings, may award the following compensation for loss of life opportunities:

(1)   Job skills training for at least one year through an appropriate State program; and

(2)   Expenses for tuition and fees at any public North Carolina community college or constituent institution of The University of North Carolina for any degree or program of the claimant's choice that is available from one or more of the applicable institutions. Claimants are also entitled to assistance in meeting any admission standards or criteria required at any of those institutions, including assistance in satisfying requirements for a certificate of equivalency of completion of secondary education. A claimant may apply for aid under this subdivision within 10 years of the claimant's release from incarceration, and aid shall continue for up to a total of five years when initiated within the 10-year

period, provided the claimant makes satisfactory progress in the courses or degree program in which the claimant is enrolled. (1947, c. 465, s. 3; 1963, c. 1174, s. 4; 1973, c. 1262, s. 10; 1997-388, s. 3; 2001-424, s. 25.12(a); 2008-173, ss. 1, 2; 2009-570, s. 24; 2010-171, s. 4.)

Article 9.

Prison Advisory Council.

§§ 148-85 through 148-88. Repealed by Session Laws 1957, c. 349, s. 11.

Article 10.

Interstate Agreement on Detainers.

§§ 148-89 through 148-95. Transferred to §§ 15A-761 to 15A-767 by Session Laws 1973, c. 1286, s. 22, as amended by Session Laws 1975, c. 573.

§§ 148-96 through 148-100. Reserved for future codification purposes.

Article 11.

Inmate Grievance Commission.

§§ 148-101 through 148-118: Repealed by Session Laws 1987, c. 746, s. 1.

Article 11A.

Corrections Administrative Remedy Procedure.

§ 148-118.1. Authority.

The Division of Adult Correction of the Department of Public Safety shall adopt an Administrative Remedy Procedure in compliance with 42 U.S.C. 1997, the "Civil Rights of Institutionalized Persons Act". The Administrative Remedy Procedure and any amendments or changes thereto shall be adopted only after prior consultation with the Grievance Resolution Board. (1987, c. 746, s. 2; 2011-145, s. 19.1(h).)

§ 148-118.2. Effect.

(a)   Upon approval of the Administrative Remedy Procedure by a federal court as authorized and required by 42 U.S.C. 1997(e)(a), and the implementation of the procedure, this procedure shall constitute the administrative remedies available to a prisoner for the purpose of preserving any cause of action under the purview of the Administrative Remedy Procedure, which a prisoner may claim to have against the State of North Carolina, the Division of Adult Correction of the Department of Public Safety, or its employees.

(b)   No State court shall entertain a prisoner's grievance or complaint which falls under the purview of the Administrative Remedy Procedure unless and until the prisoner shall have exhausted the remedies as provided in said procedure. If the prisoner has failed to pursue administrative remedies through this procedure, any petition or complaint he files shall be stayed for 90 days to allow the prisoner to file a grievance and for completion of the procedure. If at the end of 90 days the prisoner has failed to timely file his grievance, then the petition or complaint shall be dismissed. Provided, however, that the court can waive the exhaustion requirement if it finds such waiver to be in the interest of justice. (1987, c. 746, s. 2; 2011-145, s. 19.1(h).)

§ 148-118.3. Publication of procedure.

The Administrative Remedy Procedure shall be published in the North Carolina Register. (1987, c. 746, s. 2.)

§ 148-118.4. Definitions.

For purposes of this Article, "prisoner" shall refer to all prisoners in the physical custody of the Division of Adult Correction of the Department of Public Safety. (1987, c. 746, s. 2; 2011-145, s. 19.1(h).)

§ 148-118.5. Records confidentiality.

All reports, investigations, and like supporting documents prepared by the Division for purposes of responding to the prisoner's request for an administrative remedy shall be deemed to be confidential. All formal written responses to the prisoner's request shall be furnished to the prisoner as a matter of course as required by the procedure. The Grievance Resolution Board shall have access to all relevant records developed by the Division of Adult Correction of the Department of Public Safety. (1987, c. 746, s. 2; 2011-145, s. 19.1(h).)

§ 148-118.6. Grievance Resolution Board.

The Grievance Resolution Board is established as a separate agency within the Division of Adult Correction of the Department of Public Safety. It shall consist of five members appointed by the Governor to serve four-year terms. Of the members so appointed, three shall be attorneys selected from a list of 10 persons recommended by the Council of the North Carolina State Bar. The remaining two members shall be persons of knowledge and experience in one or more fields under the jurisdiction of the Secretary of Public Safety. In the event a vacancy occurs on the Board prior to the expiration of a member's term, the Governor shall appoint a new Board member to serve the unexpired term. If the vacancy occurs in one of the positions designated for an attorney, the Governor shall select another attorney from a list of five persons recommended by the Council of the North Carolina State Bar. The Board shall perform those functions assigned to it by the Governor and shall review the grievance procedure. The Grievance Resolution Board shall meet not less then quarterly to review summaries of grievances. All members of the Inmate Grievance Commission, appointed by the Governor pursuant to G.S. 148-101, may complete their terms as members of the Board. Each member of the Board shall receive per diem and travel expenses as authorized for members of State commissions and boards under G.S. 138-5. (1987, c. 746, s. 2; 2011-145, s. 19.1(h), (i).)

148-118.7. Removal of members.

The Governor may remove any member of the Grievance Resolution Board for one or more of the following reasons:

(1) Conviction of a crime involving moral turpitude or of any criminal offense the effect of which is to prevent or interfere with the performance of Board duties.

(2) Failure to regularly attend meetings of the Board.

(3) Failure to carry out duties assigned by the Board or its chairman.

(4) Acceptance of another office or the conduct of other business conflicting with or tending to conflict with the performance of Board duties.

(5) Any other ground that, under law, necessitates or justifies the removal of a State employee. (1987, c. 746, s. 2.)

§ 148-118.8. Appointment, salary, and authority of Executive Director and inmate grievance examiners.

(a) The Grievance Resolution Board shall appoint an Executive Director and grievance examiners after consultation with the Secretary of Public Safety. The Executive Director shall manage the staff and perform such other functions as are assigned to him by the Grievance Resolution Board. The Executive Director and the grievance examiners shall serve at the pleasure of the Grievance Resolution Board. However, if a grievance examiner is removed from his position for other than just cause, he shall have priority for any position that becomes available for which he is qualified according to rules regulating and defining priority as promulgated by the State Human Resources Commission. The grievance examiners shall be subject to Article 2 of Chapter 126 of the North Carolina General Statutes for purposes of salary and leave. Support staff, equipment, and facilities for the Board shall be provided by the Division of Adult Correction of the Department of Public Safety.

(b) The inmate grievance examiners shall investigate inmate grievances pursuant to the procedures established by the Administrative Remedy Procedure. Examiners shall attempt to resolve grievances through mediation with all parties. Otherwise, the inmate grievance examiners shall either (i) order such relief as is appropriate; or (ii) deny the grievance. The decision of the grievance examiner shall be binding, unless the Secretary of Public Safety (i) finds that such relief is not appropriate, (ii) gives a written explanation for this finding, and (iii) makes an alternative order of relief or denies the grievance. (1987, c. 746, s. 2; 2011-145, s. 19.1(h), (i); 2013-382, s. 9.1(c).)

§ 148-118.9. Investigatory power of the Grievance Resolution Board.

The Secretary of Public Safety may request that the Grievance Resolution Board investigate matters involving broad policy concerns. The Grievance Resolution Board may convene a fact-finding hearing to consider the issues presented for investigation. A record of testimony presented at such hearing shall be maintained by the Board. The Board shall report the findings of its investigation to the Secretary within a reasonable time. In no event shall such a request on the part of the Secretary result in a delay of the resolution of an inmate's grievance beyond the 90 day period. (1987, c. 746, s. 2; 2011-145, s. 19.1(i).)

Article 12.

Interstate Corrections Compact.

§ 148-119. Short title.

This Article shall be known and may be cited as the Interstate Corrections Compact. (1979, c. 623.)

§ 148-120. Governor to execute; form of compact.

The Governor of North Carolina is hereby authorized and requested to execute, on behalf of the State of North Carolina, with any other state or states legally joining therein a compact which shall be in form substantially as follows:

The contracting states solemnly agree that:

(1) The party states, desiring by common action to fully utilize and improve their institutional facilities and provide adequate programs for the confinement, treatment and rehabilitation of various types of offenders, declare that it is the policy of each of the party states to provide such facilities and programs on a basis of cooperation with one another, and with the federal government, thereby serving the best interest of such offenders and of society and effecting economies in capital expenditures and operational costs. The purpose of this compact is to provide for the mutual development and execution of such programs of cooperation for the confinement, treatment and rehabilitation of offenders with the most economical use of human and material resources.

(2)   As used in this compact, unless the context clearly requires otherwise:

a.   "State" means a state of the United States; the United States of America; a territory or possession of the United States; the District of Columbia; the Commonwealth of Puerto Rico.

b.   "Sending state" means a state party to this compact in which conviction or court commitment was had.

c.   "Receiving state" means a state party to this compact to which an inmate is sent for confinement other than a state in which conviction or court commitment was had.

d.   "Inmate" means a male or female offender who is committed, under sentence to or confined in a penal or correctional institution.

e.   "Institution" means any penal or correctional facility, including but not limited to a facility for the mentally ill or mentally defective, in which inmates as defined in (2)d. above may lawfully be confined.

(3)   a.   Each party state may make one or more contracts with any one or more of the other party states, or with the federal government, for the confinement of inmates on behalf of a sending state in institutions situated within receiving states. Any such contract shall provide for:

1.   Its duration;

2.   Payments to be made to the receiving state or to the federal government, by the sending state for inmate maintenance, extraordinary medical and dental expenses, and any participation in or receipt by inmates of

rehabilitative or correctional services, facilities, programs or treatment not reasonably included as part of normal maintenance;

3. Participation in programs of inmate employment, if any; the disposition or crediting of any payments received by inmates on account thereof; and the crediting of proceeds from or disposal of any products resulting therefrom;

4. Delivery and retaking of inmates;

5. Such other matters as may be necessary and appropriate to fix the obligations, responsibilities and rights of the sending and receiving states.

b. The terms and provisions of this compact shall be a part of any contract entered into by the authority of or pursuant thereto and nothing in any such contract shall be inconsistent therewith.

(4) a. Whenever the duly constituted authorities in a state party to this compact, and which has entered into a contract pursuant to Article III, Subsection (1) [paragraph a. of subdivision (3)] shall decide that confinement in, or transfer of an inmate to, an institution within the territory of another party state is necessary or desirable in order to provide adequate quarters and care or an appropriate program of rehabilitation or treatment, said officials may direct that the confinement be within an institution within the territory of said other party state, the receiving state to act in that regard solely as agent for the sending state.

b. The appropriate officials of any state party to this compact shall have access, at all reasonable times, to any institution in which it has a contractual right to confine inmates for the purpose of inspecting the facilities thereof and visiting such of its inmates as may be confined in the institution.

c. Inmates confined in an institution pursuant to the terms of this compact shall at all times be subject to the jurisdiction of the sending state and may at any time be removed therefrom for transfer to a prison or other institution within the sending state, for transfer to another institution in which the sending state may have a contractual or other right to confine inmates, for release on probation or parole, for discharge, or for any other purpose permitted by the laws of the sending state, provided that the sending state shall continue to be obligated to such payments as may be required pursuant to the terms of any contract entered into under the terms of Article III, Subsection (1) [paragraph a. of subdivision (3)].

d. Each receiving state shall provide regular reports to each sending state on the inmates of that sending state in institutions pursuant to this compact including a conduct record of each inmate and certify said record to the official designated by the sending state, in order that each inmate may have official review of his or her record in determining and altering the disposition of said inmate in accordance with the law which may obtain in the sending state and in order that the same may be a source of information for the sending state.

e. All inmates who may be confined in an institution pursuant to the provisions of this compact shall be treated in a reasonable and humane manner and shall be treated equally with such similar inmates of the receiving state as may be confined in the same institution. The fact of confinement in a receiving state shall not deprive any inmate so confined of any legal rights which said inmate would have had if confined in an appropriate institution of the sending state.

f. Any hearing or hearings to which an inmate confined pursuant to this compact may be entitled by the laws of the sending state may be had before the appropriate authorities of the sending state, or of the receiving state if authorized by the sending state. The receiving state shall provide adequate facilities for such hearings as may be conducted by the appropriate officials of a sending state. In the event such hearing or hearings are had before officials of the receiving state, the governing law shall be that of the sending state and a record of the hearing or hearings as prescribed by the sending state shall be made. Said record, together with any recommendations of the hearing officials, shall be transmitted forthwith to the official or officials before whom the hearing would have been had if it had taken place in the sending state. In any and all proceedings had pursuant to the provisions of this subdivision, the officials of the receiving state shall act solely as agents of the sending state and no final determination shall be made in any matter except by the appropriate officials of the sending state.

g. Any inmate confined pursuant to this compact shall be released within the territory of the sending state unless the inmate, and the sending and receiving states, shall agree upon release in some other place. The sending state shall bear the cost of such return to its territory.

h. Any inmate confined pursuant to the terms of this compact shall have any and all rights to participate in and derive any benefits or incur or be relieved of any obligations or have such obligations modified or his status changed on account of any action or proceeding in which he could have participated if confined in any appropriate institution of the sending state located within such state.

i. The parents, guardian, trustee, or other person or persons entitled under the laws of the sending state to act for, advise or otherwise function with respect to any inmate shall not be deprived of or restricted in his exercise of any power in respect of any inmate confined pursuant to the terms of this compact.

(5) a. Any decision of the sending state in respect to any matter over which it retains jurisdiction pursuant to this compact shall be conclusive upon and not reviewable within the receiving state, but if at the time the sending state seeks to remove an inmate from an institution in the receiving state there is pending against the inmate within such state any criminal charge or if the inmate is formally accused of having committed within such state a criminal offense, the inmate shall not be returned without the consent of the receiving state until discharge from prosecution or other form of proceeding, imprisonment or detention for such offense. The duly accredited officers of the sending state shall be permitted to transport inmates pursuant to this compact through any and all states party to this compact without interference.

b. An inmate who escapes from an institution in which he is confined pursuant to this compact shall be deemed a fugitive from the sending state and from the state in which the institution is situated. In the case of an escape to a jurisdiction other than the sending or receiving state, the responsibility for institution of extradition or rendition proceedings shall be that of the sending state, but nothing contained herein shall be construed to prevent or affect the activities of officers and agencies of any jurisdiction directed toward the apprehension and return of an escapee.

(6) Any state party to this compact may accept federal aid for use in connection with any institution or program, the use of which is or may be affected by this compact or any contract pursuant hereto; and any inmate in a receiving state pursuant to this compact may participate in any such federally-aided program or activity for which the sending and receiving states have made contractual provision, provided that if such program or activity is not part of the customary correctional regimen, the express consent of the appropriate official of the sending state shall be required therefor.

(7) This compact shall enter into force and become effective and binding upon the states so acting when it has been enacted into law by any two states.

Thereafter, this compact shall enter into force and become effective and binding as to any other of said states upon similar action by such state.

(8) This compact shall continue in force and remain binding upon a party state until it shall have enacted a statute repealing the same and providing for the sending of formal written notice of withdrawal from the compact to the appropriate official of all other party states. An actual withdrawal shall not take effect until one year after the notice provided in said statute has been sent. Such withdrawal shall not relieve the withdrawing state from its obligations assumed hereunder prior to the effective date of withdrawal. Before effective date of withdrawal, a withdrawing state shall remove to its territory, at its own expense, such inmates as it may have confined pursuant to the provisions of this compact.

(9) Nothing contained in this compact shall be construed to abrogate or impair any agreement or other arrangement which a party state may have with a nonparty state for the confinement, rehabilitation or treatment of inmates nor to repeal any other laws of a party state authorizing the making of cooperative institutional arrangements.

(10) The provisions of this compact shall be liberally construed and shall be severable. If any phrase, clause, sentence or provision of this compact is declared to be contrary to the constitution of any participating state or of the United States or the applicability thereof to any government, agency, person or circumstance is held invalid, the validity of the remainder of this compact and the applicability thereof to any government, agency, person or circumstance shall not be affected thereby. If this compact shall be held contrary to the constitution of any state participating therein, the compact shall remain in full force and effect as to the remaining states and in full force and effect as to the state affected as to all severable matters. (1979, c. 623.)

§ 148-121. Proceedings to be open; all documents public records; exception.

(a) Except as provided in subsection (c) of this section, at least 30 days before a transfer of a North Carolina inmate to another state system pursuant to this Article is approved, the Secretary of Public Safety shall give notice that the transfer is being considered. The Secretary shall give notice of the proposed transfer by:

(1) Notifying the district attorney of the district where the prisoner was convicted, the judge who presided at the prisoner's trial, the law-enforcement agency that arrested the prisoner, and the victim of the prisoner's crime;

(2) Posting notice at the courthouse in the county in which the prisoner was convicted; and

(3) Notifying any other person who has made a written request to receive notice of a transfer of the prisoner.

(b) Except as provided in subsection (c) of this section, all written comments regarding a transfer are public records under General Statutes Chapter 132.

(c) If, in the discretion of the Secretary, such notice or disclosure requirements provided for in this section would jeopardize the safety of persons or property, the provisions of this section do not apply. (1983, c. 874, s. 1; 2011-145, s. 19.1(i).)

Article 13.

Transfer of Convicted Foreign Citizens Under Federal Treaty.

§ 148-122. Transfer of convicted foreign citizens under treaty; consent by Governor.

If a treaty in effect between the United States and a foreign country provides for the transfer or exchange of convicted offenders to the country of which the offenders are citizens or nationals, the Governor may, on behalf of the State and subject to the terms of the treaty, authorize the Secretary of Public Safety to consent to the transfer or exchange of offenders and take any other action necessary to initiate the participation of the State in the treaty. (2002-166, s. 4; 2011-145, s. 19.1(i).)

§ 148-123: Reserved for future codification purposes.

§ 148-124: Reserved for future codification purposes.

§ 148-125: Reserved for future codification purposes.

§ 148-126: Reserved for future codification purposes.

§ 148-127: Reserved for future codification purposes.

Article 14.

Correction Enterprises.

§ 148-128. Authorization for Correction Enterprises.

The Section of Correction Enterprises of the Division of Adult Correction is established as a division of the Division of Adult Correction of the Department of Public Safety. The Section of Correction Enterprises of the Division of Adult Correction may develop and operate industrial, agricultural, and service enterprises that employ incarcerated offenders in an effort to provide them with meaningful work experiences and rehabilitative opportunities that will increase their employability upon release from prison. Enterprises operated under this Article shall be known as "Correction Enterprises." (2007-280, s. 1; 2011-145, s. 19.1(h), (j).)

§ 148-129. Purposes of Correction Enterprises.

Correction Enterprises shall serve all of the following purposes to:

(1)   Provide incarcerated offenders a work and training environment that emulates private industry.

(2)   Provide incarcerated offenders with training opportunities that allow them to increase work skills and employability upon release from prison.

(3)   Provide quality goods and services.

(4)   Aid victims by contributing a portion of its proceeds to the Crime Victims Compensation Fund.

(5) Generate sufficient funds from the sale of goods and services to be a self-supporting operation. (2007-280, s. 1.)

§ 148-130. Correction Enterprises Fund.

(a) All revenues from the sale of articles and commodities manufactured or produced by Correction Enterprises shall be deposited with the State Treasurer to be kept and maintained as a special revolving working-capital fund designated "Correction Enterprises Fund."

(b) Revenue in the Correction Enterprises Fund shall be applied first to capital and operating expenditures, including salaries and wages of personnel necessary to develop and operate Correction Enterprises and incentive wages for inmates employed by Correction Enterprises or participating in work assignments established by the Section of Prisons of the Division of Adult Correction. Of the remaining revenue in the Fund, five percent (5%) of the net proceeds, before expansion costs, shall be credited to the Crime Victims Compensation Fund established in G.S. 15B-23 as soon as practicable after net proceeds have been determined for the previous year. At the direction of the Governor, the remainder shall be used for other purposes within the State prison system or shall be transferred to the General Fund.

(c) The Correction Enterprises Fund shall be the source of all incentive wages and allowances paid to inmates employed by Correction Enterprises and inmates participating in work assignments established by the Section of Prisons of the Division of Adult Correction. (2007-280, s. 1; 2011-145, s. 19.1(j).)

§ 148-131. Powers and responsibilities.

In order to fulfill the purposes set forth in G.S. 148-129, the Section of Correction Enterprises of the Division of Adult Correction is authorized and empowered to take all actions necessary in the operation of its enterprises, including any of the following actions to:

(1) Develop and operate industrial, agricultural, and service enterprises either within prison facilities or outside the prison facilities.

(2) Plan and establish new industrial, agricultural, and service enterprises so long as any new enterprise is specifically approved by the Governor as required by G.S. 66-58(f).

(3) Employ inmates and any other personnel that may be necessary in the operation of Correction Enterprises.

(4) Expand, diminish, or discontinue any enterprise operating under its authority.

(5) Purchase any machinery, equipment, materials, and supplies required in the operation of its enterprises.

(6) Market and sell the goods and services produced by Correction Enterprises.

(7) Determine the prices at which products and services produced by inmate labor shall be sold.

(8) Execute and enter into contracts.

(9) Establish and operate an enterprise that complies with all applicable federal laws and guidelines required by the federal Prison Industry Enhancement Certification Program (Justice Assistance Act of 1984: Public Law 98-473, Section 819).

(10) Establish policies and procedures regarding the operation of Correction Enterprises.

(11) Take any action necessary and appropriate for the effective operation of its enterprises, so long as that action complies with applicable State and federal laws. (2007-280, s. 1; 2011-145, s. 19.1(j).)

§ 148-132. Distribution of products and services.

The Section of Correction Enterprises of the Division of Adult Correction is empowered and authorized to market and sell products and services produced by Correction Enterprises to any of the following entities:

(1) Any public agency or institution owned, managed, or controlled by the State.

(2) Any county, city, or town in this State.

(3) Any federal, state, or local public agency or institution in any other state of the union.

(4) An entity or organization that has tax-exempt status pursuant to section 501(c)(3) of the Internal Revenue Code. Products purchased by an entity pursuant to this subdivision may not be resold.

(5) Any current employee or retiree of the State of North Carolina or of a unit of local government of this State, verified through State-issued identification, or through proof of retirement status, but purchases by a State or local governmental employee or retiree may not exceed two thousand five hundred dollars ($2,500) during any calendar year. Products purchased by State and local governmental employees and retirees under this section may not be resold.

(6) Private contractors when the goods purchased will be used to perform work under a contract with a public agency. (2007-280, s. 1; 2009-451, s. 19.16; 2011-145, ss. 18.14, 19.1(j); 2013-289, s. 6.)

§ 148-133. Inmate wages and conditions of employment.

(a) The Secretary shall adopt rules for the administration and management of personnel policies for inmates who work for Correction Enterprises, including wages, working hours, training requirements, and conditions of employment. The Secretary shall adopt rules to ensure that inmates participating in the Prison Industry Enhancement Certification Program comply with all applicable federal rules and regulations.

(b) No inmate working for Correction Enterprises shall be paid more than three dollars ($3.00) per day unless applicable State or federal laws require a higher salary. Inmates who are employed as part of the Prison Industry Enhancement Certification Program shall be paid in accordance with applicable federal rules and regulations. (2007-280, s. 1.)

§ 148-134. Preference for Division of Adult Correction of the Department of Public Safety products.

All departments, institutions, and agencies of this State that are supported in whole or in part by the State shall give preference to Correction Enterprises products in purchasing articles, products, and commodities that these departments, institutions, and agencies require and that are manufactured or produced within the State prison system and offered for sale to them by Correction Enterprises. No article or commodity available from Correction Enterprises shall be purchased by any State department, institution, or agency from any other source unless the prison product does not meet the standard specifications and the reasonable requirements of the department, institution, or agency as determined by the Secretary of Administration or the requisition cannot be complied with because of an insufficient supply of the articles or commodities required. The provisions of Article 3 of Chapter 143 of the General Statutes respecting contracting for the purchase of all supplies, materials, and equipment required by the State government or any of its departments, institutions, or agencies under competitive bidding shall not apply to articles or commodities available from Correction Enterprises. The Section of Correction Enterprises of the Division of Adult Correction shall be required to keep the price of such articles or commodities substantially in accord with that paid by governmental agencies for similar articles and commodities of equivalent quality. (2007-280, s. 1; 2011-145, s. 19.1(h), (j).)

Chapter 149.

State Song and Toast.

§ 149-1. "The Old North State."

The song known as "The Old North State," as hereinafter written, is adopted and declared to be the official song of the State of North Carolina, said song being in words as follows:

"Carolina! Carolina! Heaven's blessings attend her!

While we live we will cherish, protect and defend her;

Though the scorner may sneer at and witlings defame her,

Our hearts swell with gladness whenever we name her.

    Hurrah! Hurrah! The Old North State forever!

    Hurrah! Hurrah! The good Old North State!

Though she envies not others their merited glory,

Say, whose name stands the foremost in Liberty's story!

Though too true to herself e'er to crouch to oppression,

Who can yield to just rule more loyal submission?

Plain and artless her sons, but whose doors open faster

At the knock of a stranger, or the tale of disaster?

How like to the rudeness of their dear native mountains,

With rich ore in their bosoms and life in their fountains.

And her daughters, the Queen of the Forest resembling-

So graceful, so constant, yet to gentlest breath trembling;

And true lightwood at heart, let the match be applied them,

How they kindle and flame! Oh! none know but who've tried them.

Then let all who love us, love the land that we live in

(As happy a region on this side of Heaven),

(Where Plenty and Freedom, Love and Peace smile before us,

Raise aloud, raise together, the heart-thrilling chorus!"

(1927, c. 26, s. 1.)

§ 149-2. "A Toast" to North Carolina.

The song referred to as "A Toast" to North Carolina is hereby adopted and declared to be the official toast to the State of North Carolina, said toast being in words as follows:

"Here's to the land of the long leaf pine,

The summer land where the sun doth shine,

Where the weak grow strong and the strong grow great,

Here's to 'Down Home,' the Old North State!

"Here's to the land of the cotton bloom white,

Where the scuppernong perfumes the breeze at night,

Where the soft southern moss and jessamine mate,

'Neath the murmuring pines of the Old North State!

"Here's to the land where the galax grows,

Where the rhododendron's rosette glows,

Where soars Mount Mitchell's summit great,

In the 'Land of the Sky,' in the Old North State!

"Here's to the land where maidens are fair,

Where friends are true and cold hearts rare,

The near land, the dear land whatever fate,

The blest land, the best land, the Old North State!"

(1957, c. 777.)

Chapter 150.
Uniform Revocation of Licenses.

§§ 150-1 through 150-34. Repealed by Session Laws 1973, c. 1331, as amended by Session Laws 1975, c. 69, s. 4.

Chapter 150A.

Administrative Procedure Act.

§§ 150A-1 through 150A-64. Recodified as §§ 150B-1 to 150B-64, effective January 1, 1986.

Chapter 150B.

Administrative Procedure Act.

Article 1.

General Provisions.

§ 150B-1. Policy and scope.

(a)   Purpose. - This Chapter establishes a uniform system of administrative rule making and adjudicatory procedures for agencies. The procedures ensure that the functions of rule making, investigation, advocacy, and adjudication are not all performed by the same person in the administrative process.

(b)   Rights. - This Chapter confers procedural rights.

(c)   Full Exemptions. - This Chapter applies to every agency except:

(1)   The North Carolina National Guard in exercising its court-martial jurisdiction.

(2)   The Department of Health and Human Services in exercising its authority over the Camp Butner reservation granted in Article 6 of Chapter 122C of the General Statutes.

(3) The Utilities Commission.
(4) Repealed by Session Laws 2011-287, s. 21(a), effective June 24, 2011, and applicable to rules adopted on or after that date.

(5) Repealed by Session Laws 2011-401, s. 1.10(a), effective November 1, 2011.

(6) The State Board of Elections in administering the HAVA Administrative Complaint Procedure of Article 8A of Chapter 163 of the General Statutes.

(7) The North Carolina State Lottery.

(8) [Expired June 30, 2012.]

(d) Exemptions from Rule Making. - Article 2A of this Chapter does not apply to the following:

(1) The Commission.

(2) Repealed by Session Laws 2000-189, s. 14, effective July 1, 2000.

(3) Repealed by Session Laws 2001-474, s. 34, effective November 29, 2001.

(4) The Department of Revenue, with respect to the notice and hearing requirements contained in Part 2 of Article 2A. With respect to the Secretary of Revenue's authority to redetermine the State net taxable income of a corporation under G.S. 105-130.5A, the Department is subject to the rule-making requirements of G.S. 105-262.1.

(5) The North Carolina Global TransPark Authority with respect to the acquisition, construction, operation, or use, including fees or charges, of any portion of a cargo airport complex.

(6) The Division of Adult Correction of the Department of Public Safety, with respect to matters relating solely to persons in its custody or under its supervision, including prisoners, probationers, and parolees.

(7) The State Health Plan for Teachers and State Employees in administering the provisions of Article 3B of Chapter 135 of the General Statutes.

(8) The North Carolina Federal Tax Reform Allocation Committee, with respect to the adoption of the annual qualified allocation plan required by 26 U.S.C. § 42(m), and any agency designated by the Committee to the extent necessary to administer the annual qualified allocation plan.

(9) The Department of Health and Human Services in adopting new or amending existing medical coverage policies for the State Medicaid and NC Health Choice programs pursuant to G.S. 108A-54.2.

(10) The Economic Investment Committee in developing criteria for the Job Development Investment Grant Program under Part 2F of Article 10 of Chapter 143B of the General Statutes.

(11) The North Carolina State Ports Authority with respect to fees established pursuant to G.S. 136-262(a)(11).

(12) The Department of Commerce and the Economic Investment Committee in developing criteria and administering the Site Infrastructure Development Program under G.S. 143B-437.02.

(13) The Department of Commerce and the Governor's Office in developing guidelines for the One North Carolina Fund under Part 2H of Article 10 of Chapter 143B of the General Statutes.

(14) Repealed by Session Laws 2011-145, s. 8.18(a), as amended by Session Laws 2011-391, s. 19, effective June 15, 2011.

(15) Repealed by Session Laws 2009-445, s. 41(b), effective August 7, 2009.

(16) The State Ethics Commission with respect to Chapter 138A and Chapter 120C of the General Statutes.

(17) The Department of Commerce in developing guidelines for the NC Green Business Fund under Part 2B of Article 10 of Chapter 143B of the General Statutes.

(18) The Department of Commerce and the Economic Investment Committee in developing criteria and administering the Job Maintenance and Capital Development Fund under G.S. 143B-437.012.

(19)   Repealed by Session Laws 2011-145, s. 8.18(a), as amended by Session Laws 2011-391, s. 19, effective June 15, 2011.

(20)   The Department of Health and Human Services in implementing, operating, or overseeing new 1915(b)/(c) Medicaid Waiver programs or amendments to existing 1915(b)/(c) Medicaid Waiver programs.

(21)   Reserved for future codification purposes.

(22)   The Department of Health and Human Services with respect to the content of State Plans, State Plan Amendments, and Waivers approved by the Centers for Medicare and Medicaid Services (CMS) for the North Carolina Medicaid Program and the NC Health Choice program.

(23)   The Department of Cultural Resources with respect to admission fees or related activity fees at historic sites and museums pursuant to G.S. 121-7.3.

(24)   Tryon Palace Commission with respect to admission fees or related activity fees pursuant to G.S. 143B-71.

(25)   U.S.S. Battleship Commission with respect to admission fees or related activity fees pursuant to G.S. 143B-73.

(e)   Exemptions From Contested Case Provisions. - The contested case provisions of this Chapter apply to all agencies and all proceedings not expressly exempted from the Chapter. The contested case provisions of this Chapter do not apply to the following:

(1)   The Department of Health and Human Services and the Department of Environment and Natural Resources in complying with the procedural safeguards mandated by Section 680 of Part H of Public Law 99-457 as amended (Education of the Handicapped Act Amendments of 1986).

(2)   Repealed by Session Laws 1993, c. 501, s. 29.

(3),   (4) Repealed by Session Laws 2001-474, s. 35, effective November 29, 2001.

(5)   Hearings required pursuant to the Rehabilitation Act of 1973, (Public Law 93-122), as amended and federal regulations promulgated thereunder.

G.S. 150B-51(a) is considered a contested case hearing provision that does not apply to these hearings.

(6)   Repealed by Session Laws 2007-491, s. 2, effective January 1, 2008.

(7)   The Division of Adult Correction of the Department of Public Safety.

(8)   The Department of Transportation, except as provided in G.S. 136-29.

(9)   The North Carolina Occupational Safety and Health Review Commission.

(10)   The North Carolina Global TransPark Authority with respect to the acquisition, construction, operation, or use, including fees or charges, of any portion of a cargo airport complex.

(11)   Hearings that are provided by the Department of Health and Human Services regarding the eligibility and provision of services for eligible assaultive and violent children, as defined in G.S. 122C-3(13a), shall be conducted pursuant to the provisions outlined in G.S. 122C, Article 4, Part 7.

(12)   The State Health Plan for Teachers and State Employees respect to disputes involving the performance, terms, or conditions of a contract between the Plan and an entity under contract with the Plan.

(13)   The State Health Plan for Teachers and State Employees with respect to determinations by the Executive Administrator and Board of Trustees, the Plan's designated utilization review organization, or a self-funded health maintenance organization under contract with the Plan that an admission, availability of care, continued stay, or other health care service has been reviewed and, based upon the information provided, does not meet the Plan's requirements for medical necessity, appropriateness, health care setting, or level of care or effectiveness, and the requested service is therefore denied, reduced, or terminated.

(14)   The Department of Public Safety for hearings and appeals authorized under Chapter 20 of the General Statutes.

(15)   The Wildlife Resources Commission with respect to determinations of whether to authorize or terminate the authority of a person to sell licenses and permits as a license agent of the Wildlife Resources Commission.

(16) Repealed by Session Laws 2011-399, s. 3, effective July 25, 2011.

(17) The Department of Health and Human Services with respect to the review of North Carolina Health Choice Program determinations regarding delay, denial, reduction, suspension, or termination of health services, in whole or in part, including a determination about the type or level of services.

(18) Hearings provided by the Department of Health and Human Services to decide appeals pertaining to adult care home resident discharges initiated by adult care homes under G.S. 131D-4.8.

(19) The Industrial Commission.

(20) The Department of Commerce for hearings and appeals authorized under Chapter 96 of the General Statutes.

(21) The Department of Health and Human Services for actions taken under G.S. 122C-124.2.

(f) Exemption for the University of North Carolina. - Except as provided in G.S. 143-135.3, no Article in this Chapter except Article 4 applies to The University of North Carolina.

(g) Exemption for the State Board of Community Colleges. - Except as provided in G.S. 143-135.3, no Article in this Chapter except Article 4 applies to the State Board of Community Colleges. (1973, c. 1331, s. 1; 1975, c. 390; c. 716, s. 5; c. 721, s. 1; c. 742, s. 4; 1981, c. 614, s. 22; 1983, c. 147, s. 2; c. 927, s. 13; 1985, c. 746, ss. 1, 19; 1987, c. 112, s. 2; c. 335, s. 2; c. 536, s. 1; c. 847, s. 2; c. 850, s. 20; 1987 (Reg. Sess., 1988), c. 1082, s. 14; c. 1111, s. 9; 1989, c. 76, s. 29; c. 168, s. 33; c. 373, s. 2; c. 538, s. 1; c. 751, s. 7(44); 1989 (Reg. Sess., 1990), c. 1004, s. 36; 1991, c. 103, s. 1; c. 418, s. 2; c. 477, s. 1; c. 749, ss. 9, 10; 1991 (Reg. Sess., 1992), c. 1030, s. 46; 1993, c. 501, s. 29; 1993 (Reg. Sess., 1994), c. 777, ss. 4(j), 4(k); 1995, c. 249, s. 4; c. 507, s. 27.8(m); 1997-35, s. 2; 1997-278, s. 1; 1997-412, s. 8; 1997-443, ss. 11A.110, 11A.119(a); 2000-189, s. 14; 2001-192, s. 1; 2001-299, s. 1; 2001-395, s. 6(c); 2001-424, ss. 6.20(b), 21.20(c); 2001-446, s. 5(d); 2001-474, ss. 34, 35; 2001-496, s. 8(c); 2002-99, s. 7(b); 2002-159, ss. 31.5(b), 49; 2002-172, s. 2.6; 2002-190, s. 16; 2003-226, s. 17(b); 2003-416, s. 2; 2003-435, 2nd Ex. Sess., s. 1.3; 2004-88, s. 1(e); 2005-133, s. 10; 2005-276, s. 31.1(ff); 2005-300, s. 1; 2005-344, s. 11.1; 2005-455, s. 3.3; 2006-66, ss. 12.8(c), 8.10(d); 2006-201, s. 2(a); 2007-323, ss. 13.2(c), 28.22A(o); 2007-345, s. 12; 2007-491, s. 2; 2007-552,

1st. Ex. Sess., s. 3; 2008-107, s. 10.15A(f); 2008-168, s. 5(a); 2008-187, s. 26(b); 2009-445, s. 41(b); 2009-475, s. 4; 2009-523, s. 2(a); 2010-70, s. 2; 2011-85, s. 2.11(a); 2011-145, ss. 8.18(a), (b), 14.6(j), 19.1(g), (h); 2011-264, s. 4; 2011-272, s. 5; 2011-287, s. 21(a), (b); 2011-391, s. 19; 2011-399, ss. 2, 3; 2011-401, ss. 1.10(a), (b); 2012-43, s. 3; 2013-85, s. 10; 2013-360, ss. 19.2(d), 12H.6(c), 12H.9(c).)

§ 150B-2. Definitions.

As used in this Chapter,

(1) "Administrative law judge" means a person appointed under G.S. 7A-752, 7A-753, or 7A-757.

(1a) "Agency" means an agency or an officer in the executive branch of the government of this State and includes the Council of State, the Governor's Office, a board, a commission, a department, a division, a council, and any other unit of government in the executive branch. A local unit of government is not an agency.

(1b) "Adopt" means to take final action to create, amend, or repeal a rule.

(1c) "Codifier of Rules" means the Chief Administrative Law Judge of the Office of Administrative Hearings or a designated representative of the Chief Administrative Law Judge.

(1d) "Commission" means the Rules Review Commission.

(2) "Contested case" means an administrative proceeding pursuant to this Chapter to resolve a dispute between an agency and another person that involves the person's rights, duties, or privileges, including licensing or the levy of a monetary penalty. "Contested case" does not include rulemaking, declaratory rulings, or the award or denial of a scholarship, a grant, or a loan.

(2a) Repealed by Session Laws 1991, c. 418, s. 3.

(2b) "Hearing officer" means a person or group of persons designated by an agency that is subject to Article 3A of this Chapter to preside in a contested case hearing conducted under that Article.

(3) "License" means any certificate, permit or other evidence, by whatever name called, of a right or privilege to engage in any activity, except licenses issued under Chapter 20 and Subchapter I of Chapter 105 of the General Statutes and occupational licenses.

(4) "Licensing" means any administrative action issuing, failing to issue, suspending, or revoking a license or occupational license. "Licensing" does not include controversies over whether an examination was fair or whether the applicant passed the examination.

(4a) "Occupational license" means any certificate, permit, or other evidence, by whatever name called, of a right or privilege to engage in a profession, occupation, or field of endeavor that is issued by an occupational licensing agency.

(4b) "Occupational licensing agency" means any board, commission, committee or other agency of the State of North Carolina which is established for the primary purpose of regulating the entry of persons into, and/or the conduct of persons within a particular profession, occupation or field of endeavor, and which is authorized to issue and revoke licenses. "Occupational licensing agency" does not include State agencies or departments which may as only a part of their regular function issue permits or licenses.

(5) "Party" means any person or agency named or admitted as a party or properly seeking as of right to be admitted as a party and includes the agency as appropriate.

(6) "Person aggrieved" means any person or group of persons of common interest directly or indirectly affected substantially in his or its person, property, or employment by an administrative decision.

(7) "Person" means any natural person, partnership, corporation, body politic and any unincorporated association, organization, or society which may sue or be sued under a common name.

(7a) "Policy" means any nonbinding interpretive statement within the delegated authority of an agency that merely defines, interprets, or explains the meaning of a statute or rule. The term includes any document issued by an agency which is intended and used purely to assist a person to comply with the law, such as a guidance document.

(8) "Residence" means domicile or principal place of business.

(8a) "Rule" means any agency regulation, standard, or statement of general applicability that implements or interprets an enactment of the General Assembly or Congress or a regulation adopted by a federal agency or that describes the procedure or practice requirements of an agency. The term includes the establishment of a fee and the amendment or repeal of a prior rule. The term does not include the following:

a. Statements concerning only the internal management of an agency or group of agencies within the same principal office or department enumerated in G.S. 143A-11 or 143B-6, including policies and procedures manuals, if the statement does not directly or substantially affect the procedural or substantive rights or duties of a person not employed by the agency or group of agencies.

b. Budgets and budget policies and procedures issued by the Director of the Budget, by the head of a department, as defined by G.S. 143A-2 or G.S. 143B-3, by an occupational licensing board, as defined by G.S. 93B-1, or by the State Board of Elections.

c. Nonbinding interpretative statements within the delegated authority of an agency that merely define, interpret, or explain the meaning of a statute or rule.

d. A form, the contents or substantive requirements of which are prescribed by rule or statute.

e. Statements of agency policy made in the context of another proceeding, including:

1. Declaratory rulings under G.S. 150B-4.

2. Orders establishing or fixing rates or tariffs.

f. Requirements, communicated to the public by the use of signs or symbols, concerning the use of public roads, bridges, ferries, buildings, or facilities.

g. Statements that set forth criteria or guidelines to be used by the staff of an agency in performing audits, investigations, or inspections; in settling financial disputes or negotiating financial arrangements; or in the defense, prosecution, or settlement of cases.

h. Scientific, architectural, or engineering standards, forms, or procedures, including design criteria and construction standards used to construct or maintain highways, bridges, or ferries.

i. Job classification standards, job qualifications, and salaries established for positions under the jurisdiction of the State Human Resources Commission.

j. Establishment of the interest rate that applies to tax assessments under G.S. 105-241.21 and the variable component of the excise tax on motor fuel under G.S. 105-449.80.

k. The State Medical Facilities Plan, if the Plan has been prepared with public notice and hearing as provided in G.S. 131E-176(25), reviewed by the Commission for compliance with G.S. 131E-176(25), and approved by the Governor.

l. Standards adopted by the Office of Information Technology Services applied to information technology as defined by G.S. 147-33.81.

(8b) Repealed by Session Laws 2011-398, s. 61.2, effective July 25, 2011.

(8c) "Substantial evidence" means relevant evidence a reasonable mind might accept as adequate to support a conclusion.

(9) Repealed by Session Laws 1991, c. 418, s. 3. (1973, c. 1331, s. 1; 1975, 2nd Sess., c. 983, ss. 61, 62; 1977, c. 915, s. 5; 1983, c. 641, s. 1; 1985, c. 746, s. 1; 1985 (Reg. Sess., 1986), c. 1022, s. 1(2)-1(5); 1987, c. 878, ss. 1, 2, 21; 1987 (Reg. Sess., 1988), c. 1111, s. 17; 1991, c. 418, s. 3; c. 477, ss. 3.1, 3.2, 9; 1995, c. 390, s. 29; 1996, 2nd Ex. Sess., c. 18, s. 7.10(g); 1997-456, s. 27; 2003-229, s. 12; 2007-491, s. 44(1)b; 2011-13, s. 2; 2011-398, ss. 15, 61.2; 2013-188, s. 7; 2013-382, s. 9.1(c); 2013-413, s. 1.)

§ 150B-3. Special provisions on licensing.

(a) When an applicant or a licensee makes a timely and sufficient application for issuance or renewal of a license or occupational license, including the payment of any required license fee, the existing license or occupational license does not expire until a decision on the application is finally made by the agency, and if the application is denied or the terms of the new license or occupational license are limited, until the last day for applying for judicial review of the agency order. This subsection does not affect agency action summarily suspending a license or occupational license under subsections (b) and (c) of this section.

(b) Before the commencement of proceedings for the suspension, revocation, annulment, withdrawal, recall, cancellation, or amendment of any license other than an occupational license, the agency shall give notice to the licensee, pursuant to the provisions of G.S. 150B-23. Before the commencement of such proceedings involving an occupational license, the agency shall give notice pursuant to the provisions of G.S. 150B-38. In either case, the licensee shall be given an opportunity to show compliance with all lawful requirements for retention of the license or occupational license.

(c) If the agency finds that the public health, safety, or welfare requires emergency action and incorporates this finding in its order, summary suspension of a license or occupational license may be ordered effective on the date specified in the order or on service of the certified copy of the order at the last known address of the licensee, whichever is later, and effective during the proceedings. The proceedings shall be promptly commenced and determined.

Nothing in this subsection shall be construed as amending or repealing any special statutes, in effect prior to February 1, 1976, which provide for the summary suspension of a license.

(d) This section does not apply to the following:

(1) Revocations of occupational licenses based solely on a court order of child support delinquency or a Department of Health and Human Services determination of child support delinquency issued pursuant to G.S. 110-142, 110-142.1, or 110-142.2.

(2) Refusal to renew an occupational license pursuant to G.S. 87-10.1, 87-22.2, 87-44.2, or 89C-18.1, based solely on a Department of Revenue determination that the licensee owes a delinquent income tax debt. (1973, c. 1331, s. 1; 1985, c. 746, s. 1; 1995, c. 538, s. 2(i); 1997-443, s. 11A.118(a); 1998-162, s. 8.)

§ 150B-4. Declaratory rulings.

(a) On request of a person aggrieved, an agency shall issue a declaratory ruling as to the validity of a rule or as to the applicability to a given state of facts of a statute administered by the agency or of a rule or order of the agency. Upon request, an agency shall also issue a declaratory ruling to resolve a conflict or inconsistency within the agency regarding an interpretation of the law or a rule adopted by the agency. The agency shall prescribe in its rules the procedure for requesting a declaratory ruling and the circumstances in which rulings shall or shall not be issued. A declaratory ruling is binding on the agency and the person requesting it unless it is altered or set aside by the court. An agency may not retroactively change a declaratory ruling, but nothing in this section prevents an agency from prospectively changing a declaratory ruling.

(a1) An agency shall respond to a request for a declaratory ruling as follows:

(1) Within 30 days of receipt of the request for a declaratory ruling, the agency shall make a written decision to grant or deny the request. If the agency fails to make a written decision to grant or deny the request within 30 days, the failure shall be deemed a decision to deny the request.

(2) If the agency denies the request, the decision is immediately subject to judicial review in accordance with Article 4 of this Chapter.

(3) If the agency grants the request, the agency shall issue a written ruling on the merits within 45 days of the decision to grant the request. A declaratory ruling is subject to judicial review in accordance with Article 4 of this Chapter.

(4) If the agency fails to issue a declaratory ruling within 45 days, the failure shall be deemed a denial on the merits, and the person aggrieved may seek judicial review pursuant to Article 4 of this Chapter. Upon review of an agency's failure to issue a declaratory ruling, the court shall not consider any basis for the denial that was not presented in writing to the person aggrieved.

(b) Repealed by Session Laws 1997-34, s. 1. (1973, c. 1331, s. 1; 1985, c. 746, s. 1; 1991, c. 418, s. 4; c. 477, s. 2.1; 1997-34, s. 1; 2011-398, s. 56.)

§§ 150B-5 through 150B-8. Reserved for future codification purposes.

Article 2.

Rule Making.

§§ 150B-9 through 150B-16: Repealed by Session Laws 1991, c. 418, s. 5.

§ 150B-17: Recodified as § 150B-4 by Session Laws 1991, c. 418, s. 4.

Article 2A.

Rules.

Part 1. General Provisions.

§ 150B-18. Scope and effect.

This Article applies to an agency's exercise of its authority to adopt a rule. A rule is not valid unless it is adopted in substantial compliance with this Article. An agency shall not seek to implement or enforce against any person a policy, guideline, or other interpretive statement that meets the definition of a rule contained in G.S. 150B-2(8a) if the policy, guideline, or other interpretive statement has not been adopted as a rule in accordance with this Article. (1991, c. 418, s. 1; 2011-398, s. 1; 2012-187, s. 2.)

§ 150B-19. Restrictions on what can be adopted as a rule.

An agency may not adopt a rule that does one or more of the following:

(1) Implements or interprets a law unless that law or another law specifically authorizes the agency to do so.

(2) Enlarges the scope of a profession, occupation, or field of endeavor for which an occupational license is required.

(3) Imposes criminal liability or a civil penalty for an act or omission, including the violation of a rule, unless a law specifically authorizes the agency

to do so or a law declares that violation of the rule is a criminal offense or is grounds for a civil penalty.

(4) Repeats the content of a law, a rule, or a federal regulation. A brief statement that informs the public of a requirement imposed by law does not violate this subdivision and satisfies the "reasonably necessary" standard of review set in G.S. 150B-21.9(a)(3).

(5) Establishes a fee or other charge for providing a service in fulfillment of a duty unless a law specifically authorizes the agency to do so or the fee or other charge is for one of the following:

a. A service to a State, federal, or local governmental unit.

b. A copy of part or all of a State publication or other document, the cost of mailing a document, or both.

c. A transcript of a public hearing.

d. A conference, workshop, or course.

e. Data processing services.

(6) Allows the agency to waive or modify a requirement set in a rule unless a rule establishes specific guidelines the agency must follow in determining whether to waive or modify the requirement.

(7) Repealed by Session Laws 2011-398, s. 61.2, effective July 25, 2011. (1973, c. 1331, s. 1; 1985, c. 746, s. 1; 1991, c. 418, s. 1; 1996, 2nd Ex. Sess., c. 18, s. 7.10(a); 2011-13, s. 1; 2011-398, s. 61.2.)

§ 150B-19.1. Requirements for agencies in the rule-making process.

(a) In developing and drafting rules for adoption in accordance with this Article, agencies shall adhere to the following principles:

(1) An agency may adopt only rules that are expressly authorized by federal or State law and that are necessary to serve the public interest.

(2) An agency shall seek to reduce the burden upon those persons or entities who must comply with the rule.

(3) Rules shall be written in a clear and unambiguous manner and must be reasonably necessary to implement or interpret federal or State law.

(4) An agency shall consider the cumulative effect of all rules adopted by the agency related to the specific purpose for which the rule is proposed. The agency shall not adopt a rule that is unnecessary or redundant.

(5) When appropriate, rules shall be based on sound, reasonably available scientific, technical, economic, and other relevant information. Agencies shall include a reference to this information in the notice of text required by G.S. 150B-21.2(c).

(6) Rules shall be designed to achieve the regulatory objective in a cost-effective and timely manner.

(b) Each agency subject to this Article shall conduct an annual review of its rules to identify existing rules that are unnecessary, unduly burdensome, or inconsistent with the principles set forth in subsection (a) of this section. The agency shall repeal any rule identified by this review.

(c) Each agency subject to this Article shall post on its Web site, no later than the publication date of the notice of text in the North Carolina Register, all of the following:

(1) The text of a proposed rule.

(2) An explanation of the proposed rule and the reason for the proposed rule.

(3) The federal certification required by subsection (g) of this section.

(4) Instructions on how and where to submit oral or written comments on the proposed rule, including a description of the procedure by which a person can object to a proposed rule and subject the proposed rule to legislative review.

(5) Any fiscal note that has been prepared for the proposed rule.

If an agency proposes any change to a rule or fiscal note prior to the date it proposes to adopt a rule, the agency shall publish the proposed change on its Web site as soon as practicable after the change is drafted. If an agency's staff proposes any such change to be presented to the rule-making agency, the staff shall publish the proposed change on the agency's Web site as soon as practicable after the change is drafted.

(d) Each agency shall determine whether its policies and programs overlap with the policies and programs of another agency. In the event two or more agencies' policies and programs overlap, the agencies shall coordinate the rules adopted by each agency to avoid unnecessary, unduly burdensome, or inconsistent rules.

(e) Each agency shall quantify the costs and benefits to all parties of a proposed rule to the greatest extent possible. Prior to submission of a proposed rule for publication in accordance with G.S. 150B-21.2, the agency shall review the details of any fiscal note prepared in connection with the proposed rule and approve the fiscal note before submission.

(f) If the agency determines that a proposed rule will have a substantial economic impact as defined in G.S. 150B-21.4(b1), the agency shall consider at least two alternatives to the proposed rule. The alternatives may have been identified by the agency or by members of the public.

(g) Whenever an agency proposes a rule that is purported to implement a federal law, or required by or necessary for compliance with federal law, or on which the receipt of federal funds is conditioned, the agency shall:

(1) Prepare a certification identifying the federal law requiring adoption of the proposed rule. The certification shall contain a statement setting forth the reasons why the proposed rule is required by federal law. If all or part of the proposed rule is not required by federal law or exceeds the requirements of federal law, then the certification shall state the reasons for that opinion.

(2) Post the certification on the agency Web site in accordance with subsection (c) of this section.

(3) Maintain a copy of the federal law and provide to the Office of State Budget and Management the citation to the federal law requiring or pertaining to the proposed rule.

(h) Before an agency that is within the Governor's cabinet submits the proposed text of a permanent rule change for publication in the North Carolina Register, the agency must submit the text of the proposed rule change and an analysis of the proposed rule change to the Office of State Budget and Management and obtain a certification from the Office that the agency adhered to the principles set forth in this section. Before an agency that is within the departments of the Council of State, other than the Governor, submits the proposed text of a permanent rule change for publication in the North Carolina Register, the agency must submit the text of the proposed rule change and an analysis of the proposed rule change to the Commission and obtain a certification from the Commission, or the Commission's designee, as described in G.S. 150B-21.1(b), that the agency adhered to the principles set forth in this section. The Office of State Budget and Management or the Commission, respectively, must respond to an agency's request for certification within 20 business days of receipt of the request. (2011-398, s. 2; 2012-187, s. 3; 2013-143, s. 1.1.)

§ 150B-19.2: Repealed by Session Laws 2013-413, s. 3(c). For effective date, see editor's note.

§ 150B-19.3. Limitation on certain environmental rules.

(a) An agency authorized to implement and enforce State and federal environmental laws may not adopt a rule for the protection of the environment or natural resources that imposes a more restrictive standard, limitation, or requirement than those imposed by federal law or rule, if a federal law or rule pertaining to the same subject matter has been adopted, unless adoption of the rule is required by one of the following:

(1) A serious and unforeseen threat to the public health, safety, or welfare.

(2) An act of the General Assembly or United States Congress that expressly requires the agency to adopt rules.

(3) A change in federal or State budgetary policy.

(4) A federal regulation required by an act of the United States Congress to be adopted or administered by the State.

(5) A court order.

(b) For purposes of this section, "an agency authorized to implement and enforce State and federal environmental laws" means any of the following:

(1) The Department of Environment and Natural Resources created pursuant to G.S. 143B-279.1.

(2) The Environmental Management Commission created pursuant to G.S. 143B-282.

(3) The Coastal Resources Commission established pursuant to G.S. 113A-104.

(4) The Marine Fisheries Commission created pursuant to G.S. 143B-289.51.

(5) The Wildlife Resources Commission created pursuant to G.S. 143-240.

(6) The Commission for Public Health created pursuant to G.S. 130A-29.

(7) The Sedimentation Control Commission created pursuant to G.S. 143B-298.

(8) The North Carolina Mining and Energy Commission created pursuant to G.S. 143B-293.1.

(9) The Pesticide Board created pursuant to G.S. 143-436. (2011-398, s. 2; 2012-143, s. 1(d).)

§ 150B-20. Petitioning an agency to adopt a rule.

(a) Petition. - A person may petition an agency to adopt a rule by submitting to the agency a written rule-making petition requesting the adoption. A person may submit written comments with a rule-making petition. If a rule-making petition requests the agency to create or amend a rule, the person must submit the proposed text of the requested rule change and a statement of the effect of the requested rule change. Each agency must establish by rule the procedure for submitting a rule-making petition to it and the procedure the agency follows in considering a rule-making petition.

(b)   Time. - An agency must grant or deny a rule-making petition submitted to it within 30 days after the date the rule-making petition is submitted, unless the agency is a board or commission. If the agency is a board or commission, it must grant or deny a rule-making petition within 120 days after the date the rule-making petition is submitted.

(c)   Action. - If an agency denies a rule-making petition, it must send the person who submitted the petition a written statement of the reasons for denying the petition. If an agency grants a rule-making petition, it must inform the person who submitted the rule-making petition of its decision and must initiate rule-making proceedings. When an agency grants a rule-making petition, the notice of text it publishes in the North Carolina Register may state that the agency is initiating rule making as the result of a rule-making petition and state the name of the person who submitted the rule-making petition. If the rule-making petition requested the creation or amendment of a rule, the notice of text the agency publishes may set out the text of the requested rule change submitted with the rule-making petition and state whether the agency endorses the proposed text.

(d)   Review. - Denial of a rule-making petition is a final agency decision and is subject to judicial review under Article 4 of this Chapter. Failure of an agency to grant or deny a rule-making petition within the time limits set in subsection (b) is a denial of the rule-making petition.

(e)   Repealed by Session Laws 1996, Second Extra Session, c. 18, s. 7.10(b). (1973, c. 1331, s. 1; 1985, c. 746, s. 1; 1991, c. 418, s. 1; c. 477, s. 2; 1996, 2nd Ex. Sess., c. 18, s. 7.10(b); 1997-34, s. 2; 2003-229, s. 1.)

§ 150B-21. Agency must designate rule-making coordinator; duties of coordinator.

(a)   Each agency must designate one or more rule-making coordinators to oversee the agency's rule-making functions. The coordinator shall serve as the liaison between the agency, other agencies, units of local government, and the public in the rule-making process. The coordinator shall report directly to the agency head.

(b)   The rule-making coordinator shall be responsible for the following:

(1)   Preparing notices of public hearings.

(2)   Coordinating access to the agency's rules.

(3)   Screening all proposed rule actions prior to publication in the North Carolina Register to assure that an accurate fiscal note has been completed as required by G.S. 150B-21.4(b).

(4)   Consulting with the North Carolina Association of County Commissioners and the North Carolina League of Municipalities to determine which local governments would be affected by any proposed rule action.

(5)   Providing the North Carolina Association of County Commissioners and the North Carolina League of Municipalities with copies of all fiscal notes required by G.S. 150B-21.4(b), prior to publication in the North Carolina Register of the proposed text of a permanent rule change.

(6)   Coordinating the submission of proposed rules to the Governor as provided by G.S. 150B-21.26.

(c)   At the earliest point in the rule-making process and in consultation with the North Carolina Association of County Commissioners, the North Carolina League of Municipalities, and with samples of county managers or city managers, as appropriate, the rule-making coordinator shall lead the agency's efforts in the development and drafting of any rules or rule changes that could:

(1)   Require any unit of local government, including a county, city, school administrative unit, or other local entity funded by or through a unit of local government to carry out additional or modified responsibilities;

(2)   Increase the cost of providing or delivering a public service funded in whole or in part by any unit of local government; or

(3)   Otherwise affect the expenditures or revenues of a unit of local government.

(d) The rule-making coordinator shall send to the Office of State Budget and Management for compilation a copy of each final fiscal note prepared pursuant to G.S. 150B-21.4(b).

(e) The rule-making coordinator shall compile a schedule of the administrative rules and amendments expected to be proposed during the next fiscal year. The coordinator shall provide a copy of the schedule to the Office of State Budget and Management in a manner proposed by that Office.

(f) Repealed by Session Laws 2011-398, s. 3, effective October 1, 2011, and applicable to rules adopted on or after that date. (1991, c. 418, s. 1; 1995, c. 415, s. 1; c. 507, s. 27.8(v); 2000-140, s. 93.1(a); 2001-424, s. 12.2(b); 2011-398, s. 3.)

Part 2. Adoption of Rules.

§ 150B-21.1. Procedure for adopting a temporary rule.

(a) Adoption. - An agency may adopt a temporary rule when it finds that adherence to the notice and hearing requirements of G.S. 150B-21.2 would be contrary to the public interest and that the immediate adoption of the rule is required by one or more of the following:

(1) A serious and unforeseen threat to the public health, safety, or welfare.

(2) The effective date of a recent act of the General Assembly or the United States Congress.

(3) A recent change in federal or State budgetary policy.

(4) A recent federal regulation.

(5) A recent court order.

(6) The need for a rule establishing review criteria as authorized by G.S. 131E-183(b) to complement or be made consistent with the State Medical Facilities Plan approved by the Governor, if the rule addresses a matter included in the State Medical Facilities Plan, and the proposed rule and a notice

of public hearing is submitted to the Codifier of Rules prior to the effective date of the Plan.

(7) The need for the Wildlife Resources Commission to establish any of the following:

a. No wake zones.

b. Hunting or fishing seasons, including provisions for manner of take or any other conditions required for the implementation of such season.

c. Hunting or fishing bag limits.

d. Management of public game lands as defined in G.S. 113-129(8a).

(8) The need for the Secretary of State to implement the certification technology provisions of Article 11A of Chapter 66 of the General Statutes, to adopt uniform Statements of Policy that have been officially adopted by the North American Securities Administrators Association, Inc., for the purpose of promoting uniformity of state securities regulation, and to adopt rules governing the conduct of hearings pursuant to this Chapter.

(9) The need for the Commissioner of Insurance to implement the provisions of G.S. 58-2-205.

(10) The need for the Chief Information Officer to implement the information technology procurement provisions of Article 3D of Chapter 147 of the General Statutes.

(11) The need for the State Board of Elections to adopt a temporary rule after prior notice or hearing or upon any abbreviated notice or hearing the agency finds practical for one or more of the following:

a. In accordance with the provisions of G.S. 163-22.2.

b. To implement any provisions of state or federal law for which the State Board of Elections has been authorized to adopt rules.

c. The need for the rule to become effective immediately in order to preserve the integrity of upcoming elections and the elections process.

(12) The need for an agency to adopt a temporary rule to implement the provisions of any of the following acts until all rules necessary to implement the provisions of the act have become effective as either temporary or permanent rules:

    a. Repealed by Session Laws 2000-148, s. 5, effective July 1, 2002.

    b. Repealed by Session Laws 2000-69, s. 5, effective July 1, 2003.

(13), (14) Reserved.

(15) Expired pursuant to Session Laws 2002-164, s. 5, effective October 1, 2004.

(16) Expired pursuant to Session Laws 2003-184, s. 3, effective July 1, 2005.

(17) To maximize receipt of federal funds for the Medicaid or NC Health Choice programs within existing State appropriations, to reduce Medicaid or NC Health Choice expenditures, and to reduce Medicaid and NC Health Choice fraud and abuse.

(a1) Recodified as subdivision (a)(16) of this section by Session Laws 2004-156, s. 1.

(a2) A recent act, change, regulation, or order as used in subdivisions (2) through (5) of subsection (a) of this section means an act, change, regulation, or order occurring or made effective no more than 210 days prior to the submission of a temporary rule to the Rules Review Commission. Upon written request of the agency, the Commission may waive the 210-day requirement upon consideration of the degree of public benefit, whether the agency had control over the circumstances that required the requested waiver, notice to and opposition by the public, the need for the waiver, and previous requests for waivers submitted by the agency.

(a3) Unless otherwise provided by law, the agency shall:

(1) At least 30 business days prior to adopting a temporary rule, submit the rule and a notice of public hearing to the Codifier of Rules, and the Codifier of Rules shall publish the proposed temporary rule and the notice of public hearing on the Internet to be posted within five business days.

(2) At least 30 business days prior to adopting a temporary rule, notify persons on the mailing list maintained pursuant to G.S. 150B-21.2(d) and any other interested parties of its intent to adopt a temporary rule and of the public hearing.

(3) Accept written comments on the proposed temporary rule for at least 15 business days prior to adoption of the temporary rule.

(4) Hold at least one public hearing on the proposed temporary rule no less than five days after the rule and notice have been published.

(a4) An agency must also prepare a written statement of its findings of need for a temporary rule stating why adherence to the notice and hearing requirements in G.S. 150B-21.2 would be contrary to the public interest and why the immediate adoption of the rule is required. If the temporary rule establishes a new fee or increases an existing fee, the agency shall include in the written statement that it has complied with the requirements of G.S. 12-3.1. The statement must be signed by the head of the agency adopting the temporary rule.

(b) Review. - When an agency adopts a temporary rule it must submit the rule and the agency's written statement of its findings of the need for the rule to the Rules Review Commission. Within 15 business days after receiving the proposed temporary rule, the Commission shall review the agency's written statement of findings of need for the rule and the rule to determine whether the statement meets the criteria listed in subsection (a) of this section and the rule meets the standards in G.S. 150B-21.9. The Commission shall direct a member of its staff who is an attorney licensed to practice law in North Carolina to review the statement of findings of need and the rule. The staff member shall make a recommendation to the Commission, which must be approved by the Commission or its designee. The Commission's designee shall be a panel of at least three members of the Commission. In reviewing the statement, the Commission or its designee may consider any information submitted by the agency or another person. If the Commission or its designee finds that the statement meets the criteria listed in subsection (a) of this section and the rule meets the standards in G.S. 150B-21.9, the Commission or its designee must approve the temporary rule and deliver the rule to the Codifier of Rules within two business days of approval. The Codifier of Rules must enter the rule into the North Carolina Administrative Code on the sixth business day following receipt from the Commission or its designee.

(b1)   If the Commission or its designee finds that the statement does not meet the criteria listed in subsection (a) of this section or that the rule does not meet the standards in G.S. 150B-21.9, the Commission or its designee must immediately notify the head of the agency. The agency may supplement its statement of need with additional findings or submit a new statement. If the agency provides additional findings or submits a new statement, the Commission or its designee must review the additional findings or new statement within five business days after the agency submits the additional findings or new statement. If the Commission or its designee again finds that the statement does not meet the criteria listed in subsection (a) of this section or that the rule does not meet the standards in G.S. 150B-21.9, the Commission or its designee must immediately notify the head of the agency and return the rule to the agency.

(b2)   If an agency decides not to provide additional findings or submit a new statement when notified by the Commission or its designee that the agency's findings of need for a rule do not meet the required criteria or that the rule does not meet the required standards, the agency must notify the Commission or its designee of its decision. The Commission or its designee shall then return the rule to the agency. When the Commission returns a rule to an agency in accordance with this subsection, the agency may file an action for declaratory judgment in Wake County Superior Court pursuant to Article 26 of Chapter 1 of the General Statutes.

(b3)   Notwithstanding any other provision of this subsection, if the agency has not complied with the provisions of G.S. 12-3.1, the Codifier of Rules shall not enter the rule into the Code.

(c)   Standing. - A person aggrieved by a temporary rule adopted by an agency may file an action for declaratory judgment in Wake County Superior Court pursuant to Article 26 of Chapter 1 of the General Statutes. In the action, the court shall determine whether the agency's written statement of findings of need for the rule meets the criteria listed in subsection (a) of this section and whether the rule meets the standards in G.S. 150B-21.9. The court shall not grant an ex parte temporary restraining order.

(c1)   Filing a petition for rule making or a request for a declaratory ruling with the agency that adopted the rule is not a prerequisite to filing an action under this subsection. A person who files an action for declaratory judgment under this subsection must serve a copy of the complaint on the agency that adopted the rule being contested, the Codifier of Rules, and the Commission.

(d)   Effective Date and Expiration. - A temporary rule becomes effective on the date specified in G.S. 150B-21.3. A temporary rule expires on the earliest of the following dates:

(1)   The date specified in the rule.

(2)   The effective date of the permanent rule adopted to replace the temporary rule, if the Commission approves the permanent rule.

(3)   The date the Commission returns to an agency a permanent rule the agency adopted to replace the temporary rule.

(4)   The effective date of an act of the General Assembly that specifically disapproves a permanent rule adopted to replace the temporary rule.

(5)   270 days from the date the temporary rule was published in the North Carolina Register, unless the permanent rule adopted to replace the temporary rule has been submitted to the Commission.

(e)   Publication. - When the Codifier of Rules enters a temporary rule in the North Carolina Administrative Code, the Codifier must publish the rule in the North Carolina Register. (1973, c. 1331, s. 1; 1981, c. 688, s. 12; 1981 (Reg. Sess., 1982), c. 1232, s. 1; 1983, c. 857; c. 927, ss. 4, 8; 1985, c. 746, s. 1; 1985 (Reg. Sess., 1986), c. 1022, s. 1(1), 1(8); 1987, c. 285, ss. 10-12; 1991, c. 418, s. 1; 1991 (Reg. Sess., 1992), c. 900, s. 149; 1993, c. 553, s. 54; 1995, c. 507, s. 27.8(c); 1996, 2nd Ex. Sess., c. 18, ss. 7.10(c), (d); 1997-403, ss. 1-3; 1998-127, s. 2; 1998-212, s. 26B(h); 1999-434, s. 16; 1999-453, s. 5(a); 2000-69, ss. 3, 5; 2000-148, ss. 4, 5; 2001-126, s. 12; 2001-421, ss. 2.3, 5.3; 2001-424, ss. 27.17(b), (c), 27.22(a), (b); 2001-487, s. 21(g); 2002-97, ss. 2, 3; 2002-164, s. 4.6; 2003-184, s. 3; 2003-229, s. 2; 2003-413, ss. 27, 29; 2004-156, s. 1; 2011-398, s. 4; 2013-360, s. 12H.9(d); 2013-413, s. 39.)

§ 150B-21.1A. Adoption of an emergency rule.

(a)   Adoption. - An agency may adopt an emergency rule without prior notice or hearing or upon any abbreviated notice or hearing the agency finds practical when it finds that adherence to the notice and hearing requirements of this Part would be contrary to the public interest and that the immediate adoption of the rule is required by a serious and unforeseen threat to the public health or safety. When an agency adopts an emergency rule, it must simultaneously commence the process for adopting a temporary rule by submitting the rule to the Codifier of Rules for publication on the Internet in accordance with G.S. 150B-21.1(a3). The Department of Health and Human Services or the appropriate rule-making agency within the Department may adopt emergency rules in accordance with this section when a recent act of the General Assembly or the United States Congress or a recent change in federal regulations authorizes new or increased services or benefits for children and families and the emergency rule is necessary to implement the change in State or federal law.

(b) Review. - An agency must prepare a written statement of its findings of need for an emergency rule. The statement must be signed by the head of the agency adopting the rule. When an agency adopts an emergency rule, it must submit the rule and the agency's written statement of its findings of the need for the rule to the Codifier of Rules. Within two business days after an agency submits an emergency rule, the Codifier of Rules must review the agency's written statement of findings of need for the rule to determine whether the statement of need meets the criteria in subsection (a) of this section. In reviewing the statement, the Codifier of Rules may consider any information submitted by the agency or another person. If the Codifier of Rules finds that the statement meets the criteria, the Codifier of Rules must notify the head of the agency and enter the rule in the North Carolina Administrative Code on the sixth business day following approval by the Codifier of Rules.

If the Codifier of Rules finds that the statement does not meet the criteria in subsection (a) of this section, the Codifier of Rules must immediately notify the head of the agency. The agency may supplement its statement of need with additional findings or submit a new statement. If the agency provides additional findings or submits a new statement, the Codifier of Rules must review the additional findings or new statement within one business day after the agency submits the additional findings or new statement. If the Codifier of Rules again finds that the statement does not meet the criteria in subsection (a) of this section, the Codifier of Rules must immediately notify the head of the agency.

If an agency decides not to provide additional findings or submit a new statement when notified by the Codifier of Rules that the agency's findings of need for a rule do not meet the required criteria, the agency must notify the Codifier of Rules of its decision. The Codifier of Rules must then enter the rule in the North Carolina Administrative Code on the sixth business day after receiving notice of the agency's decision. Notwithstanding any other provision of this subsection, if the agency has not complied with the provisions of G.S. 12-3.1, the Codifier of Rules shall not enter the rule into the Code.

(c)   Standing. - A person aggrieved by an emergency rule adopted by an agency may file an action for declaratory judgment in Wake County Superior Court pursuant to Article 26 of Chapter 1 of the General Statutes. In the action, the court shall determine whether the agency's written statement of findings of need for the rule meets the criteria listed in subsection (a) of this section and whether the rule meets the standards in G.S. 150B-21.9. The court shall not grant an ex parte temporary restraining order.

Filing a petition for rule making or a request for a declaratory ruling with the agency that adopted the rule is not a prerequisite to filing an action under this subsection. A person who files an action for declaratory judgment under this subsection must serve a copy of the complaint on the agency that adopted the rule being contested, the Codifier of Rules, and the Commission.

(d)   Effective Date and Expiration. - An emergency rule becomes effective on the date specified in G.S. 150B-21.3. An emergency rule expires on the earliest of the following dates:

(1)   The date specified in the rule.

(2)   The effective date of the temporary rule adopted to replace the emergency rule, if the Commission approves the temporary rule.

(3)   The date the Commission returns to an agency a temporary rule the agency adopted to replace the emergency rule.

(4)   Sixty days from the date the emergency rule was published in the North Carolina Register, unless the temporary rule adopted to replace the emergency rule has been submitted to the Commission.

(e)   Publication. - When the Codifier of Rules enters an emergency rule in the North Carolina Administrative Code, the Codifier of Rules must publish the rule in the North Carolina Register. (2003-229, s. 3.)

§ 150B-21.1B: Expired pursuant to Session Laws 2009-475, s. 16, effective June 30, 2012.

§ 150B-21.2. Procedure for adopting a permanent rule.

(a) Steps. - Before an agency adopts a permanent rule, the agency must comply with the requirements of G.S. 150B-19.1, and it must take the following actions:

(1) Publish a notice of text in the North Carolina Register.

(2) When required by G.S. 150B-21.4, prepare or obtain a fiscal note for the proposed rule.

(3) Repealed by Session Laws 2003-229, s. 4, effective July 1, 2003.

(4) When required by subsection (e) of this section, hold a public hearing on the proposed rule after publication of the proposed text of the rule.

(5) Accept oral or written comments on the proposed rule as required by subsection (f) of this section.

(b) Repealed by Session Laws 2003-229, s. 4, effective July 1, 2003.

(c) Notice of Text. - A notice of the proposed text of a rule must include all of the following:

(1) The text of the proposed rule, unless the rule is a readoption without substantive changes to the existing rule proposed in accordance with G.S. 150B-21.3A.

(2) A short explanation of the reason for the proposed rule.

(2a) A link to the agency's Web site containing the information required by G.S. 150B-19.1(c).

(3) A citation to the law that gives the agency the authority to adopt the rule.

(4) The proposed effective date of the rule.

(5) The date, time, and place of any public hearing scheduled on the rule.

(6) Instructions on how a person may demand a public hearing on a proposed rule if the notice does not schedule a public hearing on the proposed

rule and subsection (e) of this section requires the agency to hold a public hearing on the proposed rule when requested to do so.

(7) The period of time during which and the person within the agency to whom written comments may be submitted on the proposed rule.

(8) If a fiscal note has been prepared for the rule, a statement that a copy of the fiscal note can be obtained from the agency.

(9) Repealed by Session Laws 2013-143, s. 1, effective June 19, 2013.

(d) Mailing List. - An agency must maintain a mailing list of persons who have requested notice of rule making. When an agency publishes in the North Carolina Register a notice of text of a proposed rule, it must mail a copy of the notice or text to each person on the mailing list who has requested notice on the subject matter described in the notice or the rule affected. An agency may charge an annual fee to each person on the agency's mailing list to cover copying and mailing costs.

(e) Hearing. - An agency must hold a public hearing on a rule it proposes to adopt if the agency publishes the text of the proposed rule in the North Carolina Register and the agency receives a written request for a public hearing on the proposed rule within 15 days after the notice of text is published. The agency must accept comments at the public hearing on both the proposed rule and any fiscal note that has been prepared in connection with the proposed rule.

An agency may hold a public hearing on a proposed rule and fiscal note in other circumstances. When an agency is required to hold a public hearing on a proposed rule or decides to hold a public hearing on a proposed rule when it is not required to do so, the agency must publish in the North Carolina Register a notice of the date, time, and place of the public hearing. The hearing date of a public hearing held after the agency publishes notice of the hearing in the North Carolina Register must be at least 15 days after the date the notice is published. If notice of a public hearing has been published in the North Carolina Register and that public hearing has been cancelled, the agency shall publish notice in the North Carolina Register at least 15 days prior to the date of any rescheduled hearing.

(f) Comments. - An agency must accept comments on the text of a proposed rule that is published in the North Carolina Register and any fiscal note that has been prepared in connection with the proposed rule for at least 60 days after the text is published or until the date of any public hearing held on the proposed rule, whichever is longer. An agency must consider fully all written and oral comments received.

(g)   Adoption. - An agency shall not adopt a rule until the time for commenting on the proposed text of the rule has elapsed and shall not adopt a rule if more than 12 months have elapsed since the end of the time for commenting on the proposed text of the rule. Prior to adoption, an agency shall review any fiscal note that has been prepared for the proposed rule and consider any public comments received in connection with the proposed rule or the fiscal note. An agency shall not adopt a rule that differs substantially from the text of a proposed rule published in the North Carolina Register unless the agency publishes the text of the proposed different rule in the North Carolina Register and accepts comments on the proposed different rule for the time set in subsection (f) of this section.

An adopted rule differs substantially from a proposed rule if it does one or more of the following:

(1)   Affects the interests of persons who, based on the proposed text of the rule published in the North Carolina Register, could not reasonably have determined that the rule would affect their interests.

(2)   Addresses a subject matter or an issue that is not addressed in the proposed text of the rule.

(3)   Produces an effect that could not reasonably have been expected based on the proposed text of the rule.

When an agency adopts a rule, it shall not take subsequent action on the rule without following the procedures in this Part. An agency must submit an adopted rule to the Rules Review Commission within 30 days of the agency's adoption of the rule.

(h)   Explanation. - An agency must issue a concise written statement explaining why the agency adopted a rule if, within 15 days after the agency adopts the rule, a person asks the agency to do so. The explanation must state the principal reasons for and against adopting the rule and must discuss why the agency rejected any arguments made or considerations urged against the adoption of the rule. The agency must issue the explanation within 15 days after receipt of the request for an explanation.

(i) Record. - An agency must keep a record of a rule-making proceeding. The record must include all written comments received, a transcript or recording of any public hearing held on the rule, any fiscal note that has been prepared for the rule, and any written explanation made by the agency for adopting the rule. (1973, c. 1331, s. 1; 1975, 2nd Sess., c. 983, s. 63; 1977, c. 915, s. 2; 1983, c. 927, ss. 3, 7; 1985, c. 746, s. 1; 1985 (Reg. Sess., 1986), c. 1022, s. 1(1), (7); 1987, c. 285, ss. 7-9; 1989, c. 5, s. 1; 1991, c. 418, s. 1; 1995, c. 507, s. 27.8(d); 1996, 2nd Ex. Sess., c. 18, s. 7.10(e); 2003-229, s. 4; 2011-398, s. 5; 2013-143, s. 1; 2013-413, s. 3(a).)

§ 150B-21.3. Effective date of rules.

(a) Temporary and Emergency Rules. - A temporary rule or an emergency rule becomes effective on the date the Codifier of Rules enters the rule in the North Carolina Administrative Code.

(b) Permanent Rule. - A permanent rule approved by the Commission becomes effective on the first day of the month following the month the rule is approved by the Commission, unless the Commission received written objections to the rule in accordance with subsection (b2) of this section, or unless the agency that adopted the rule specifies a later effective date.

(b1) Delayed Effective Dates. - If the Commission received written objections to the rule in accordance with subsection (b2) of this section, the rule becomes effective on the earlier of the thirty-first legislative day or the day of adjournment of the next regular session of the General Assembly that begins at least 25 days after the date the Commission approved the rule, unless a different effective date applies under this section. If a bill that specifically disapproves the rule is introduced in either house of the General Assembly before the thirty-first legislative day of that session, the rule becomes effective on the earlier of either the day an unfavorable final action is taken on the bill or the day that session of the General Assembly adjourns without ratifying a bill that specifically disapproves the rule. If the agency adopting the rule specifies a later effective date than the date that would otherwise apply under this subsection, the later date applies. A permanent rule that is not approved by the Commission or that is specifically disapproved by a bill enacted into law before it becomes effective does not become effective.

A bill specifically disapproves a rule if it contains a provision that refers to the rule by appropriate North Carolina Administrative Code citation and states that the rule is disapproved. Notwithstanding any rule of either house of the General Assembly, any member of the General Assembly may introduce a bill during the first 30 legislative days of any regular session to disapprove a rule that has been approved by the Commission and that either has not become effective or has become effective by executive order under subsection (c) of this section.

(b2)   Objection. - Any person who objects to the adoption of a permanent rule may submit written comments to the agency. If the objection is not resolved prior to adoption of the rule, a person may submit written objections to the Commission. If the Commission receives written objections from 10 or more persons, no later than 5:00 P.M. of the day following the day the Commission approves the rule, clearly requesting review by the legislature in accordance with instructions contained in the notice pursuant to G.S. 150B-21.2(c)(9), and the Commission approves the rule, the rule will become effective as provided in subsection (b1) of this section. The Commission shall notify the agency that the rule is subject to legislative disapproval on the day following the day it receives 10 or more written objections. When the requirements of this subsection have been met and a rule is subject to legislative disapproval, the agency may adopt the rule as a temporary rule if the rule would have met the criteria listed in G.S. 150B-21.1(a) at the time the notice of text for the permanent rule was published in the North Carolina Register. If the Commission receives objections from 10 or more persons clearly requesting review by the legislature, and the rule objected to is one of a group of related rules adopted by the agency at the same time, the agency that adopted the rule may cause any of the other rules in the group to become effective as provided in subsection (b1) of this section by submitting a written statement to that effect to the Commission before the other rules become effective.

(c)   Executive Order Exception. - The Governor may, by executive order, make effective a permanent rule that has been approved by the Commission but the effective date of which has been delayed in accordance with subsection (b1) of this section upon finding that it is necessary that the rule become effective in order to protect public health, safety, or welfare. A rule made effective by executive order becomes effective on the date the order is issued or at a later date specified in the order. When the Codifier of Rules enters in the North Carolina Administrative Code a rule made effective by executive order, the entry must reflect this action.

A rule that is made effective by executive order remains in effect unless it is specifically disapproved by the General Assembly in a bill enacted into law on or before the day of adjournment of the regular session of the General Assembly that begins at least 25 days after the date the executive order is issued. A rule that is made effective by executive order and that is specifically disapproved by a bill enacted into law is repealed as of the date specified in the bill. If a rule that is made effective by executive order is not specifically disapproved by a bill enacted into law within the time set by this subsection, the Codifier of Rules must note this in the North Carolina Administrative Code.

(c1)   Fees. - Notwithstanding any other provision of this section, a rule that establishes a new fee or increases an existing fee shall not become effective until the agency has complied with the requirements of G.S. 12-3.1.

(d)   Legislative Day and Day of Adjournment. - As used in this section:

(1)   A "legislative day" is a day on which either house of the General Assembly convenes in regular session.

(2)   The "day of adjournment" of a regular session held in an odd-numbered year is the day the General Assembly adjourns by joint resolution or by operation of law for more than 30 days.

(3)   The "day of adjournment" of a regular session held in an even-numbered year is the day the General Assembly adjourns sine die.

(e)   OSHA Standard. - A permanent rule concerning an occupational safety and health standard that is adopted by the Occupational Safety and Health Division of the Department of Labor and is identical to a federal regulation promulgated by the Secretary of the United States Department of Labor becomes effective on the date the Division delivers the rule to the Codifier of Rules, unless the Division specifies a later effective date. If the Division specifies a later effective date, the rule becomes effective on that date.

(f)   Technical Change. - A permanent rule for which no notice or hearing is required under G.S. 150B-21.5(a)(1) through (a)(5) or G.S. 150B-21.5(b) becomes effective on the first day of the month following the month the rule is approved by the Rules Review Commission. (1991, c. 418, s. 1; 1995, c. 507, s. 27.8(e); 1995 (Reg. Sess., 1996), c. 742, s. 43; 1996, 2nd Ex. Sess., c. 18, s. 7.10(f); 1997-34, s. 3; 2001-487, s. 80(b); 2002-97, s. 5; 2003-229, s. 5; 2004-156, ss. 2, 3; 2012-194, s. 66.5(b).)

§ 150B-21.3A. Periodic review and expiration of existing rules.

(a) Definitions. - For purposes of this section, the following definitions apply:

(1) Commission. - Means the Rules Review Commission.

(2) Committee. - Means the Joint Legislative Administrative Procedure Oversight Committee.

(3) Necessary with substantive public interest. - Means any rule for which the agency has received public comments within the past two years. A rule is also "necessary with substantive public interest" if the rule affects the property interest of the regulated public and the agency knows or suspects that any person may object to the rule.

(4) Necessary without substantive public interest. - Means a rule for which the agency has not received a public comment concerning the rule within the past two years. A "necessary without substantive public interest" rule includes a rule that merely identifies information that is readily available to the public, such as an address or a telephone number.

(5) Public comment. - Means written comments objecting to the rule, in whole or in part, received by an agency from any member of the public, including an association or other organization representing the regulated community or other members of the public.

(6) Unnecessary rule. - Means a rule that the agency determines to be obsolete, redundant, or otherwise not needed.

(b) Automatic Expiration. - Except as provided in subsection (e) of this section, any rule for which the agency that adopted the rule has not conducted a review in accordance with this section shall expire on the date set in the schedule established by the Commission pursuant to subsection (d) of this section.

(c) Review Process. - Each agency subject to this Article shall conduct a review of the agency's existing rules at least once every 10 years in accordance with the following process:

(1) Step 1: The agency shall conduct an analysis of each existing rule and make an initial determination as to whether the rule is (i) necessary with

substantive public interest, (ii) necessary without substantive public interest, or (iii) unnecessary. The agency shall then post the results of the initial determination on its Web site and invite the public to comment on the rules and the agency's initial determination. The agency shall also submit the results of the initial determination to the Office of Administrative Hearings for posting on its Web site. The agency shall accept public comment for no less than 60 days following the posting. The agency shall review the public comments and prepare a brief response addressing the merits of each comment. After completing this process, the agency shall submit a report to the Commission. The report shall include the following items:

a. The agency's initial determination.

b. All public comments received in response to the agency's initial determination.

c. The agency's response to the public comments.

(2) Step 2: The Commission shall review the reports received from the agencies pursuant to subdivision (1) of this subsection. If a public comment relates to a rule that the agency determined to be necessary and without substantive public interest or unnecessary, the Commission shall determine whether the public comment has merit and, if so, designate the rule as necessary with substantive public interest. For purposes of this subsection, a public comment has merit if it addresses the specific substance of the rule and relates to any of the standards for review by the Commission set forth in G.S. 150B-21.9(a). The Commission shall prepare a final determination report and submit the report to the Committee for consultation in accordance with subdivision (3) of this subsection. The report shall include the following items:

a. The agency's initial determination.

b. All public comments received in response to the agency's initial determination.

c. The agency's response to the public comments.

d. A summary of the Commission's determinations regarding public comments.

e. A determination that all rules that the agency determined to be necessary and without substantive public interest and for which no public comment was received or for which the Commission determined that the public comment was without merit be allowed to remain in effect without further action.

f. A determination that all rules that the agency determined to be unnecessary and for which no public comment was received or for which the Commission determined that the public comment was without merit shall expire on the first day of the month following the date the report becomes effective in accordance with this section.

g. A determination that all rules that the agency determined to be necessary with substantive public interest or that the Commission designated as necessary with public interest as provided in this subdivision shall be readopted as though the rules were new rules in accordance with this Article.

(3) Step 3: The final determination report shall not become effective until the agency has consulted with the Committee. The determinations contained in the report pursuant to sub-subdivisions e., f., and g. of subdivision (2) of this subsection shall become effective on the date the report is reviewed by the Committee. If the Committee does not hold a meeting to hear the consultation required by this subdivision within 60 days of receipt of the final determination report, the consultation requirement is deemed satisfied, and the determinations contained in the report become effective on the 61st day following the date the Committee received the report. If the Committee disagrees with a determination regarding a specific rule contained in the report, the Committee may recommend that the General Assembly direct the agency to conduct a review of the specific rule in accordance with this section in the next year following the consultation.

(d) Timetable. - The Commission shall establish a schedule for the review of existing rules in accordance with this section on a decennial basis by assigning each Title of the Administrative Code a date by which the review required by this section must be completed. In establishing the schedule, the Commission shall consider the scope and complexity of rules subject to this section and the resources required to conduct the review required by this section. The Commission shall have broad authority to modify the schedule and extend the time for review in appropriate circumstances. Except as provided in subsection (e) of this section, if the agency fails to conduct the review by the date set by the Commission, the rules contained in that Title which have not been reviewed will expire. The Commission may exempt rules that have been adopted or amended within the previous 10 years from the review required by this section. However, any rule exempted on this basis must be reviewed in accordance with this section no more than 10 years following the last time the rule was amended.

(e)   Rules to Conform to or Implement Federal Law. - Rules adopted to conform to or implement federal law shall not expire as provided by this section. The Commission shall report annually to the Committee on any rules that do not expire pursuant to this subsection.

(f)   Other Reviews. - Notwithstanding any provision of this section, an agency may subject a rule that it determines to be unnecessary to review under this section at any time by notifying the Commission that it wishes to be placed on the schedule for the current year. The Commission may also subject a rule to review under this section at any time by notifying the agency that the rule has been placed on the schedule for the current year. (2013-413, s. 3(b).)

§ 150B-21.4. Fiscal notes on rules.

(a)   State Funds. - Before an agency adopts a permanent rule change that would require the expenditure or distribution of funds subject to the State Budget Act, Chapter 143C of the General Statutes it must obtain certification from the Office of State Budget and Management that the funds that would be required by the proposed rule change are available. The agency shall submit the text of the proposed rule change, an analysis of the proposed rule change, and a fiscal note on the proposed rule change to the Office at the same time as the agency submits the notice of text for publication pursuant to G.S. 150B-21.2. The fiscal note must state the amount of funds that would be expended or distributed as a result of the proposed rule change and explain how the amount was computed. The Office of State Budget and Management must certify a proposed rule change if funds are available to cover the expenditure or distribution required by the proposed rule change.

(a1)   DOT Analyses. - In addition to the requirements of subsection (a) of this section, any agency that adopts a rule affecting environmental permitting of Department of Transportation projects shall conduct an analysis to determine if the rule will result in an increased cost to the Department of Transportation. The analysis shall be conducted and submitted to the Board of Transportation when the agency submits the notice of text for publication. The agency shall consider any recommendations offered by the Board of Transportation prior to adopting the rule. Once a rule subject to this subsection is adopted, the Board of Transportation may submit any objection to the rule it may have to the Rules Review Commission. If the Rules Review Commission receives an objection to a rule from the Board of Transportation no later than 5:00 P.M. of the day following the day the Commission approves the rule, then the rule shall only become effective as provided in G.S. 150B-21.3(b1).

(b) Local Funds. - Before an agency adopts a permanent rule change that would affect the expenditures or revenues of a unit of local government, it must submit the text of the proposed rule change and a fiscal note on the proposed rule change to the Office of State Budget and Management as provided by G.S. 150B-21.26, the Fiscal Research Division of the General Assembly, the North Carolina Association of County Commissioners, and the North Carolina League of Municipalities. The fiscal note must state the amount by which the proposed rule change would increase or decrease expenditures or revenues of a unit of local government and must explain how the amount was computed.

(b1) Substantial Economic Impact. - Before an agency adopts a permanent rule change that would have a substantial economic impact and that is not identical to a federal regulation that the agency is required to adopt, the agency shall prepare a fiscal note for the proposed rule change and have the note approved by the Office of State Budget and Management. The agency may request the Office of State Budget and Management to prepare the fiscal note only after, working with the Office, it has exhausted all resources, internal and external, to otherwise prepare the required fiscal note. If an agency requests the Office of State Budget and Management to prepare a fiscal note for a proposed rule change, that Office must prepare the note within 90 days after receiving a written request for the note. If the Office of State Budget and Management fails to prepare a fiscal note within this time period, the agency proposing the rule change shall prepare a fiscal note. A fiscal note prepared in this circumstance does not require approval of the Office of State Budget and Management.

If an agency prepares the required fiscal note, the agency must submit the note to the Office of State Budget and Management for review. The Office of State Budget and Management shall review the fiscal note within 14 days after it is submitted and either approve the note or inform the agency in writing of the reasons why it does not approve the fiscal note. After addressing these reasons, the agency may submit the revised fiscal note to that Office for its review. If an agency is not sure whether a proposed rule change would have a substantial economic impact, the agency shall ask the Office of State Budget and Management to determine whether the proposed rule change has a substantial economic impact. Failure to prepare or obtain approval of the fiscal note as required by this subsection shall be a basis for objection to the rule under G.S. 150B-21.9(a)(4).

As used in this subsection, the term "substantial economic impact" means an aggregate financial impact on all persons affected of at least one million dollars ($1,000,000) in a 12-month period. In analyzing substantial economic impact, an agency shall do the following:

(1)   Determine and identify the appropriate time frame of the analysis.

(2)   Assess the baseline conditions against which the proposed rule is to be measured.

(3)   Describe the persons who would be subject to the proposed rule and the type of expenditures these persons would be required to make.

(4)   Estimate any additional costs that would be created by implementation of the proposed rule by measuring the incremental difference between the baseline and the future condition expected after implementation of the rule. The analysis should include direct costs as well as opportunity costs. Cost estimates must be monetized to the greatest extent possible. Where costs are not monetized, they must be listed and described.

(5)   For costs that occur in the future, the agency shall determine the net present value of the costs by using a discount factor of seven percent (7%).

(b2)   Content. - A fiscal note required by subsection (b1) of this section must contain the following:

(1)   A description of the persons who would be affected by the proposed rule change.

(2)   A description of the types of expenditures that persons affected by the proposed rule change would have to make to comply with the rule and an estimate of these expenditures.

(3)   A description of the purpose and benefits of the proposed rule change.

(4)   An explanation of how the estimate of expenditures was computed.

(5) A description of at least two alternatives to the proposed rule that were considered by the agency and the reason the alternatives were rejected. The alternatives may have been identified by the agency or by members of the public.

(c) Errors. - An erroneous fiscal note prepared in good faith does not affect the validity of a rule.

(d) If an agency proposes the repeal of an existing rule, the agency is not required to prepare a fiscal note on the proposed rule change as provided by this section. (1973, c. 1331, s. 1; 1979, 2nd Sess., c. 1137, s. 41.1; 1983, c. 761, s. 185; 1985, c. 746, s. 1; 1987, c. 827, s. 54; 1991, c. 418, s. 1; 1995, c. 415, s. 2; c. 507, s. 27.8(b); 2000-140, s. 93.1(a); 2001-424, s. 12.2(b); 2003-229, s. 6; 2005-276, s. 28.8(a); 2006-203, s. 124; 2011-398, s. 6; 2012-187, s. 4; 2013-149, s. 1; 2013-413, s. 2.)

§ 150B-21.5. Circumstances when notice and rule-making hearing not required.

(a) Amendment. - An agency is not required to publish a notice of text in the North Carolina Register or hold a public hearing when it proposes to amend a rule to do one of the following:

(1) Reletter or renumber the rule or subparts of the rule.

(2) Substitute one name for another when an organization or position is renamed.

(3) Correct a citation in the rule to another rule or law when the citation has become inaccurate since the rule was adopted because of the repeal or renumbering of the cited rule or law.

(4) Change information that is readily available to the public, such as an address or a telephone number.

(5) Correct a typographical error in the North Carolina Administrative Code.

(6) Change a rule in response to a request or an objection by the Commission, unless the Commission determines that the change is substantial.

(b)   Repeal. - An agency is not required to publish a notice of text in the North Carolina Register or hold a public hearing when it proposes to repeal a rule as a result of any of the following:

(1)   The law under which the rule was adopted is repealed.

(2)   The law under which the rule was adopted or the rule itself is declared unconstitutional.

(3)   The rule is declared to be in excess of the agency's statutory authority.

(c)   OSHA Standard. - The Occupational Safety and Health Division of the Department of Labor is not required to publish a notice of text in the North Carolina Register or hold a public hearing when it proposes to adopt a rule that concerns an occupational safety and health standard and is identical to a federal regulation promulgated by the Secretary of the United States Department of Labor. The Occupational Safety and Health Division is not required to submit to the Commission for review a rule for which notice and hearing is not required under this subsection.

(d)   State Building Code. - The Building Code Council is not required to publish a notice of text in the North Carolina Register when it proposes to adopt a rule that concerns the North Carolina State Building Code. The Building Code Council is required to publish a notice in the North Carolina Register when it proposes to adopt a rule that concerns the North Carolina State Building Code. The notice must include all of the following:

(1)   A statement of the subject matter of the proposed rule making.

(2)   A short explanation of the reason for the proposed action.

(3)   A citation to the law that gives the agency the authority to adopt a rule on the subject matter of the proposed rule making.

(4)   The person to whom questions or written comments may be submitted on the subject matter of the proposed rule making.

The Building Code Council is required to submit to the Commission for review a rule for which notice of text is not required under this subsection. In adopting a rule, the Council shall comply with the procedural requirements of G.S. 150B-

21.3. (1991, c. 418, s. 1; 1995, c. 504, s. 12; 1997-34, s. 4; 2001-141, s. 5; 2001-421, s. 1.3; 2003-229, s. 7.)

§ 150B-21.6. Incorporating material in a rule by reference.

An agency may incorporate the following material by reference in a rule without repeating the text of the referenced material:

(1)   Another rule or part of a rule adopted by the agency.

(2)   All or part of a code, standard, or regulation adopted by another agency, the federal government, or a generally recognized organization or association.

(3)   Repealed by Session Laws 1997-34, s. 5.

In incorporating material by reference, the agency must designate in the rule whether or not the incorporation includes subsequent amendments and editions of the referenced material. The agency can change this designation only by a subsequent rule-making proceeding. The agency must have copies of the incorporated material available for inspection and must specify in the rule both where copies of the material can be obtained and the cost on the date the rule is adopted of a copy of the material.

A statement in a rule that a rule incorporates material by reference in accordance with former G.S. 150B-14(b) is a statement that the rule does not include subsequent amendments and editions of the referenced material. A statement in a rule that a rule incorporates material by reference in accordance with former G.S. 150B-14(c) is a statement that the rule includes subsequent amendments and editions of the referenced material. (1973, c. 1331, s. 1; 1975, 2nd Sess., c. 983, s. 64; 1981 (Reg. Sess., 1982), c. 1359, s. 5; 1983, c. 641, s. 3; c. 768, s. 19; 1985, c. 746, s. 1; 1987, c. 285, s. 13; 1991, c. 418, s. 1; 1997-34, s. 5.)

§ 150B-21.7. Effect of transfer of duties or termination of agency on rules.

(a)   When a law that authorizes an agency to adopt a rule is repealed and another law gives the same or another agency substantially the same authority to adopt a rule, the rule remains in effect until the agency with authority over the rule amends or repeals the rule. When a law that authorizes an agency to adopt a rule is repealed and another law does not give the same or another agency substantially the same authority to adopt a rule, a rule adopted under the repealed law is repealed as of the date the law is repealed. The agency that adopted the rule shall notify the Codifier of Rules that the rule is repealed pursuant to this subsection.

(b) When an executive order abolishes part or all of an agency and transfers a function of that agency to another agency, a rule concerning the transferred function remains in effect until the agency to which the function is transferred amends or repeals the rule. When an executive order abolishes part or all of an agency and does not transfer a function of that agency to another agency, a rule concerning a function abolished by the executive order is repealed as of the effective date of the executive order. The agency that adopted the rule shall notify the Codifier of Rules that the rule is repealed pursuant to this subsection.

(c) When notified of a rule repealed under this section, the Codifier of Rules must enter the repeal of the rule in the North Carolina Administrative Code. (1973, c. 1331, s. 1; 1985, c. 746, s. 1; 1991, c. 418, s. 1; 2013-143, s. 2.)

Part 3. Review by Commission.

§ 150B-21.8. Review of rule by Commission.

(a) Emergency Rule. - The Commission does not review an emergency rule.

(b) Temporary and Permanent Rules. - An agency must submit temporary and permanent rules adopted by it to the Commission before the rule can be included in the North Carolina Administrative Code. The Commission reviews a temporary or permanent rule in accordance with the standards in G.S. 150B-21.9 and follows the procedure in this Part in its review of a rule.

(c) Scope. - When the Commission reviews an amendment to a permanent rule, it may review the entire rule that is being amended. The procedure in G.S. 150B-21.12 applies when the Commission objects to a part of a permanent rule that is within its scope of review but is not changed by a rule amendment.

(d) Judicial Review. - When the Commission returns a permanent rule to an agency in accordance with G.S. 150B-21.12(d), the agency may file an action for declaratory judgment in Wake County Superior Court pursuant to Article 26 of Chapter 1 of the General Statutes. (1991, c. 418, s. 1; 2003-229, s. 8.)

§ 150B-21.9. Standards and timetable for review by Commission.

(a) Standards. - The Commission must determine whether a rule meets all of the following criteria:

(1) It is within the authority delegated to the agency by the General Assembly.

(2) It is clear and unambiguous.

(3) It is reasonably necessary to implement or interpret an enactment of the General Assembly, or of Congress, or a regulation of a federal agency. The Commission shall consider the cumulative effect of all rules adopted by the agency related to the specific purpose for which the rule is proposed.

(4) It was adopted in accordance with Part 2 of this Article.

The Commission shall not consider questions relating to the quality or efficacy of the rule but shall restrict its review to determination of the standards set forth in this subsection.

The Commission may ask the Office of State Budget and Management to determine if a rule has a substantial economic impact and is therefore required to have a fiscal note. The Commission must ask the Office of State Budget and Management to make this determination if a fiscal note was not prepared for a rule and the Commission receives a written request for a determination of whether the rule has a substantial economic impact.

(a1) Entry of a rule in the North Carolina Administrative Code after review by the Commission creates a rebuttable presumption that the rule was adopted in accordance with Part 2 of this Article.

(b) Timetable. - The Commission must review a permanent rule submitted to it on or before the twentieth of a month by the last day of the next month. The Commission must review a rule submitted to it after the twentieth of a month by the last day of the second subsequent month. The Commission must review a temporary rule in accordance with the timetable and procedure set forth in G.S. 150B-21.1. (1991, c. 418, s. 1; 1995, c. 507, s. 27.8(f); 2000-140, s. 93.1(a); 2001-424, s. 12.2(b); 2003-229, s. 9.)

§ 150B-21.10. Commission action on permanent rule.

At the first meeting at which a permanent rule is before the Commission for review, the Commission must take one of the following actions:

(1) Approve the rule, if the Commission determines that the rule meets the standards for review.

(2) Object to the rule, if the Commission determines that the rule does not meet the standards for review.

(3) Extend the period for reviewing the rule, if the Commission determines it needs additional information on the rule to be able to decide whether the rule meets the standards for review.

In reviewing a new rule or an amendment to an existing rule, the Commission may request an agency to make technical changes to the rule and may condition its approval of the rule on the agency's making the requested technical changes. (1991, c. 418, s. 1.)

§ 150B-21.11. Procedure when Commission approves permanent rule.

When the Commission approves a permanent rule, it must notify the agency that adopted the rule of the Commission's approval, and deliver the approved rule to the Codifier of Rules. Regulatory Reform

If the approved rule will increase or decrease expenditures or revenues of a unit of local government, the Commission must also notify the Governor of the Commission's approval of the rule and deliver a copy of the approved rule to the

Governor by the end of the month in which the Commission approved the rule. (1991, c. 418, s. 1; 1995, c. 415, s. 4; c. 507, s. 27.8(g); 2011-291, s. 2.59; 2011-398, s. 7.)

§ 150B-21.12. Procedure when Commission objects to a permanent rule.

(a) Action. - When the Commission objects to a permanent rule, it must send the agency that adopted the rule a written statement of the objection and the reason for the objection. The agency that adopted the rule must take one of the following actions:

(1) Change the rule to satisfy the Commission's objection and submit the revised rule to the Commission.

(2) Submit a written response to the Commission indicating that the agency has decided not to change the rule.

(b) Time Limit. - An agency that is not a board or commission must take one of the actions listed in subsection (a) of this section within 30 days after receiving the Commission's statement of objection. A board or commission must take one of these actions within 30 days after receiving the Commission's statement of objection or within 10 days after the board or commission's next regularly scheduled meeting, whichever comes later.

(c) Changes. - When an agency changes a rule in response to an objection by the Commission, the Commission must determine whether the change satisfies the Commission's objection. If it does, the Commission must approve the rule. If it does not, the Commission must send the agency a written statement of the Commission's continued objection and the reason for the continued objection. The Commission must also determine whether the change is substantial. In making this determination, the Commission shall use the standards set forth in G.S. 150B-21.2(g). If the change is substantial, the revised rule shall be published and reviewed in accordance with the procedure set forth in G.S. 150B-21.1(a3) and (b).

(d) Return of Rule. - A rule to which the Commission has objected remains under review by the Commission until the agency that adopted the rule decides not to satisfy the Commission's objection and makes a written request to the Commission to return the rule to the agency. When the Commission returns a rule to which it has objected, it must notify the Codifier of Rules of its action. If the rule that is returned would have increased or decreased expenditures or revenues of a unit of local government, the Commission must also notify the Governor of its action and must send a copy of the record of the Commission's review of the rule to the Governor. The record of review consists of the rule, the Commission's letter of objection to the rule, the agency's written response to the Commission's letter, and any other relevant documents before the Commission when it decided to object to the rule.

Regulatory Reform (1991, c. 418, s. 1; 1995, c. 415, s. 5; c. 507, s. 27.8(h), (y); 2003-229, s. 10; 2011-291, s. 2.60; 2011-398, s. 8.)

§ 150B-21.13. Procedure when Commission extends period for review of permanent rule.

When the Commission extends the period for review of a permanent rule, it must notify the agency that adopted the rule of the extension and the reason for the extension. After the Commission extends the period for review of a rule, it may call a public hearing on the rule. Within 70 days after extending the period for review of a rule, the Commission must decide whether to approve the rule, object to the rule, or call a public hearing on the rule. (1991, c. 418, s. 1.)

§ 150B-21.14. Public hearing on a rule.

The Commission may call a public hearing on a rule when it extends the period for review of the rule. At the request of an agency, the Commission may call a public hearing on a rule that is not before it for review. Calling a public hearing on a rule not already before the Commission for review places the rule before the Commission for review. When the Commission decides to call a public hearing on a rule, it must publish notice of the public hearing in the North Carolina Register.

After a public hearing on a rule, the Commission must approve the rule or object to the rule in accordance with the standards and procedures in this Part. The Commission must make its decision of whether to approve or object to the rule within 70 days after the public hearing. (1991, c. 418, s. 1.)

§ 150B-21.15: Repealed by Session Laws 1995, c. 507, s. 27

§ 150B-21.16: Repealed by Session Laws 2011-398, s. 9, effec 2011, and applicable to rules adopted on or after that date.

Part 4. Publication of Code and Register.

§ 150B-21.17. North Carolina Register.

(a) Content. - The Codifier of Rules must publish the North Register. The North Carolina Register must be published at lea month and must contain the following:

(1) Temporary rules entered in the North Carolina Adminis

(1a) The text of proposed rules and the text of permanent ru the Commission.

(1b) Emergency rules entered into the North Carolina Admir

(2) Repealed by Session Laws 2011-398, s. 10, effective and applicable to rules adopted on or after that date

(3) Executive orders of the Governor.

(4) Final decision letters from the United States Attorney G concerning changes in laws that affect voting in a jurisdiction s 5 of the Voting Rights Act of 1965, as required by G.S. 120-30.

(5) Repealed by Session Laws 2011-330, s. 33(c), effective and by Session Laws 2011-398, s. 10, effective October 1, 20 applicable to rules adopted on or after that date.

(6) Other information the Codifier determines to be helpful

(b) Form. - When an agency publishes notice in the North of the proposed text of a new rule, the Codifier of Rules must p complete text of the proposed new rule. In publishing the text o rule, the Codifier must indicate the rule is new by underlining th of the rule.

When an agency publishes notice in the North Carolina Register of the proposed text of an amendment to an existing rule, the Codifier must publish the complete text of the rule that is being amended unless the Codifier determines that publication of the complete text of the rule being amended is not necessary to enable the reader to understand the proposed amendment. In publishing the text of a proposed amendment to a rule, the Codifier must indicate deleted text with overstrikes and added text with underlines.

When an agency publishes notice in the North Carolina Register of the proposed repeal of an existing rule, the Codifier must publish the complete text of the rule the agency proposes to repeal unless the Codifier determines that publication of the complete text is impractical. In publishing the text of a rule the agency proposes to repeal, the Codifier must indicate the rule is to be repealed.

(c) The Codifier may authorize and license the private indexing, marketing, sales, reproduction, and distribution of the Register. (1991, c. 418, s. 1; 1995, c. 507, s. 27.8(k); 2001-141, s. 6; 2001-421, s. 1.4; 2003-229, s. 11; 2006-66, s. 18.1; 2011-330, s. 33(c); 2011-398, s. 10.)

§ 150B-21.18. North Carolina Administrative Code.

The Codifier of Rules must compile all rules into a Code known as the North Carolina Administrative Code. The format and indexing of the Code must conform as nearly as practical to the format and indexing of the North Carolina General Statutes. The Codifier must publish printed copies of the Code and may publish the Code in other forms. The Codifier may authorize and license the private indexing, marketing, sales, reproduction, and distribution of the Code. The Codifier must keep superseded rules. (1973, c. 1331, s. 1; 1979, c. 69, ss. 3, 7; c. 541, s. 2; c. 688, s. 1; 1979, 2nd Sess., c. 1266, ss. 1-3; 1981 (Reg. Sess., 1982), c. 1359, s. 6; 1983, c. 641, s. 6; 1985, c. 746, s. 1; 1985 (Reg. Sess., 1986), c. 1003, s. 2; c. 1022, s. 1(1), (19); c. 1032, s. 12; 1987, c. 774, ss. 2-4; 1987 (Reg. Sess., 1988), c. 1111, s. 3; 1989, c. 500, s. 43(a); 1991, c. 418, s. 1; 1993 (Reg. Sess., 1994), c. 777, s. 2; 2011-398, s. 11.)

§ 150B-21.19. Requirements for including rule in Code.

To be acceptable for inclusion in the North Carolina Administrative Code, a rule must:

(1)　Cite the law under which the rule is adopted.

(2)　Be signed by the head of the agency or the rule-making coordinator for the agency that adopted the rule.

(3)　Be in the physical form specified by the Codifier of Rules.

(4)　Have been approved by the Commission, if the rule is a permanent rule.

(5)　Have complied with the provisions of G.S. 12-3.1, if the rule establishes a new fee or increases an existing fee. (1973, c. 1331, s. 1; 1979, c. 571, s. 1; 1981, c. 688, s. 14; 1983, c. 927, ss. 6, 9; 1985, c. 746, s. 1; 1985 (Reg. Sess., 1986), c. 1022, s. 1(1); c. 1028, s. 35; 1987, c. 285, s. 16; 1991, c. 418, s. 1; 1995, c. 507, s. 27.8(l); 2002-97, s. 4.)

§ 150B-21.20.　Codifier's authority to revise form of rules.

(a)　Authority. - After consulting with the agency that adopted the rule, the Codifier of Rules may revise the form of a rule submitted for inclusion in the North Carolina Administrative Code to do one or more of the following:

(1)　Rearrange the order of the rule in the Code or the order of the subsections, subdivisions, or other subparts of the rule.

(2)　Provide a catch line or heading for the rule or revise the catch line or heading of the rule.

(3)　Reletter or renumber the rule or the subparts of the rule in accordance with a uniform system.

(4)　Rearrange definitions and lists.

(5)　Make other changes in arrangement or in form that do not change the substance of the rule and are necessary or desirable for a clear and orderly arrangement of the rule.

(6) Omit from the published rule a map, a diagram, an illustration, a chart, or other graphic material, if the Codifier of Rules determines that the Office of Administrative Hearings does not have the capability to publish the material or that publication of the material is not practicable. When the Codifier of Rules omits graphic material from the published rule, the Codifier must insert a reference to the omitted material and information on how to obtain a copy of the omitted material.

(b) Effect. - Revision of a rule by the Codifier of Rules under this section does not affect the effective date of the rule or require the agency to readopt or resubmit the rule. When the Codifier of Rules revises the form of a rule, the Codifier of Rules must send the agency that adopted the rule a copy of the revised rule. The revised rule is the official rule, unless the rule was revised under subdivision (a)(6) of this section to omit graphic material. When a rule is revised under that subdivision, the official rule is the published text of the rule plus the graphic material that was not published. (1973, c. 1331, s. 1; 1979, c. 571, s. 1; 1981, c. 688, s. 14; 1983, c. 927, ss. 6, 9; 1985, c. 746, s. 1; 1985 (Reg. Sess., 1986), c. 1022, s. 1(1); c. 1028, s. 35; 1987, c. 285, s. 16; 1987 (Reg. Sess., 1988), c. 1111, s. 23; 1991, c. 418, s. 1; 1997-34, s. 6; 2013-143, s. 3.)

§ 150B-21.21. Publication of rules of North Carolina State Bar, Building Code Council, and exempt agencies.

(a) State Bar. - The North Carolina State Bar must submit a rule adopted or approved by it and entered in the minutes of the North Carolina Supreme Court to the Codifier of Rules for inclusion in the North Carolina Administrative Code. The State Bar must submit a rule within 30 days after it is entered in the minutes of the Supreme Court. The Codifier of Rules must compile, make available for public inspection, and publish a rule included in the North Carolina Administrative Code under this subsection in the same manner as other rules in the Code.

(a1) Building Code Council. - The Building Code Council shall publish the North Carolina State Building Code as provided in G.S. 143-138(g). The Codifier of Rules is not required to publish the North Carolina State Building Code in the North Carolina Administrative Code.

(b) Exempt Agencies. - Notwithstanding any other provision of law, an agency that is exempted from this Article by G.S. 150B-1 or any other statute must submit a temporary or permanent rule adopted by it to the Codifier of Rules for inclusion in the North Carolina Administrative Code. These exempt agencies must submit a rule to the Codifier of Rules within 30 days after adopting the rule.

(c) Publication. - A rule submitted to the Codifier of Rules under this section must be in the physical form specified by the Codifier of Rules. The Codifier of Rules must compile, make available for public inspection, and publish a rule submitted under this section in the same manner as other rules in the North Carolina Administrative Code. (1991, c. 418, s. 1; 1997-34, s. 7; 2001-141, s. 7; 2011-398, s. 12.)

§ 150B-21.22. Effect of inclusion in Code.

Official or judicial notice can be taken of a rule in the North Carolina Administrative Code and shall be taken when appropriate. (1973, c. 1331, s. 1; 1985, c. 746, s. 1; 1991, c. 418, s. 1; 1997-34, s. 8.)

§ 150B-21.23: Repealed by Session Laws 2011-398, s. 13, effective October 1, 2011, and applicable to rules adopted on or after that date.

§ 150B-21.24. Access to Register and Code.

(a) Register. - The Codifier of Rules shall make available the North Carolina Register on the Internet at no charge.

(b) Code. - The Codifier of Rules shall make available the North Carolina Administrative Code on the Internet at no charge. (1973, c. 1331, s. 1; c. 69, ss. 3, 7; c. 688, s. 1; 1979, c. 541, s. 2; 1979, 2nd Sess., c. 1266, ss. 1-3; 1981 (Reg. Sess., 1982), c. 1359, s. 6; 1983, c. 641, s. 6; 1985, c. 746, s. 1; 1985 (Reg. Sess., 1986), c. 1003, s. 2; c. 1022, s. 1(1), (19); c. 1032, s. 12; 1987, c. 774, ss. 2-4; 1987 (Reg. Sess., 1988), c. 1111, s. 3; 1989, c. 500, s. 43(a); 1991, c. 418, s. 1; 2002-97, s. 1; 2011-145, s. 24.1.)

§ 150B-21.25. Paid copies of Register and Code.

A person who is not entitled to a free copy of the North Carolina Administrative Code or North Carolina Register may obtain a copy by paying a fee set by the Codifier of Rules. The Codifier must set separate fees for the North Carolina Register and the North Carolina Administrative Code in amounts that cover publication, copying, and mailing costs. All monies received under this section must be credited to the General Fund. (1991, c. 418, s. 1.)

Part 5. Rules Affecting Local Governments.

§ 150B-21.26. Office of State Budget and Management to conduct preliminary review of certain administrative rules.

(a)   Preliminary Review. - At least 60 days before an agency publishes in the North Carolina Register the proposed text of a permanent rule change that would affect the expenditures or revenues of a unit of local government, the agency must submit all of the following to the Office of State Budget and Management for preliminary review:

(1)   The text of the proposed rule change.

(2)   A short explanation of the reason for the proposed change.

(3)   A fiscal note stating the amount by which the proposed rule change would increase or decrease expenditures or revenues of a unit of local government and explaining how the amount was computed.

(b)   Scope. - The preliminary review of a proposed permanent rule change that would affect the expenditures or revenues of a unit of local government shall include consideration of the following:

(1)   The agency's explanation of the reason for the proposed change.

(2)   Any unanticipated effects of the proposed change on local government budgets.

(3)   The potential costs of the proposed change weighed against the potential risks to the public of not taking the proposed change. (1995, c. 415, s. 3; c. 507, s. 27.8(w); 2011-398, s. 14.)

§ 150B-21.27. Minimizing the effects of rules on local budgets.

In adopting permanent rules that would increase or decrease the expenditures or revenues of a unit of local government, the agency shall consider the timing for implementation of the proposed rule as part of the preparation of the fiscal note required by G.S. 150B-21.4(b). If the computation of costs in a fiscal note indicates that the proposed rule change will disrupt the budget process as set out in the Local Government Budget and Fiscal Control Act, Article 3 of Chapter 159 of the General Statutes, the agency shall specify the effective date of the change as July 1 following the date the change would otherwise become effective under G.S. 150B-21.3. (1995, c. 415, s. 3; c. 507, s. 27.8(x).)

§ 150B-21.28. Role of the Office of State Budget and Management.

The Office of State Budget and Management shall:

(1)   Compile an annual summary of the projected fiscal impact on units of local government of State administrative rules adopted during the preceding fiscal year.

(2)   Compile from information provided by each agency schedules of anticipated rule actions for the upcoming fiscal year.

(3)   Provide the Governor, the General Assembly, the North Carolina Association of County Commissioners, and the North Carolina League of Municipalities with a copy of the annual summary and schedules by no later than March 1 of each year. (1995, c. 415, s. 3; 2000-140, s. 93.1(a); 2001-424, s. 12.2(b).)

Article 3.

Administrative Hearings.

§ 150B-22. Settlement; contested case.

It is the policy of this State that any dispute between an agency and another person that involves the person's rights, duties, or privileges, including licensing or the levy of a monetary penalty, should be settled through informal procedures. In trying to reach a settlement through informal procedures, the agency may not conduct a proceeding at which sworn testimony is taken and witnesses may be cross-examined. If the agency and the other person do not agree to a resolution of the dispute through informal procedures, either the agency or the person may commence an administrative proceeding to determine the person's rights, duties, or privileges, at which time the dispute becomes a "contested case." (1985 (Reg. Sess., 1986), c. 1022, s. 1(11); 1991, c. 418, s. 16.)

§ 150B-22.1. Special education petitions.

(a) Notwithstanding any other provision of this Chapter, timelines and other procedural safeguards required to be provided under IDEA and Article 9 of Chapter 115C of the General Statutes must be followed in an impartial due process hearing initiated when a petition is filed under G.S. 115C-109.6 with the Office of Administrative Hearings.

(b) The administrative law judge who conducts a hearing under G.S. 115C-109.6 shall not be a person who has a personal or professional interest that conflicts with the judge's objectivity in the hearing. Furthermore, the judge must possess knowledge of, and the ability to understand, IDEA and legal interpretations of IDEA by federal and State courts. The judges are encouraged to participate in training developed and provided by the State Board of Education under G.S. 115C-107.2(h)[(g)].

(c) For the purpose of this section, the term "IDEA" means The Individuals with Disabilities Education Improvement Act, 20 U.S.C. § 1400, et seq., (2004), as amended, and its regulations. (2006-69, s. 5.)

§ 150B-23. Commencement; assignment of administrative law judge; hearing required; notice; intervention.

(a) A contested case shall be commenced by paying a fee in an amount established in G.S. 150B-23.2 and by filing a petition with the Office of Administrative Hearings and, except as provided in Article 3A of this Chapter, shall be conducted by that Office. The party who files the petition shall serve a copy of the petition on all other parties and, if the dispute concerns a license, the person who holds the license. A party who files a petition shall file a certificate of service together with the petition. A petition shall be signed by a party, an attorney representing a party, or other representative of the party as may specifically be authorized by law, and, if filed by a party other than an agency, shall state facts tending to establish that the agency named as the respondent has deprived the petitioner of property, has ordered the petitioner to pay a fine or civil penalty, or has otherwise substantially prejudiced the petitioner's rights and that the agency:

(1) Exceeded its authority or jurisdiction;

(2) Acted erroneously;

(3) Failed to use proper procedure;

(4) Acted arbitrarily or capriciously; or

(5) Failed to act as required by law or rule.

The parties in a contested case shall be given an opportunity for a hearing without undue delay. Any person aggrieved may commence a contested case hereunder.

A local government employee, applicant for employment, or former employee to whom Chapter 126 of the General Statutes applies may commence a contested case under this Article in the same manner as any other petitioner. The case shall be conducted in the same manner as other contested cases under this Article.

(a1) Repealed by Session Laws 1985 (Regular Session, 1986), c. 1022, s. 1(9).

(a2) An administrative law judge assigned to a contested case may require a party to the case to file a prehearing statement. A party's prehearing statement must be served on all other parties to the contested case.

(a3) A Medicaid enrollee, or network provider authorized in writing to act on behalf of the enrollee, who appeals a notice of resolution issued by an LME/MCO under Chapter 108D of the General Statutes may commence a contested case under this Article in the same manner as any other petitioner. The case shall be conducted in the same manner as other contested cases under this Article. Solely and only for the purposes of contested cases commenced as Medicaid managed care enrollee appeals under Chapter 108D of the General Statutes, an LME/MCO is considered an agency as defined in G.S. 150B-2(1a). The LME/MCO shall not be considered an agency for any other purpose.

(b) The parties to a contested case shall be given a notice of hearing not less than 15 days before the hearing by the Office of Administrative Hearings. If prehearing statements have been filed in the case, the notice shall state the date, hour, and place of the hearing. If prehearing statements have not been filed in the case, the notice shall state the date, hour, place, and nature of the hearing, shall list the particular sections of the statutes and rules involved, and shall give a short and plain statement of the factual allegations.

(c) Notice shall be given by one of the methods for service of process under G.S. 1A-1, Rule 4(j) or Rule 4(j3). If given by registered or certified mail, by signature confirmation as provided by the United States Postal Service, or by designated delivery service authorized pursuant to 26 U.S.C. § 7502(f)(2) with delivery receipt, notice shall be deemed to have been given on the delivery date appearing on the return receipt, copy of the proof of delivery provided by the United States Postal Service, or delivery receipt. If giving of notice cannot be accomplished by a method under G.S. 1A-1, Rule 4(j) or Rule 4(j3), notice shall then be given in the manner provided in G.S. 1A-1, Rule 4(j1).

(d) Any person may petition to become a party by filing a motion to intervene in the manner provided in G.S. 1A-1, Rule 24. In addition, any person interested in a contested case may intervene and participate in that proceeding to the extent deemed appropriate by the administrative law judge.

(e) All hearings under this Chapter shall be open to the public. Hearings shall be conducted in an impartial manner. Hearings shall be conducted according to the procedures set out in this Article, except to the extent and in the particulars that specific hearing procedures and time standards are governed by another statute.

(f) Unless another statute or a federal statute or regulation sets a time limitation for the filing of a petition in contested cases against a specified agency, the general limitation for the filing of a petition in a contested case is 60 days. The time limitation, whether established by another statute, federal statute, or federal regulation, or this section, shall commence when notice is given of the agency decision to all persons aggrieved who are known to the agency by personal delivery or by the placing of the notice in an official depository of the United States Postal Service wrapped in a wrapper addressed to the person at the latest address given by the person to the agency. The notice shall be in writing, and shall set forth the agency action, and shall inform the persons of the right, the procedure, and the time limit to file a contested case petition. When no informal settlement request has been received by the agency prior to issuance of the notice, any subsequent informal settlement request shall not suspend the time limitation for the filing of a petition for a contested case hearing. (1973, c. 1331, s. 1; 1975, 2nd Sess., c. 983, s. 65; 1985, c. 746, s. 1; 1985 (Reg. Sess., 1986), c. 1022, ss. 1(9), (10), 6(2), (3); 1987, c. 878, ss. 3-5; c. 879, s. 6.1; 1987 (Reg. Sess., 1988), c. 1111, s. 5; 1991, c. 35, s. 1; 1993 (Reg. Sess., 1994), c. 572, s. 2; 2009-451, s. 21A.1(a); 2011-332, s. 2.1; 2011-398, s. 16; 2012-187, s. 6; 2013-397, s. 4.)

§ 150B-23.1. Mediated settlement conferences.

(a) Purpose. - This section authorizes a mediation program in the Office of Administrative Hearings in which the chief administrative law judge may require the parties in a contested case to attend a prehearing settlement conference conducted by a mediator. The purpose of the program is to determine whether a system of mediated settlement conferences may make the operation of the Office of Administrative Hearings more efficient, less costly, and more satisfying to the parties.

(b) Definitions. - The following definitions apply in this section:

(1) Mediated settlement conference. - A conference ordered by the chief administrative law judge involving the parties to a contested case and conducted by a mediator prior to a contested case hearing.

(2) Mediator. - A neutral person who acts to encourage and facilitate a resolution of a contested case but who does not make a decision on the merits of the contested case.

(c) Conference. - The chief administrative law judge may order a mediated settlement conference for all or any part of a contested case to which an administrative law judge is assigned to preside. All aspects of the mediated settlement conference shall be conducted insofar as possible in accordance with the rules adopted by the Supreme Court for the court-ordered mediation pilot program under G.S. 7A-38.

(d)   Attendance. - The parties to a contested case in which a mediated settlement conference is ordered, their attorneys, and other persons having authority to settle the parties' claims shall attend the settlement conference unless excused by the presiding administrative law judge.

(e)   Mediator. - The parties shall have the right to stipulate to a mediator. Upon the failure of the parties to agree within a time limit established by the presiding administrative law judge, a mediator shall be appointed by the presiding administrative law judge.

(f)   Sanctions. - Upon failure of a party or a party's attorney to attend a mediated settlement conference ordered under this section, the presiding administrative law judge may impose any sanction authorized by G.S. 150B-33(b)(8) or (10).

(g)   Standards. - Mediators authorized to conduct mediated settlement conferences under this section shall comply with the standards adopted by the Supreme Court for the court-ordered mediation pilot program under G.S. 7A-38.

(h)   Immunity. - A mediator acting pursuant to this section shall have judicial immunity in the same manner and to the same extent as a judge of the General Court of Justice.

(i)   Costs. - Costs of a mediated settlement conference shall be paid one share by the petitioner, one share by the respondent, and an equal share by any intervenor, unless otherwise apportioned by the administrative law judge.

(j)   Inadmissibility of Negotiations. - All conduct or communications made during a mediated settlement conference are presumed to be made in compromise negotiations and shall be governed by Rule 408 of the North Carolina Rules of Evidence.

(k)   Right to Hearing. - Nothing in this section restricts the right to a contested case hearing. (1993, c. 321, s. 25(b); c. 363, ss. 1, 3; 1995, c. 145, s. 1.)

§ 150B-23.2. Fee for filing a contested case hearing.

(a) Filing Fee. - In every contested case commenced in the Office of Administrative Hearings by a person aggrieved, the petitioner shall pay a filing fee, and the administrative law judge shall have the authority to assess that filing fee against the losing party, in the amount of one hundred twenty-five dollars ($125.00), unless the Office of Administrative Hearings establishes a lesser filing fee by rule.

(b) Time of Collection. - All fees that are required to be assessed, collected, and remitted under subsection (a) of this section shall be collected by the Office of Administrative Hearings at the time of commencement of the contested case except as may be allowed by rule to permit or complete late payment or in suits in forma pauperis.

(c) Forms of Payment. - The Office of Administrative Hearings may by rule provide for the acceptable forms for payment and transmission of the filing fee.

(d) Wavier or Refund. - The Office of Administrative Hearings shall by rule provide for the fee to be waived in a contested case in which the petition is filed in forma pauperis and supported by such proofs as are required in G.S. 1-110 and in a contested case involving a mandated federal cause of action. The Office of Administrative Hearings shall by rule provide for the fee to be refunded in a contested case in which the losing party is the State. (2009-451, s. 21A.1(b); 2012-187, s. 5.)

§ 150B-24. Venue of hearing.

(a) The hearing of a contested case shall be conducted:

(1) In the county in this State in which any person whose property or rights are the subject matter of the hearing maintains his residence;

(2) In the county where the agency maintains its principal office if the property or rights that are the subject matter of the hearing do not affect any person or if the subject matter of the hearing is the property or rights of residents of more than one county; or

(3) In any county determined by the administrative law judge in his discretion to promote the ends of justice or better serve the convenience of witnesses.

(b) Any person whose property or rights are the subject matter of the hearing waives his objection to venue by proceeding in the hearing. (1973, c. 1331, s. 1; 1985, c. 746, s. 1; 1987, c. 878, s. 6.)

§ 150B-25. Conduct of hearing; answer.

(a) If a party fails to appear in a contested case after proper service of notice, and if no adjournment or continuance is granted, the administrative law judge may proceed with the hearing in the absence of the party.

(b) Repealed by Session Laws 1991, c. 35, s. 2.

(c) The parties shall be given an opportunity to present arguments on issues of law and policy and an opportunity to present evidence on issues of fact.

(d) A party may cross-examine any witness, including the author of a document prepared by, on behalf of, or for use of the agency and offered in evidence. Any party may submit rebuttal evidence. (1973, c. 1331, s. 1; 1985, c. 746, s. 1; 1985 (Reg. Sess., 1986), c. 1022, s. 1(13); 1987, c. 878, s. 6; 1991, c. 35, s. 2.)

§ 150B-26. Consolidation.

When contested cases involving a common question of law or fact or multiple proceedings involving the same or related parties are pending, the Director of the Office of Administrative Hearings may order a joint hearing of any matters at issue in the cases, order the cases consolidated, or make other orders to reduce costs or delay in the proceedings. (1973, c. 1331, s. 1; 1985, c. 746, s. 1; 1985, (Reg. Sess., 1986), c. 1022, s. 1(1), 1(14).)

§ 150B-27. Subpoena.

After the commencement of a contested case, subpoenas may be issued and served in accordance with G.S. 1A-1, Rule 45. In addition to the methods of service in G.S. 1A-1, Rule 45, a State law enforcement officer may serve a subpoena on behalf of an agency that is a party to the contested case by any method by which a sheriff may serve a subpoena under that Rule. Upon a motion, the administrative law judge may quash a subpoena if, upon a hearing, the administrative law judge finds that the evidence the production of which is required does not relate to a matter in issue, the subpoena does not describe with sufficient particularity the evidence the production of which is required, or for any other reason sufficient in law the subpoena may be quashed.

Witness fees shall be paid by the party requesting the subpoena to subpoenaed witnesses in accordance with G.S. 7A-314. However, State officials or employees who are subpoenaed shall not be entitled to witness fees, but they shall receive their normal salary and they shall not be required to take any annual leave for the witness days. Travel expenses of State officials or employees who are subpoenaed shall be reimbursed as provided in G.S. 138-6. (1973, c. 1331, s. 1; 1975, 2nd Sess., c. 983, s. 66; 1985, c. 746, s. 1; 1987, c. 878, s. 6; 1991, c. 35, s. 3.)

§ 150B-28. Depositions and discovery.

(a)   A deposition may be used in lieu of other evidence when taken in compliance with the Rules of Civil Procedure, G.S. 1A-1. Parties in contested cases may engage in discovery pursuant to the provisions of the Rules of Civil Procedure, G.S. 1A-1.

(b)   Repealed by Session Laws 2007-491, s. 2, effective January 1, 2008. (1973, c. 1331, s. 1; 1985, c. 746, s. 1; 2007-491, s. 2.)

§ 150B-29. Rules of evidence.

(a)   In all contested cases, irrelevant, immaterial and unduly repetitious evidence shall be excluded. Except as otherwise provided, the rules of evidence as applied in the trial division of the General Court of Justice shall be followed;

but, when evidence is not reasonably available under the rules to show relevant facts, then the most reliable and substantial evidence available shall be admitted. On the judge's own motion, an administrative law judge may exclude evidence that is inadmissible under this section. The party with the burden of proof in a contested case must establish the facts required by G.S. 150B-23(a) by a preponderance of the evidence. It shall not be necessary for a party or his attorney to object at the hearing to evidence in order to preserve the right to object to its consideration by the administrative law judge in making a decision or by the court on judicial review.

(b) Evidence in a contested case, including records and documents, shall be offered and made a part of the record. Factual information or evidence not made a part of the record shall not be considered in the determination of the case, except as permitted under G.S. 150B-30. Documentary evidence may be received in the form of a copy or excerpt or may be incorporated by reference, if the materials so incorporated are available for examination by the parties. Upon timely request, a party shall be given an opportunity to compare the copy with the original if available. (1973, c. 1331, s. 1; 1985, c. 746, s. 1; 1987, c. 878, s. 7; 1991, c. 35, s. 4; 2000-190, s. 4; 2012-187, s. 7.1.)

§ 150B-30. Official notice.

Official notice may be taken of all facts of which judicial notice may be taken and of other facts within the specialized knowledge of the agency. The noticed fact and its source shall be stated and made known to affected parties at the earliest practicable time, and any party shall on timely request be afforded an opportunity to dispute the noticed fact through submission of evidence and argument. (1973, c. 1331, s. 1; 1985, c. 746, s. 1.)

§ 150B-31. Stipulations.

(a) The parties in a contested case may, by a stipulation in writing filed with the administrative law judge, agree upon any fact involved in the controversy, which stipulation shall be used as evidence at the hearing and be binding on the parties thereto. Parties should agree upon facts when practicable.

(b) Except as otherwise provided by law, disposition may be made of a contested case by stipulation, agreed settlement, consent order, waiver, default, or other method agreed upon by the parties. (1973, c. 1331, s. 1; 1985, c. 746, s. 1; 1987, c. 878, s. 6.)

§ 150B-31.1. Contested tax cases.

(a) Application. - This section applies only to contested tax cases. A contested tax case is a case involving a disputed tax matter arising under G.S. 105-241.15. To the extent any provision in this section conflicts with another provision in this Article, this section controls.

(b) Simple Procedures. - The Chief Administrative Law Judge may limit and simplify the procedures that apply to a contested tax case involving a taxpayer who is not represented by an attorney. An administrative law judge assigned to a contested tax case must make reasonable efforts to assist a taxpayer who is not represented by an attorney in order to assure a fair hearing.

(c) Venue. - A hearing in a contested tax case must be conducted in Wake County, unless the parties agree to hear the case in another county.

(d) Reports. - The following agency reports are admissible without testimony from personnel of the agency:

(1) Law enforcement reports.

(2) Government agency lab reports used for the enforcement of motor fuel tax laws.

(e) Confidentiality. - The record, proceedings, and decision in a contested tax case are confidential until the final decision is issued in the case. (2007-491, s. 42; 2008-134, s. 9.)

§ 150B-32. Designation of administrative law judge.

(a) The Director of the Office of Administrative Hearings shall assign himself or another administrative law judge to preside over a contested case.

(a1) Repealed by Sessions Laws 1985 (Reg. Sess., 1986), c. 1022, s. 1(15), effective July 15, 1986.

(b) On the filing in good faith by a party of a timely and sufficient affidavit of personal bias or disqualification of an administrative law judge, the administrative law judge shall determine the matter as a part of the record in the case, and this determination shall be subject to judicial review at the conclusion of the proceeding.

(c) When an administrative law judge is disqualified or it is impracticable for him to continue the hearing, the Director shall assign another administrative law judge to continue with the case unless it is shown that substantial prejudice to any party will result, in which event a new hearing shall be held or the case dismissed without prejudice. (1973, c. 1331, s. 1; 1985, c. 746, s. 1; 1985 (Reg. Sess., 1986), c. 1022, s. 1(1), 1(12), 1(15), c. 1028, s. 40; 1987, c. 878, s. 8.)

§ 150B-33. Powers of administrative law judge.

(a) An administrative law judge shall stay any contested case under this Article on motion of an agency which is a party to the contested case, if the agency shows by supporting affidavits that it is engaged in other litigation or administrative proceedings, by whatever name called, with or before a federal agency, and this other litigation or administrative proceedings will determine the position, in whole or in part, of the agency in the contested case. At the conclusion of the other litigation or administrative proceedings, the contested case shall proceed and be determined as expeditiously as possible.

(b) An administrative law judge may:

(1) Administer oaths and affirmations;

(2) Sign, issue, and rule on subpoenas in accordance with G.S. 150B-27 and G.S. 1A-1, Rule 45;

(3) Provide for the taking of testimony by deposition and rule on all objections to discovery in accordance with G.S. 1A-1, the Rules of Civil Procedure;

(3a)   Rule on all prehearing motions that are authorized by G.S. 1A-1, the Rules of Civil Procedure;

(4)   Regulate the course of the hearings, including discovery, set the time and place for continued hearings, and fix the time for filing of briefs and other documents;

(5)   Direct the parties to appear and confer to consider simplification of the issues by consent of the parties;

(6)   Stay the contested action by the agency pending the outcome of the case, upon such terms as he deems proper, and subject to the provisions of G.S. 1A-1, Rule 65;

(7)   Determine whether the hearing shall be recorded by a stenographer or by an electronic device; and

(8)   Enter an order returnable in the General Court of Justice, Superior Court Division, to show cause why the person should not be held in contempt. The Court shall have the power to impose punishment as for contempt for any act which would constitute direct or indirect contempt if the act occurred in an action pending in Superior Court.

(9)   Determine that a rule as applied in a particular case is void because (1) it is not within the statutory authority of the agency, (2) is not clear and unambiguous to persons it is intended to direct, guide, or assist, or (3) is not reasonably necessary to enable the agency to fulfill a duty delegated to it by the General Assembly.

(10)   Impose the sanctions provided for in G.S. 1A-1 or Chapter 3 of Title 26 of the North Carolina Administrative Code for noncompliance with applicable procedural rules.

(11)   Order the assessment of reasonable attorneys' fees and witnesses' fees against the State agency involved in contested cases decided under this Article where the administrative law judge finds that the State agency named as respondent has substantially prejudiced the petitioner's rights and has acted arbitrarily or capriciously or under Chapter 126 where the administrative law judge finds discrimination, harassment, or orders reinstatement or back pay.

(12) Repealed by Session Laws 2011-398, s. 17. For effective date and applicability, see editor's note. (1973, c. 1331, s. 1; 1985, c. 746, s. 1; 1987, c. 878, ss. 5, 9, 10, 26; 1987 (Reg. Sess., 1988), c. 1111, ss. 18, 19; 1991, c. 35, s. 5; 2000-190, s. 5; 2004-156, s. 4; 2011-398, s. 17; 2012-187, s. 7.2.)

§ 150B-34. Final decision or order.

(a) In each contested case the administrative law judge shall make a final decision or order that contains findings of fact and conclusions of law. The administrative law judge shall decide the case based upon the preponderance of the evidence, giving due regard to the demonstrated knowledge and expertise of the agency with respect to facts and inferences within the specialized knowledge of the agency.

(b) Repealed by Session Laws 1991, c. 35, s. 6.

(c) Repealed by Session Laws 2011-398, s. 18. For effective date and applicability, see editor's note.

(d) Except for the exemptions contained In G.S. 150B-1, the provisions of this section regarding the decision of the administrative law judge shall apply only to agencies subject to Article 3 of this Chapter, notwithstanding any other provisions to the contrary relating to recommended decisions by administrative law judges.

(e) An administrative law judge may grant judgment on the pleadings, pursuant to a motion made in accordance with G.S. 1A-1, Rule 12(c), or summary judgment, pursuant to a motion made in accordance with G.S. 1A-1, Rule 56, that disposes of all issues in the contested case. Notwithstanding subsection (a) of this section, a decision granting a motion for judgment on the pleadings or summary judgment need not include findings of fact or conclusions of law, except as determined by the administrative law judge to be required or allowed by G.S. 1A-1, Rule 12(c), or Rule 56. (1973, c. 1331, s. 1; 1985, c. 746, s. 1; 1987, c. 878, ss. 5, 23; 1987 (Reg. Sess., 1988), c. 1111, s. 21; 1991, c. 35, s. 6; 2000-190, s. 6; 2011-398, s. 18.)

§ 150B-35. No ex parte communication; exceptions.

Unless required for disposition of an ex parte matter authorized by law, the administrative law judge assigned to a contested case may not communicate, directly or indirectly, in connection with any issue of fact, or question of law, with any person or party or his representative, except on notice and opportunity for all parties to participate. (1973, c. 1331, s. 1; 1985, c. 746, s. 1; 1987, c. 878, s. 11; 2011-398, s. 19.)

§ 150B-36: Repealed by Session Laws 2011-398, s. 20. For effective date and applicability, see editor's note.

§ 150B-37. Official record.

(a)   In a contested case, the Office of Administrative Hearings shall prepare an official record of the case that includes:

(1)   Notices, pleadings, motions, and intermediate rulings;

(2)   Questions and offers of proof, objections, and rulings thereon;

(3)   Evidence presented;

(4)   Matters officially noticed, except matters so obvious that a statement of them would serve no useful purpose; and

(5)   Repealed by Session Laws 1987, c. 878, s. 25.

(6)   The administrative law judge's final decision or order.

(b)   Proceedings at which oral evidence is presented shall be recorded, but need not be transcribed unless requested by a party. Each party shall bear the cost of the transcript or part thereof or copy of said transcript or part thereof which said party requests, and said transcript or part thereof shall be added to the official record as an exhibit.

(c)   The Office of Administrative Hearings shall forward a copy of the administrative law judge's final decision to each party. (1973, c. 1331, s. 1; 1985, c. 746, s. 1; 1987, c. 878, ss. 13, 25; 2000-190, s. 8; 2011-398, s. 21.)

Article 3A.

Other Administrative Hearings.

§ 150B-38. Scope; hearing required; notice; venue.

(a)   The provisions of this Article shall apply to:

(1)   Occupational licensing agencies.

(2)   The State Banking Commission, the Commissioner of Banks, and the Credit Union Division of the Department of Commerce.

(3)   The Department of Insurance and the Commissioner of Insurance.

(4)   The State Chief Information Officer in the administration of the provisions of Article 3D of Chapter 147 of the General Statutes.

(5)   The North Carolina State Building Code Council.

(6)   The State Board of Elections in the administration of any investigation or audit under the provisions of Article 22A of Chapter 163 of the General Statutes.

(b)   Prior to any agency action in a contested case, the agency shall give the parties in the case an opportunity for a hearing without undue delay and notice not less than 15 days before the hearing. Notice to the parties shall include:

(1)   A statement of the date, hour, place, and nature of the hearing;

(2)   A reference to the particular sections of the statutes and rules involved; and

(3)   A short and plain statement of the facts alleged.

(c)   Notice shall be given by one of the methods for service of process under G.S. 1A-1, Rule 4(j) or Rule 4(j3). If given by registered or certified mail, by signature confirmation as provided by the United States Postal Service, or by designated delivery service authorized pursuant to 26 U.S.C. § 7502(f)(2) with delivery receipt, notice shall be deemed to have been given on the delivery date appearing on the return receipt, copy of proof of delivery provided by the United States Postal Service, or delivery receipt. If notice cannot be given by one of the methods for service of process under G.S. 1A-1, Rule 4(j) or Rule 4(j3), then notice shall be given in the manner provided in G.S. 1A-1, Rule 4(j1).

(d) A party who has been served with a notice of hearing may file a written response with the agency. If a written response is filed, a copy of the response must be mailed to all other parties not less than 10 days before the date set for the hearing.

(e) All hearings conducted under this Article shall be open to the public. A hearing conducted by the agency shall be held in the county where the agency maintains its principal office. A hearing conducted for the agency by an administrative law judge requested under G.S. 150B-40 shall be held in a county in this State where any person whose property or rights are the subject matter of the hearing resides. If a different venue would promote the ends of justice or better serve the convenience of witnesses, the agency or the administrative law judge may designate another county. A person whose property or rights are the subject matter of the hearing waives his objection to venue if he proceeds in the hearing.

(f) Any person may petition to become a party by filing with the agency or hearing officer a motion to intervene in the manner provided by G.S. 1A-1, Rule 24. In addition, any person interested in a contested case under this Article may intervene and participate to the extent deemed appropriate by the agency hearing officer.

(g) When contested cases involving a common question of law or fact or multiple proceedings involving the same or related parties are pending before an agency, the agency may order a joint hearing of any matters at issue in the cases, order the cases consolidated, or make other orders to reduce costs or delay in the proceedings.

(h) Every agency shall adopt rules governing the conduct of hearings that are consistent with the provisions of this Article. (1985, c. 746, s. 1; 1985 (Reg. Sess., 1986), c. 1022, s. 6(3); 1989, c. 76, s. 30; c. 751, s. 7(45); 1991 (Reg. Sess., 1992), c. 959, s. 76; 1999-434, s. 17; 2001-141, s. 8; 2001-193, s. 12; 2001-487, s. 21(h); 2010-169, s. 7; 2011-332, s. 2.3.)

§ 150B-39. Depositions; discovery; subpoenas.

(a) A deposition may be used in lieu of other evidence when taken in compliance with the Rules of Civil Procedure, G.S. 1A-1. Parties in a contested case may engage in discovery pursuant to the provisions of the Rules of Civil Procedure, G.S. 1A-1.

(b) Upon a request for an identifiable agency record involving a material fact in a contested case, the agency shall promptly provide the record to a party, unless the record relates solely to the agency's internal procedures or is exempt from disclosure by law.

(c) In preparation for, or in the conduct of, a contested case subpoenas may be issued and served in accordance with G.S. 1A-1, Rule 45. Upon a motion, the agency may quash a subpoena if, upon a hearing, the agency finds that the evidence, the production of which is required, does not relate to a matter in issue, the subpoena does not describe with sufficient particularity the evidence the production of which is required, or for any other reason sufficient in law the subpoena may be quashed. Witness fees shall be paid by the party requesting the subpoena to subpoenaed witnesses in accordance with G.S. 7A-314. However, State officials or employees who are subpoenaed shall not be entitled to any witness fees, but they shall receive their normal salary and they shall not be required to take any annual leave for the witness days. Travel expenses of State officials or employees who are subpoenaed shall be reimbursed as provided in G.S. 138-6. (1985, c. 746, s. 1; 1991, c. 35, s. 8.)

§ 150B-40. Conduct of hearing; presiding officer; ex parte communication.

(a) Hearings shall be conducted in a fair and impartial manner. At the hearing, the agency and the parties shall be given an opportunity to present evidence on issues of fact, examine and cross-examine witnesses, including the author of a document prepared by, on behalf of or for the use of the agency and offered into evidence, submit rebuttal evidence, and present arguments on issues of law or policy.

If a party fails to appear in a contested case after he has been given proper notice, the agency may continue the hearing or proceed with the hearing and make its decision in the absence of the party.

(b) Except as provided under subsection (e) of this section, hearings under this Article shall be conducted by a majority of the agency. An agency shall designate one or more of its members to preside at the hearing. If a party files in good faith a timely and sufficient affidavit of the personal bias or other reason for disqualification of any member of the agency, the agency shall determine the matter as a part of the record in the case, and its determination shall be subject to judicial review at the conclusion of the proceeding. If a presiding officer is disqualified or it is impracticable for him to continue the hearing, another presiding officer shall be assigned to continue with the case, except that if assignment of a new presiding officer will cause substantial prejudice to any party, a new hearing shall be held or the case dismissed without prejudice.

(c) The presiding officer may:

(1) Administer oaths and affirmations;

(2) Sign and issue subpoenas in the name of the agency, requiring attendance and giving of testimony by witnesses and the production of books, papers, and other documentary evidence;

(3) Provide for the taking of testimony by deposition;

(4) Regulate the course of the hearings, set the time and place for continued hearings, and fix the time for filing of briefs and other documents;

(5) Direct the parties to appear and confer to consider simplification of the issues by consent of the parties; and

(6) Apply to any judge of the superior court resident in the district or presiding at a term of court in the county where a hearing is pending for an order to show cause why any person should not be held in contempt of the agency and its processes, and the court shall have the power to impose punishment as for contempt for acts which would constitute direct or indirect contempt if the acts occurred in an action pending in superior court.

(d) Unless required for disposition of an ex parte matter authorized by law, a member of an agency assigned to make a decision or to make findings of fact and conclusions of law in a contested case under this Article shall not communicate, directly or indirectly, in connection with any issue of fact or question of law, with any person or party or his representative, except on notice and opportunity for all parties to participate. This prohibition begins at the time of the notice of hearing. An agency member may communicate with other members of the agency and may have the aid and advice of the agency staff other than the staff which has been or is engaged in investigating or prosecuting functions in connection with the case under consideration or a factually-related case. This section does not apply to an agency employee or party representative with professional training in accounting, actuarial science, economics or financial analysis insofar as the case involves financial practices or conditions.

(e) When a majority of an agency is unable or elects not to hear a contested case, the agency shall apply to the Director of the Office of Administrative Hearings for the designation of an administrative law judge to preside at the hearing of a contested case under this Article. Upon receipt of the application, the Director shall, without undue delay, assign an administrative law judge to hear the case.

The provisions of this Article, rather than the provisions of Article 3, shall govern a contested case in which the agency requests an administrative law judge from the Office of Administrative Hearings.

The administrative law judge assigned to hear a contested case under this Article shall sit in place of the agency and shall have the authority of the presiding officer in a contested case under this Article. The administrative law judge shall make a proposal for decision, which shall contain proposed findings of fact and proposed conclusions of law.

An administrative law judge shall stay any contested case under this Article on motion of an agency which is a party to the contested case, if the agency shows by supporting affidavits that it is engaged in other litigation or administrative proceedings, by whatever name called, with or before a federal agency, and this other litigation or administrative proceedings will determine the position, in whole or in part, of the agency in the contested case. At the conclusion of the other litigation or administrative proceedings, the contested case shall proceed and be determined as expeditiously as possible.

The agency may make its final decision only after the administrative law judge's proposal for decision is served on the parties, and an opportunity is given to each party to file exceptions and proposed findings of fact and to present oral and written arguments to the agency. (1985, c. 746, s. 1; 1985 (Reg. Sess., 1986), c. 1022, ss. 1(1), 6(3), 6(4).)

§ 150B-41. Evidence; stipulations; official notice.

(a)   In all contested cases, irrelevant, immaterial, and unduly repetitious evidence shall be excluded. Except as otherwise provided, the rules of evidence as applied in the trial division of the General Court of Justice shall be followed; but, when evidence is not reasonably available under such rules to show relevant facts, they may be shown by the most reliable and substantial evidence available. It shall not be necessary for a party or his attorney to object to evidence at the hearing in order to preserve the right to object to its consideration by the agency in reaching its decision, or by the court of judicial review.

(b)   Evidence in a contested case, including records and documents shall be offered and made a part of the record. Other factual information or evidence shall not be considered in determination of the case, except as permitted under G.S. 150B-30. Documentary evidence may be received in the form of a copy or excerpt or may be incorporated by reference, if the materials so incorporated are available for examination by the parties. Upon timely request, a party shall be given an opportunity to compare the copy with the original if available.

(c)   The parties in a contested case under this Article by a stipulation in writing filed with the agency may agree upon any fact involved in the controversy, which stipulation shall be used as evidence at the hearing and be binding on the parties thereto. Parties should agree upon facts when practicable. Except as otherwise provided by law, disposition may be made of a contested case by stipulation, agreed settlement, consent order, waiver, default, or other method agreed upon by the parties.

(d)   Official notice may be taken of all facts of which judicial notice may be taken and of other facts within the specialized knowledge of the agency. The noticed fact and its source shall be stated and made known to affected parties at the earliest practicable time, and any party shall on timely request be afforded an opportunity to dispute the noticed fact through submission of evidence and argument. An agency may use its experience, technical competence, and specialized knowledge in the evaluation of evidence presented to it. (1985, c. 746, s. 1.)

§ 150B-42. Final agency decision; official record.

(a) After compliance with the provisions of G.S. 150B-40(e), if applicable, and review of the official record, as defined in subsection (b) of this section, an agency shall make a written final decision or order in a contested case. The decision or order shall include findings of fact and conclusions of law. Findings of fact shall be based exclusively on the evidence and on matters officially noticed. Findings of fact, if set forth in statutory language, shall be accompanied by a concise and explicit statement of the underlying facts supporting them. A decision or order shall not be made except upon consideration of the record as a whole or such portion thereof as may be cited by any party to the proceeding and shall be supported by substantial evidence admissible under G.S. 150B-41. A copy of the decision or order shall be served upon each party by one of the methods for service of process under G.S. 1A-1, Rule 5(b). If service is by registered, certified, or first-class mail, by signature confirmation as provided by the United States Postal Service, or by designated delivery service authorized pursuant to 26 U.S.C. § 7502(f)(2) with delivery receipt, the copy shall be addressed to the party at the latest address given by the party to the agency. Service by one of the additional methods provided in G.S. 1A-1, Rule 5(b), is effective as provided therein and shall be accompanied by a certificate of service as provided in G.S. 1A-1, Rule 5(b1). G.S. 1A-1, Rule 6(e), applies if service is by first-class mail. A copy shall be furnished to the party's attorney of record.

(b) An agency shall prepare an official record of a hearing that shall include:

(1) Notices, pleadings, motions, and intermediate rulings;

(2) Questions and offers of proof, objections, and rulings thereon;

(3) Evidence presented;

(4) Matters officially noticed, except matters so obvious that a statement of them would serve no useful purpose;

(5) Proposed findings and exceptions; and

(6) Any decision, opinion, order, or report by the officer presiding at the hearing and by the agency.

(c) Proceedings at which oral evidence is presented shall be recorded, but need not be transcribed unless requested by a party. Each party shall bear the cost of the transcript or part thereof or copy of said transcript or part thereof which said party requests. (1985, c. 746, s. 1; 2011-332, s. 2.4.)

Article 4.

Judicial Review.

§ 150B-43. Right to judicial review.

Any party or person aggrieved by the final decision in a contested case, and who has exhausted all administrative remedies made available to the party or person aggrieved by statute or agency rule, is entitled to judicial review of the decision under this Article, unless adequate procedure for judicial review is provided by another statute, in which case the review shall be under such other statute. Nothing in this Chapter shall prevent any party or person aggrieved from invoking any judicial remedy available to the party or person aggrieved under the law to test the validity of any administrative action not made reviewable under this Article. Absent a specific statutory requirement, nothing in this Chapter shall require a party or person aggrieved to petition an agency for rule making or to seek or obtain a declaratory ruling before obtaining judicial review of a final decision or order made pursuant to G.S. 150B-34. (1973, c. 1331, s. 1; 1985, c. 746, s. 1; 2011-398, s. 22; 2012-194, s. 62.1.)

§ 150B-44. Right to judicial intervention when decision unreasonably delayed.

Unreasonable delay on the part of any agency or administrative law judge in taking any required action shall be justification for any person whose rights, duties, or privileges are adversely affected by such delay to seek a court order compelling action by the agency or administrative law judge. Failure of an administrative law judge subject to Article 3 of this Chapter or failure of an agency subject to Article 3A of this Chapter to make a final decision within 120 days of the close of the contested case hearing is justification for a person whose rights, duties, or privileges are adversely affected by the delay to seek a court order compelling action by the agency or by the administrative law judge. The Board of Trustees of the North Carolina State Health Plan for Teachers and State Employees is a "board" for purposes of this section. (1973, c. 1331, s. 1; 1985, c. 746, s. 1; 1985 (Reg. Sess., 1986), c. 1022, s. 1(17); 1987, c. 878, ss. 5, 27; 1991, c. 35, s. 9; 2000-190, s. 9; 2008-168, s. 5(b); 2011-398, s. 23.)

§ 150B-45. Procedure for seeking review; waiver.

(a) Procedure. - To obtain judicial review of a final decision under this Article, the person seeking review must file a petition within 30 days after the person is served with a written copy of the decision. The petition must be filed as follows:

(1) Contested tax cases. - A petition for review of a final decision in a contested tax case arising under G.S. 105-241.15 must be filed in the Superior Court of Wake County.

(2) Other final decisions. - A petition for review of any other final decision under this Article must be filed in the superior court of the county where the person aggrieved by the administrative decision resides, or in the case of a person residing outside the State, in the county where the contested case which resulted in the final decision was filed.

(b) Waiver. - A person who fails to file a petition within the required time waives the right to judicial review under this Article. For good cause shown, however, the superior court may accept an untimely petition. (1973, c. 1331, s. 1; 1985, c. 746, s. 1; 1987, c. 878, s. 16; 2007-491, s. 43; 2013-143, s. 4.)

§ 150B-46. Contents of petition; copies served on all parties; intervention.

The petition shall explicitly state what exceptions are taken to the decision or procedure and what relief the petitioner seeks. Within 10 days after the petition is filed with the court, the party seeking the review shall serve copies of the petition by personal service or by certified mail upon all who were parties of record to the administrative proceedings. Names and addresses of such parties shall be furnished to the petitioner by the agency upon request. Any party to the administrative proceeding is a party to the review proceedings unless the party withdraws by notifying the court of the withdrawal and serving the other parties with notice of the withdrawal. Other parties to the proceeding may file a response to the petition within 30 days of service. Parties, including agencies, may state exceptions to the decision or procedure and what relief is sought in the response.

Any person aggrieved may petition to become a party by filing a motion to intervene as provided in G.S. 1A-1, Rule 24. (1973, c. 1331, s. 1; 1985, c. 746, s. 1; 1991, c. 35, s. 10.)

§ 150B-47. Records filed with clerk of superior court; contents of records; costs.

Within 30 days after receipt of the copy of the petition for review, or within such additional time as the court may allow, the Office of Administrative Hearings shall transmit to the reviewing court the original or a certified copy of the official record in the contested case under review. With the permission of the court, the record may be shortened by stipulation of all parties to the review proceedings. Any party unreasonably refusing to stipulate to limit the record may be taxed by the court for such additional costs as may be occasioned by the refusal. The court may require or permit subsequent corrections or additions to the record when deemed desirable. (1973, c. 1331, s. 1; 1983, c. 919, s. 3; 1985, c. 746, s. 1; 1985 (Reg. Sess., 1986), c. 1022, s. 1(18); 1987, c. 878, s. 22; 2011-398, s. 24.)

§ 150B-48. Stay of decision.

At any time before or during the review proceeding, the person aggrieved may apply to the reviewing court for an order staying the operation of the administrative decision pending the outcome of the review. The court may grant or deny the stay in its discretion upon such terms as it deems proper and subject to the provisions of G.S. 1A-1, Rule 65. (1973, c. 1331, s. 1; 1985, c. 746, s. 1.)

§ 150B-49. New evidence.

A party or person aggrieved who files a petition in the superior court may apply to the court to present additional evidence. If the court is satisfied that the evidence is material to the issues, is not merely cumulative, and could not reasonably have been presented at the administrative hearing, the court may remand the case so that additional evidence can be taken. If an administrative law judge did not make a final decision in the case, the court shall remand the case to the agency that conducted the administrative hearing under Article 3A of this Chapter. After hearing the evidence, the agency may affirm or modify its previous findings of fact and final decision. If an administrative law judge made a final decision in the case, the court shall remand the case to the administrative law judge. After hearing the evidence, the administrative law judge may affirm or modify his previous findings of fact and final decision. The additional evidence and any affirmation or modification of a final decision shall be made part of the official record. (1973, c. 1331, s. 1; 1985, c. 746, s. 1; 1987, c. 878, s. 17; 2000-190, s. 10; 2011-398, s. 25.)

§ 150B-50. Review by superior court without jury.

The review by a superior court of administrative decisions under this Chapter shall be conducted by the court without a jury. (1973, c. 1331, s. 1; 1983, c. 919, s. 2; 1985, c. 746, s. 1; 1987, c. 878, s. 18; 2011-398, s. 26.)

§ 150B-51. Scope and standard of review.

(a), (a1) Repealed by Sessions Laws, 2011-398, s. 27. For effective date and applicability, see editor's note.

(b) The court reviewing a final decision may affirm the decision or remand the case for further proceedings. It may also reverse or modify the decision if the substantial rights of the petitioners may have been prejudiced because the findings, inferences, conclusions, or decisions are:

(1) In violation of constitutional provisions;

(2) In excess of the statutory authority or jurisdiction of the agency or administrative law judge;

(3) Made upon unlawful procedure;

(4) Affected by other error of law;

(5) Unsupported by substantial evidence admissible under G.S. 150B-29(a), 150B-30, or 150B-31 in view of the entire record as submitted; or

(6) Arbitrary, capricious, or an abuse of discretion.

(c) In reviewing a final decision in a contested case, the court shall determine whether the petitioner is entitled to the relief sought in the petition based upon its review of the final decision and the official record. With regard to asserted errors pursuant to subdivisions (1) through (4) of subsection (b) of this section, the court shall conduct its review of the final decision using the de novo standard of review. With regard to asserted errors pursuant to subdivisions (5) and (6) of subsection (b) of this section, the court shall conduct its review of the final decision using the whole record standard of review.

(d) In reviewing a final decision allowing judgment on the pleadings or summary judgment, the court may enter any order allowed by G.S. 1A-1, Rule 12(c) or Rule 56. If the order of the court does not fully adjudicate the case, the court shall remand the case to the administrative law judge for such further proceedings as are just. (1973, c. 1331, s. 1; 1983, c. 919, s. 4; 1985, c. 746, s. 1; 1987, c. 878, s. 19; 2000-140, s. 94.1; 2000-190, s. 11; 2011-398, s. 27.)

§ 150B-52. Appeal; stay of court's decision.

A party to a review proceeding in a superior court may appeal to the appellate division from the final judgment of the superior court as provided in G.S. 7A-27. The scope of review to be applied by the appellate court under this section is the same as it is for other civil cases. In cases reviewed under G.S. 150B-51(c), the court's findings of fact shall be upheld if supported by substantial evidence. Pending the outcome of an appeal, an appealing party may apply to the court that issued the judgment under appeal for a stay of that judgment or a stay of the administrative decision that is the subject of the appeal, as appropriate. (1973, c. 1331, s. 1; 1985, c. 746, s. 1; 1987, c. 878, s. 20; 2000-140, s. 94; 2000-190, s. 12.)

§§ 150B-53 through 150B-57. Reserved for future codification purposes.

Article 5.

Publication of Administrative Rules.

§§ 150B-58 through 150B-64: Repealed by Session Laws 1991, c. 418, s. 5.

Chapter 151.

Constables.

§§ 151-1 through 151-8. Repealed by Session Laws 1969, c. 1190, s. 57.

Chapter 152.

Coroners.

§ 152-1. Election; vacancies in office; appointment by clerk in special cases.

In each county a coroner shall be elected by the qualified voters thereof in the same manner and at the same time as the election of members of the General Assembly, and shall hold office for a term of four years, or until his successor is elected and qualified.

A vacancy in the office of coroner shall be filled by the county commissioners, and the person so appointed shall, upon qualification, hold office until his successor is elected and qualified. If the coroner were elected as the nominee of a political party, then the county commissioners shall consult with the county executive committee of that political party before filling the vacancy, and shall appoint the person recommended by that committee if the party makes a recommendation within 30 days of the occurrence of the vacancy; this sentence shall apply only to the counties of Alamance, Alleghany, Avery, Beaufort, Brunswick, Buncombe, Burke, Cabarrus, Caldwell, Cherokee, Clay, Cleveland, Davidson, Davie, Graham, Guilford, Haywood, Henderson, Jackson, Madison, McDowell, Mecklenburg, Moore, New Hanover, Polk, Randolph, Rockingham, Rutherford, Stanly, Stokes, Transylvania, Wake, and Yancey.

When the coroner shall be out of the county, or shall for any reason be unable to hold the necessary inquest as provided by law, or there is a vacancy existing in the office of coroner which has not been filled by the county commissioners and it is made to appear to the clerk of the superior court by satisfactory evidence that a deceased person whose body has been found within the county probably came to his death by the criminal act or default of some person, it is the duty of the clerk to appoint some suitable person to act as coroner in such special case. (Const., art. 4, s. 24; 1903, c. 661; Rev., ss. 1047, 1049; C.S., ss. 1014, 1018; Ex. Sess. 1924, c. 65; 1935, c. 376; 1981, c. 504, s. 8; c. 763, s. 5; c. 830.)

§ 152-2. Oaths to be taken.

Every coroner, before entering upon the duties of his office, shall take and subscribe to the oaths prescribed for public officers, and an oath of office. (Code, s. 661; Rev., s. 1048; C.S., s. 1015; Ex. Sess. 1924, c. 65.)

§ 152-3. Coroner's bond.

Every coroner shall execute an undertaking conditioned upon the faithful discharge of the duties of his office with good and sufficient surety in the penal sum of two thousand dollars ($2,000), payable to the State of North Carolina, and approved by the board of county commissioners. (1791, c. 342, ss. 1, 2, P. R.; 1820, c. 1047, ss. 1, 2, P. R.; R. C., c. 25, s. 2; Code, s. 661; 1899, c. 54, s. 52; Rev., s. 299; C.S., s. 1016; Ex. Sess. 1924, c. 65.)

§ 152-4. Coroners' bonds registered; certified copies evidence.

All official bonds of coroners shall be duly approved, certified, registered, and filed as sheriffs' bonds are required to be; and certified copies of the same duly certified by the register of deeds, with official seal attached, shall be received and read in evidence in the like cases and in like manner as such copies of sheriffs' bonds are now allowed to be read in evidence. (1860-1, c. 18; Code, s. 662; Rev., s. 300; C.S., s. 1017; Ex. Sess. 1924, c. 65.)

§ 152-5. Fees of coroners.

Fees of coroners shall be the same as are or may be allowed sheriffs in similar cases:

For holding an inquest over a dead body, five dollars ($5.00); if necessarily engaged more than one day, for each additional day, five dollars ($5.00).

For burying a pauper over whom an inquest has been held, all necessary and actual expenses, to be approved by the board of county commissioners, and paid by the county. (Code, s. 3743; 1903, c. 781; Rev., s. 2775; C.S., s. 3905; 1967, c. 1154, s. 6.)

§ 152-6. Powers, penalties, and liabilities of special coroner.

The special coroner appointed under the provisions of G.S. 152-1 shall be invested with all the powers and duties conferred upon the several coroners in respect to holding inquests over deceased bodies, and shall be subject to the penalties and liabilities imposed on the said coroners. (1903, c. 661, s. 2; Rev., s. 1050; C.S., s. 1019; Ex. Sess. 1924, c. 65.)

§ 152-7. Duties of coroners with respect to inquests and preliminary hearings.

The duties of the several coroners with respect to inquests and preliminary hearings shall be as follows:

(1)   Whenever it appears that the deceased probably came to his death by the criminal act or default of some person, he shall go to the place where the body of such deceased person is and make a careful investigation and inquiry as to when and by what means such deceased person came to his death and the name of the deceased, if to be found out, together with all the material circumstances attending his death, and shall make a complete record of such personal investigation: Provided, however, that the coroner shall not proceed to summon a jury as is hereinafter provided if he shall be satisfied from his personal investigation that the death of the said deceased was from natural causes, or that no person is blamable in any respect in connection with such death, and shall so find and make such finding in writing as a part of his report, giving the reason for such finding; unless an affidavit be filed with the coroner indicating blame in connection with the death of the deceased. A written report

of said investigation shall be filed by the coroner with the medical examiner and the district attorney of the superior court.

(2)   To empanel a jury of six persons, under oath, to make further inquiry as to the circumstances of death and to call witnesses as necessary to determine the circumstances. The coroner shall order that the names of at least 15 persons be drawn from the jury box in accordance with the procedure in G.S. 9-5. The coroner shall examine the jurors appearing in obedience to the summons, and may excuse jurors for whom service would be an extreme hardship, who would be unable to remain impartial in determining the issues, or are otherwise disqualified to serve as jurors. If the remaining jurors are less than six in number, the coroner shall cause sufficient additional names to be drawn from the jury box and have them summoned, so as to obtain the immediate attendance of at least six qualified jurors. The first six qualified jurors constitute the inquest jury.

(3)   If it appears that the deceased was slain, or came to his death in such manner as to indicate any person or persons guilty of the crime in connection with the said death, then the said inquiry shall ascertain who was guilty, either as principal or accessory, or otherwise, if known; and the cause and manner of his death.

(4)   Whenever in such investigations, whether preliminary or before his jury, it shall appear to the coroner or to the jury that any person or persons are culpable in the matter of such death, he shall forthwith issue his warrant for such persons and cause the same to be brought before him and the inquiry shall proceed as in the case of preliminary hearings in the district court, and in case it appears to the said coroner and the jury that such persons are probably guilty of any crime in connection with the death of the deceased, then the said coroner shall commit such persons to jail, if it appears that such persons are probably guilty of a capital crime, and in case it appears that such persons are not probably guilty of a capital crime, but are probably guilty of a lesser crime, then such coroner is to have the power and authority to fix bail for such person or persons. All such persons as are found probably guilty in such hearing shall be delivered to the keeper of the common jail for such county by the sheriff or such other officer as may perform his duties at such hearings and committed to jail unless such persons have been allowed and given the bail fixed by such coroner.

(5)   As many persons as are found to be material witnesses in the matters involved in such inquiry and hearings, and are not culpable themselves shall be

bound in recognizance with sufficient surety to appear at the next superior court to give evidence, and such as may default in giving such recognizance may be by such coroner committed to jail as is provided for State witnesses in other cases.

(6) Immediately upon information of the death of a person within his county, under such circumstances as call for an investigation as provided in G.S. 130A-383, the coroner shall notify the district attorney of the superior court and the medical examiner.

(7) If an inquest or preliminary hearing be ordered, to arrange for the examination of any and all witnesses including those who may be offered by the county medical examiner.

(8) To permit counsel for the family of the deceased, the solicitor of his district, or anyone designated by him, and counsel for any accused person to be present and participate in such hearing and examine and cross-examine witnesses and, whenever a warrant shall have been issued for any accused person, such accused person shall be entitled to counsel and to a full and complete hearing.

(9) To hold his inquiry where the body of the deceased shall be or at any other place in the county, and the body of the deceased need not be present at such hearing. The hearing may be adjourned to other times and places.

(10) To reduce to writing all of the testimony of all witnesses, and to have each witness to sign his testimony in the presence of the coroner, who shall attest the same, and, upon direction of the district attorney of the district, all of the testimony heard by the coroner and his jury shall be taken stenographically, and expense of such taking, when approved by the coroner and the district attorney of the district, shall be paid by the county. When the testimony is taken by a stenographer, the witness shall be caused to sign the same after it has been written out, and the coroner shall attest such signature. The attestation of all the signatures of witnesses who shall testify before the coroner shall include attaching his seal, and such statements, when so signed and attested, shall be received as competent evidence in all courts either for the purpose of contradiction or corroboration of witnesses who make the same, under the same rules as other evidence to contradict or corroborate may be now admitted. The coroner shall file a copy of all written testimony given at the hearing with the county medical examiner and with the district attorney of the superior court. (Code, s. 657; 1899, c. 478; 1905, c. 628; Rev., s. 1051; 1909, c. 707, s. 1;

C.S., s. 1020; Ex. Sess. 1924, c. 65; 1955, c. 972, s. 2; 1957, c. 503, ss. 1, 2; 1967, c. 1154, s. 6; 1973, c. 47, s. 2; c. 108, s. 92; c. 558; 2007-484, s. 11(d).)

§ 152-8. Acts as sheriff in certain cases; special coroner.

If at any time there is no person properly qualified to act as sheriff in any county, the coroner of such county is hereby required to execute all process and in all other things to act as sheriff, until some person is appointed sheriff in said county; and he shall be under the same rules and regulations, and subject to the same forfeitures, fines, and penalties as sheriffs are by law for neglect or disobedience of the same duties. If at any time the sheriff of any county is interested in or a party to any proceeding in any court, and there is no coroner in such county, or if the coroner is interested in any such proceeding, then the clerk of the court from which such process issues shall appoint some suitable person to act as special coroner to execute such process, and such special coroner shall be under the same rules, regulations, and penalties as hereinabove provided for. (Code, s. 658; 1891, c. 173; Rev., s. 1052; C.S., s. 1021; Ex. Sess. 1924, c. 65.)

§ 152-9. Compensation of jurors at inquest.

All persons who may be summoned to act as jurors in any inquest held by a coroner over dead bodies, and who, in obedience thereto, appear and act as such jurors, shall be entitled to the same compensation in per diem and mileage as is allowed by law to jurors acting in the superior courts. The coroners of the respective counties are authorized and empowered to take proof of the number of days of service of each juror so acting, and also of the number of miles traveled by such juror in going to and returning from such place of inquest, and shall file with the board of commissioners of the county a correct account of the same, which shall be, by such commissioners, audited and paid in the manner provided for the pay of jurors acting in the superior courts. (Code, ss. 659, 660; Rev., s. 1053; C.S., s. 1022; Ex. Sess. 1924, c. 65.)

§ 152-10. Hearing by coroner in lieu of other preliminary hearing; habeas corpus.

All hearings by a coroner and his jury, as provided herein, when the accused has been arrested and has participated in such hearing, shall be in lieu of any other preliminary hearing, and such cases shall be immediately sent to the clerk of the superior court of such county and docketed by him in the same manner as warrants from magistrates. Any accused person who shall be so committed by a coroner shall have the right, upon habeas corpus, to have a judge of the superior or district court review the action of the coroner in fixing bail or declining the same. (Ex. Sess. 1924, c. 65; 1973, c. 108, s. 93.)

§ 152-11. Service of process issued by coroner.

All process, both subpoenas and warrants for the arrest of any person or persons, and orders for the summoning of a jury, in case it may appear necessary for such coroner to issue such order, shall be served by the sheriff or other lawful officer of the county in which such dead body is found, and in case it is necessary to subpoena witnesses or to arrest persons in a county other than such county in which the body of the deceased is found, then such coroner may issue his process to any other county in the State, with his official seal attached, and such process shall be served by the sheriff or other lawful officer of the county to which it is directed, but such process shall not be served outside of the county in which such dead body is found unless attested by the official seal of such coroner. (Ex. Sess. 1924, c. 65.)

Chapter 152A.

County Medical Examiner.

§§ 152A-1 through 152A-12. Repealed by Session Laws 1967, c. 1154, s. 8.

Chapter 153.

Counties and County Commissioners.

§§ 153-1 through 153-382. Repealed by Session Laws 1973, c. 822.

Chapter 153A.

Counties.

Article 1.

Definitions and Statutory Construction.

§ 153A-1. Definitions.

Unless otherwise specifically provided, or unless otherwise clearly required by the context, the words and phrases defined in this section have the meaning indicated when used in this Chapter.

(1) "City" means a city as defined by G.S. 160A-1(2), except that it does not include a city that, without regard to its date of incorporation, would be disqualified from receiving gasoline tax allocations by G.S. 136-41.2(a).

(2) "Clerk" means the clerk to the board of commissioners.

(3) "County" means any one of the counties listed in G.S. 153A-10.

(4) "General law" means an act of the General Assembly that applies to all units of local government, to all counties, to all counties within a class defined by population or other criteria, to all cities, or to all cities within a class defined by population or other criteria, including a law that meets the foregoing standards but contains a clause or section exempting from its effect one or more counties, cities, or counties and cities.

(5) "Local act" means an act of the General Assembly that applies to one or more specific counties, cities, or counties and cities by name. "Local act" is interchangeable with the terms "special act," "special law," "public-local act," and "private act," is used throughout this Chapter in preference to those terms, and means a local act as defined in this subdivision without regard to the terminology employed in local acts or other portions of the General Statutes.

(6) "Publish," "publication," and other forms of the verb "to publish" mean insertion in a newspaper qualified under G.S. 1-597 to publish legal advertisements in the county. (1973, c. 822, s. 1.)

§ 153A-2. Effect on prior laws and actions taken pursuant to prior laws.

The provisions of this Chapter, insofar as they are the same in substance as laws in effect as of December 31, 1973, are intended to continue those laws in effect and not to be new enactments. The enactment of this Chapter does not require the readoption of any county or city ordinance adopted pursuant to laws that were in effect as of December 31, 1973, and that are restated or revised in this Chapter. The provisions of this Chapter do not affect any act heretofore done, any liability incurred, any right accrued or vested, or any suit or prosecution begun or cause of action accrued as of January 1, 1974. (1973, c. 822, s. 1.)

§ 153A-3. Effect of Chapter on local acts.

(a) Except as provided in this section, nothing in this Chapter repeals or amends a local act in effect as of January 1, 1974, or any portion of such an act, unless this Chapter or a subsequent enactment of the General Assembly clearly shows a legislative intent to repeal or supersede that local act.

(b) If this Chapter and a local act each provide a procedure that contains every action necessary for the performance or execution of a power, right, duty, function, privilege, or immunity, the two procedures may be used in the alternative, and a county may follow either one.

(c) If this Chapter and a local act each provide a procedure for the performance or execution of a power, right, duty, function, privilege, or immunity, but the local act procedure does not contain every action necessary for the performance or execution, the two procedures may be used in the alternative, and a county may follow either one; but the local act procedure shall be supplemented as necessary by this Chapter's procedure. If a local act procedure is being supplemented in such a manner, and there is a conflict or inconsistency between the local act procedure and this Chapter's procedure, the local act procedure shall be followed.

(d) If a power, right, duty, function, privilege, or immunity is conferred on counties by this Chapter, and a local act enacted earlier than this Chapter omits or expressly denies or limits the same power, right, duty, function, privilege, or immunity, this Chapter supersedes the local act. (1973, c. 822, s. 1.)

§ 153A-4. Broad construction.

It is the policy of the General Assembly that the counties of this State should have adequate authority to exercise the powers, rights, duties, functions, privileges, and immunities conferred upon them by law. To this end, the provisions of this Chapter and of local acts shall be broadly construed and grants of power shall be construed to include any powers that are reasonably expedient to the exercise of the power. (1973, c. 822, s. 1.)

§ 153A-5. Statutory references deemed amended to conform to Chapter.

If a reference is made in another portion of the General Statutes, in a local act, or in a city or county ordinance, resolution, or order to a portion of Chapter 153, and the reference is to Chapter 153 as it existed immediately before February 1, 1974, the reference is deemed amended to refer to that portion of this Chapter that most nearly corresponds to the repealed or superseded portion of Chapter 153. (1973, c. 822, s. 1.)

§§ 153A-6 through 153A-9. Reserved for future codification purposes.

Article 2.

Corporate Powers.

§ 153A-10. State has 100 counties.

North Carolina has 100 counties. They are: Alamance, Alexander, Alleghany, Anson, Ashe, Avery, Beaufort, Bertie, Bladen, Brunswick, Buncombe, Burke, Cabarrus, Caldwell, Camden, Carteret, Caswell, Catawba, Chatham, Cherokee, Chowan, Clay, Cleveland, Columbus, Craven, Cumberland, Currituck, Dare, Davidson, Davie, Duplin, Durham, Edgecombe, Forsyth, Franklin, Gaston, Gates, Graham, Granville, Greene, Guilford, Halifax, Harnett, Haywood, Henderson, Hertford, Hoke, Hyde, Iredell, Jackson, Johnston, Jones, Lee, Lenoir, Lincoln, Macon, Madison, Martin, McDowell, Mecklenburg, Mitchell, Montgomery, Moore, Nash, New Hanover, Northampton, Onslow, Orange, Pamlico, Pasquotank, Pender, Perquimans, Person, Pitt, Polk, Randolph, Richmond, Robeson, Rockingham, Rowan, Rutherford, Sampson, Scotland,

Stanly, Stokes, Surry, Swain, Transylvania, Tyrrell, Union, Vance, Wake, Warren, Washington, Watauga, Wayne, Wilkes, Wilson, Yadkin, and Yancey. (1973, c. 822, s. 1.)

§ 153A-11. Corporate powers.

The inhabitants of each county are a body politic and corporate under the name specified in the act creating the county. Under that name they are vested with all the property and rights of property belonging to the corporation; have perpetual succession; may sue and be sued; may contract and be contracted with; may acquire and hold any property and rights of property, real and personal, that may be devised, sold, or in any manner conveyed, dedicated to, or otherwise acquired by the corporation, and from time to time may hold, invest, sell, or dispose of the property and rights of property; may have a common seal and alter and renew it at will; and have and may exercise in conformity with the laws of this State county powers, rights, duties, functions, privileges, and immunities of every name and nature. (1868, c. 20, ss. 1, 2, 3, 8; 1876-7, c. 141, s. 1; Code, ss. 702, 703, 704, 707; Rev., ss. 1309, 1310, 1318; C.S., ss. 1290, 1291, 1297; 1973, c. 822, s. 1; 2011-284, s. 105.)

§ 153A-12. Exercise of corporate power.

Except as otherwise directed by law, each power, right, duty, function, privilege and immunity of the corporation shall be exercised by the board of commissioners. A power, right, duty, function, privilege, or immunity shall be carried into execution as provided by the laws of the State; a power, right, duty, function, privilege, or immunity that is conferred or imposed by law without direction or restriction as to how it is to be exercised or performed shall be carried into execution as provided by ordinance or resolution of the board of commissioners. (1868, c. 20, ss. 1, 2; 1876-7, c. 141, s. 1; Code, ss. 702, 703; Rev., s. 1309; C.S., s. 1290; 1973, c. 882, s. 1.)

§ 153A-13. Continuing contracts.

A county may enter into continuing contracts, some portion or all of which are to be performed in ensuing fiscal years. In order to enter into such a contract, the county must have sufficient funds appropriated to meet any amount to be paid under the contract in the fiscal year in which it is made. In each year, the board of commissioners shall appropriate sufficient funds to meet the amounts to be paid during the fiscal year under continuing contracts previously entered into. (1959, c. 250; 1973, c. 822, s. 1.)

§ 153A-14. Grants and loans from other governments.

A county may contract for and accept grants and loans as permitted by G.S. 160A-17.1. (1973, c. 822, s. 1; 2007-91, s. 2.)

§ 153A-15. Consent of board of commissioners necessary in certain counties before land may be condemned or acquired by a unit of local government outside the county.

(a) Notwithstanding the provisions of Chapter 40A of the General Statutes or any other general law or local act conferring the power of eminent domain, before final judgment may be entered in any action of condemnation initiated by a county, city or town, special district, or other unit of local government which is located wholly or primarily outside another county, whereby the condemnor seeks to acquire property located in the other county, the condemnor shall furnish proof that the county board of commissioners of the county where the land is located has consented to the taking.

(b) Notwithstanding the provisions of G.S. 153A-158, 160A-240.1, 130A-55, or any other general law or local act conferring the power to acquire real property, before any county, city or town, special district, or other unit of local government which is located wholly or primarily outside another county acquires any real property located in the other county by exchange, purchase or lease, it must have the approval of the county board of commissioners of the county where the land is located.

(c) This section applies to Alamance, Alleghany, Anson, Ashe, Bertie, Bladen, Brunswick, Burke, Buncombe, Cabarrus, Caldwell, Camden, Carteret, Caswell, Catawba, Chatham, Cherokee, Clay, Cleveland, Columbus, Craven,

Cumberland, Currituck, Davidson, Davie, Duplin, Durham, Edgecombe, Forsyth, Franklin, Gaston, Graham, Granville, Greene, Guilford, Halifax, Harnett, Haywood, Henderson, Hoke, Iredell, Jackson, Johnston, Jones, Lee, Lenoir, Lincoln, Macon, Madison, Martin, McDowell, Mecklenburg, Montgomery, Nash, New Hanover, Northampton, Onslow, Orange, Pamlico, Pasquotank, Pender, Perquimans, Person, Pitt, Polk, Richmond, Robeson, Rockingham, Rowan, Rutherford, Sampson, Scotland, Stanly, Stokes, Surry, Swain, Transylvania, Union, Vance, Wake, Warren, Watauga, Wayne, Wilkes, and Yancey Counties only.

(d) This section does not apply as to any condemnation or acquisition of real property or an interest in real property by a city where the property to be condemned or acquired is within the corporate limits of that city. (1981, c. 134, ss. 1, 2; c. 270, ss. 1, 2; c. 283, ss. 1-3; c. 459, s. 1; c. 941, s. 1; 1981 (Reg. Sess., 1982), c. 1150, s. 1; 1989 (Reg. Sess., 1990), c. 973, s. 1; c. 1061, s. 1; 1991, c. 615, s. 3; 1991 (Reg. Sess., 1992), c. 790, s. 1; 1993 (Reg. Sess., 1994), c. 624, s. 1; c. 628, s. 1; 1995 (Reg. Sess., 1996), c. 681, s. 1; 1997-164, s. 1; 1997-263, s. 1; 1998-110, s. 1; 1998-217, s. 47; 1999-6, s. 1; 2005-33, s. 1; 2013-174, s. 1.)

§ 153A-15.1. Agreement to make payment in lieu of future ad valorem taxes required before wetlands acquisition by a unit of local government.

(a) Condemnation. - Notwithstanding the provisions of G.S. 153A-15, Chapter 40A of the General Statutes, or any other general law or local act conferring the power of eminent domain, before a final judgment may be entered or a final condemnation resolution adopted in an action of condemnation initiated by a unit of local government whose property is exempt from tax under Section 2(3) of Article V of the North Carolina Constitution, whereby the condemnor seeks to acquire land for the purpose of wetlands mitigation, the condemnor shall agree in writing to pay to the county where the land is located a sum equal to the estimated amount of ad valorem taxes that would have accrued to the county for the next 20 years had the land not been acquired by the condemnor.

(b) Purchase. - Notwithstanding the provisions of G.S. 130A-55, 153A-15, 153A-158, 160A-240.1, or any other general law or local act conferring the power to acquire real property, before any unit of local government whose property is exempt from tax under Section 2(3) of Article V of the North Carolina

Constitution purchases any land for the purpose of wetlands mitigation, the unit shall agree in writing to pay to the county where the land is located a sum equal to the estimated amount of ad valorem taxes that would have accrued to the county for the next 20 years had the land not been acquired by the acquiring unit.

(c) Definition. - For purposes of this section, the "estimated amount of ad valorem taxes that would have accrued for the next 20 years" means the total assessed value of the acquired land excluded from the county's tax base multiplied by the tax rate set by the county board of commissioners in its most recent budget ordinance adopted under Chapter 159 of the General Statutes, and then multiplied by 20.

(d) Exception. - This section does not apply to any condemnation or acquisition of land by a city or special district if the land to be condemned or acquired is within the corporate limits of that city or special district or within the county where the city or special district is located.

(e) Application. - This section applies only to land acquired in counties designated as a development tier one area under G.S. 143B-437.08. (2004-188, s. 1; 2006-252, s. 2.17.)

§ 153A-16. Reserved for future codification purposes.

Article 3.

Boundaries.

§ 153A-17. Existing boundaries.

The boundaries of each county shall remain as presently established, until changed in accordance with law. (1973, c. 822, s. 1.)

§ 153A-18. Uncertain or disputed boundary.

(a) If two or more counties are uncertain as to the exact location of the boundary between them, they may cause the boundary to be surveyed, marked, and mapped. The counties may appoint special commissioners to supervise the surveying, marking, and mapping. A commissioner so appointed or a person surveying or marking the boundary may enter upon private property to view and survey the boundary or to erect boundary markers. Upon ratification of the survey by the board of commissioners of each county, a map showing the surveyed boundary shall be recorded in the office of the register of deeds of each county in the manner provided by law for the recordation of maps or plats and in the Secretary of State's office. The map shall contain a reference to the date of each resolution of ratification and to the page in the minutes of each board of commissioners where the resolution may be found. Upon recordation, the map is conclusive as to the location of the boundary.

(b) If two or more counties dispute the exact location of the boundary between them, and the dispute cannot be resolved pursuant to subsection (a) of this section, any of the counties may apply to a superior court judge who has jurisdiction pursuant to G.S. 7A-47.1 or 7A-48 in any of the districts or sets of districts as defined in G.S. 7A-41.1 in which any of the counties is located for appointment of a boundary commission. The application shall identify the disputed boundary and ask that a boundary commission be appointed. Upon receiving the application, the court shall set a date for a hearing on whether to appoint the commission. The court shall cause notice of the hearing to be served on the other county or counties. If, after the hearing, the court finds that the location of the boundary is disputed, it shall appoint a boundary commission.

The commission shall consist of one resident of each disputing county and a resident of some other county. The court may appoint one or more surveyors to assist the commission. The commission shall locate, survey, and map and may mark the disputed boundary. To do so it may take evidence and hear testimony, and any commissioner and any person surveying or marking the boundary may enter upon private property to view and survey the boundary or to erect boundary markers. Within 45 days after the day it is appointed, unless this time is extended by the court, the commission shall make its report (which shall include a map of the surveyed boundary) to the court. To be sufficient, the report must be concurred in by a majority of the commissioners. If the court is satisfied that the commissioners have made no error of law, it shall ratify the report, after which the map shall be recorded in the office of the register of deeds of each county in the manner provided by law for the recordation of maps or plats and in the Secretary of State's office. Upon recordation, the map is conclusive as to the location of the boundary.

The disputing counties shall divide equally the costs of locating, surveying, marking, and mapping the boundary, unless the court finds that an equal division of the costs would be unjust. In that case the court may determine the division of costs.

(c) Two or more counties may establish the boundary between them pursuant to subsection (a), above, by the use of base maps prepared from orthophotography, which base maps show the monuments of the United States Geological Survey and North Carolina State Plane Coordinate System established pursuant to Chapter 102 of the General Statutes. Upon ratification of the location of the boundary determined from orthophotography by the board of commissioners of each county, the map showing the boundary and the monuments of the United States Geological Survey and North Carolina State Plane Coordinate System shall be recorded in the Office of the Register of Deeds of each county and in the Secretary of State's office. The map shall contain a reference to the date of each resolution of ratification and to the page in the minutes of each board of commissioners where the resolution may be found. Upon recordation, the map is conclusive as to the location of the boundary. (1836, c. 3; R.C., c. 27; Code, s. 721; Rev., s. 1322; C.S., s. 1299; 1925, c. 251; 1973, c. 822, s. 1; 1987 (Reg. Sess., 1988), c. 1037, s. 121; 1997-299, s. 1.)

§ 153A-19. Establishing and naming townships.

(a) A county may by resolution establish and abolish townships, change their boundaries, and prescribe their names, except that no such resolution may become effective during the period beginning January 1, 1998, and ending January 2, 2000, and any resolution providing that the boundaries of a township shall change automatically with changes in the boundaries of a city shall not be effective during that period. The current boundaries of each township within a county shall at all times be drawn on a map, or set out in a written description, or shown by a combination of these techniques. This current delineation shall be available for public inspection in the office of the clerk.

(b) Any provision of a city charter or other local act which provides that the boundaries of a township shall change automatically upon a change in a city boundary shall not be effective during the period beginning January 1, 1998, and ending January 2, 2000.

(c)   The county manager or, where there is no county manager, the chairman of the board of commissioners, shall report township boundaries and changes in those boundaries to the United States Bureau of the Census in the Boundary and Annexations Survey. In responding to the surveys, each county manager or, if there is no manager, chairman of the board of commissioners shall consult with the county board of elections and other appropriate local agencies as to the location of township boundaries, so that the Census Bureau's mapping of township boundaries does not disagree with any county voting precinct boundaries that may be based on township boundaries. (1868, c. 20, s. 8; Code, s. 707; Rev., s. 1318; C.S., s. 1297; 1973, c. 822, s. 1; 1987, c. 715, s. 1; c. 879, s. 2; 1993, c. 352, s. 1; 1995, c. 423, s. 4.)

§ 153A-20. Map of electoral districts.

If a county is divided into electoral districts for the purpose of nominating or electing persons to the board of commissioners, the current boundaries of the electoral districts shall at all times be drawn on a map, or set out in a written description, or shown by a combination of these techniques. This current delineation shall be available for public inspection in the office of the clerk. (1973, c. 822, s. 1.)

§ 153A-21. Repealed by Session Laws 1973, c. 884.

§ 153A-22. Redefining electoral district boundaries.

(a)   If a county is divided into electoral districts for the purpose of nominating or electing persons to the board of commissioners, the board of commissioners may find as a fact whether there is substantial inequality of population among the districts.

(b)   If the board finds that there is substantial inequality of population among the districts, it may by resolution redefine the electoral districts.

(c)   Redefined electoral districts shall be so drawn that the quotients obtained by dividing the population of each district by the number of commissioners apportioned to the district are as nearly equal as practicable, and each district shall be composed of territory within a continuous boundary.

(d) No change in the boundaries of an electoral district may affect the unexpired term of office of a commissioner residing in the district and serving on the board on the effective date of the resolution. If the terms of office of members of the board do not all expire at the same time, the resolution shall state which seats are to be filled at the initial election held under the resolution.

(e) A resolution adopted pursuant to this section shall be the basis of electing persons to the board of commissioners at the first general election for members of the board of commissioners occurring after the resolution's effective date, and thereafter. A resolution becomes effective upon its adoption, unless it is adopted during the period beginning 150 days before the day of a primary and ending on the day of the next succeeding general election for membership on the board of commissioners, in which case it becomes effective on the first day after the end of the period.

(f) Not later than 10 days after the day on which a resolution becomes effective, the clerk shall file in the Secretary of State's office, in the office of the register of deeds of the county, and with the chairman of the county board of elections, a certified copy of the resolution.

(g) This section shall not apply to counties where under G.S. 153A-58(3)d. or under public or local act, districts are for residence purposes only, and the qualified voters of the entire county nominate all candidates for and elect all members of the board. (1981, c. 795.)

§§ 153A-23 through 153A-24. Reserved for future codification purposes.

Article 4.

Form of Government.

Part 1. General Provisions.

§ 153A-25. Qualifications for appointive office.

The board of commissioners may fix qualifications for any appointive office, including a requirement that a person serving in such an office reside within the county. The board may not waive qualifications fixed by law for an appointive office but may fix additional qualifications for that office. (1973, c. 822, s. 1.)

§ 153A-26. Oath of office.

Each person elected by the people or appointed to a county office shall, before entering upon the duties of the office, take and subscribe the oath of office prescribed in Article VI, Sec. 7 of the Constitution. The oath of office shall be administered by some person authorized by law to administer oaths and shall be filed with the clerk.

On the first Monday in December following each general election at which county officers are elected, the persons who have been elected to county office in that election shall assemble at the regular meeting place of the board of commissioners. At that time each such officer shall take and subscribe the oath of office. An officer not present at this time may take and subscribe the oath at a later time. (1868, c. 20, s. 8; 1874-5, c. 237, s. 3; Code, ss. 707, 708; 1895, c. 135, ss. 3, 4; Rev., ss. 1316, 1318; C.S., ss. 1295, 1297; 1965, c. 26; 1973, c. 822, s. 1.)

§ 153A-27. Vacancies on the board of commissioners.

If a vacancy occurs on the board of commissioners, the remaining members of the board shall appoint a qualified person to fill the vacancy. If the number of vacancies on the board is such that a quorum of the board cannot be obtained, the chairman of the board shall appoint enough members to make up a quorum, and the board shall then proceed to fill the remaining vacancies. If the number of vacancies on the board is such that a quorum of the board cannot be obtained and the office of chairman is vacant, the clerk of superior court of the county shall fill the vacancies upon the request of any remaining member of the board or upon the petition of any five registered voters of the county. If for any other reason the remaining members of the board do not fill a vacancy within 60 days after the day the vacancy occurs, the clerk shall immediately report the vacancy to the clerk of superior court of the county. The clerk of superior court shall, within 10 days after the day the vacancy is reported to him, fill the vacancy.

If the member being replaced was serving a two-year term, or if the member was serving a four-year term and the vacancy occurs later than 60 days before the general election held after the first two years of the term, the appointment to fill the vacancy is for the remainder of the unexpired term. Otherwise, the term of the person appointed to fill the vacancy extends to the first Monday in

December next following the first general election held more than 60 days after the day the vacancy occurs; at that general election, a person shall be elected to the seat vacated, either to the remainder of the unexpired term or, if the term has expired, to a full term.

To be eligible for appointment to fill a vacancy, a person must (i) be a member of the same political party as the member being replaced, if that member was elected as the nominee of a political party, and (ii) be a resident of the same district as the member being replaced, if the county is divided into electoral districts. The board of commissioners or the clerk of superior court, as the case may be, shall consult the county executive committee of the appropriate political party before filling a vacancy, but neither the board nor the clerk of the superior court is bound by the committee's recommendation. (Code, s. 719; 1895, c. 135, s. 7; Rev., s. 1314; 1909, c. 490, s. 1; C.S., s. 1294; 1959, c. 1325; 1965, cc. 239, 382; 1967, cc. 7, 424, 439, 1022; 1969, cc. 82, 222; 1971, c. 743, s. 1; 1973, c. 822, s. 1; 1985, c. 563, ss. 7.3, 7.4.)

§ 153A-27.1. Vacancies on board of commissioners in certain counties.

(a) If a vacancy occurs on the board of commissioners, the remaining members of the board shall appoint a qualified person to fill the vacancy. If the number of vacancies on the board is such that a quorum of the board cannot be obtained, the chairman of the board shall appoint enough members to make up a quorum, and the board shall then proceed to fill the remaining vacancies. If the number of vacancies on the board is such that a quorum of the board cannot be obtained and the office of chairman is vacant, the clerk of superior court of the county shall fill the vacancies upon the request of any remaining member of the board or upon the petition of any registered voters of the county.

(b) If the member being replaced was serving a two-year term, or if the member was serving a four-year term and the vacancy occurs later than 60 days before the general election held after the first two years of the term, the appointment to fill the vacancy is for the remainder of the unexpired term. Otherwise, the term of the person appointed to fill the vacancy extends to the first Monday in December next following the first general election held more than 60 days after the day the vacancy occurs; at that general election, a person shall be elected to the seat vacated for the remainder of the unexpired term.

(c) To be eligible for appointment to fill a vacancy, a person must (i) be a member of the same political party as the member being replaced, if that member was elected as the nominee of a political party, and (ii) be a resident of the same district as the member being replaced, if the county is divided into electoral districts.

(d) If the member who vacated the seat was elected as a nominee of a political party, the board of commissioners, the chairman of the board, or the clerk of superior court, as the case may be, shall consult the county executive committee of the appropriate political party before filling the vacancy, and shall appoint the person recommended by the county executive committee of the political party of which the commissioner being replaced was a member, if the party makes a recommendation within 30 days of the occurrence of the vacancy.

(e) Whenever because of G.S. 153A-58(3)b. or because of any local act, only the qualified voters of an area which is less than the entire county were eligible to vote in the general election for the member whose seat is vacant, the appointing authority must accept the recommendation only if the county executive committee restricted voting to committee members who represent precincts all or part of which were within the territorial area of the district of the county commissioner.

(f) The provisions of any local act which provides that a county executive committee of a political party shall fill any vacancy on a board of county commissioners are repealed.

(g) Counties subject to this section are not subject to G.S. 153A-27.

(h) This section shall apply only in the following counties: Alamance, Alexander, Alleghany, Avery, Beaufort, Brunswick, Buncombe, Burke, Cabarrus, Caldwell, Carteret, Cherokee, Clay, Cleveland, Cumberland, Dare, Davidson, Davie, Forsyth, Graham, Guilford, Haywood, Henderson, Hyde, Jackson, Lee, Lincoln, Macon, Madison, McDowell, Mecklenburg, Moore, Pender, Polk, Randolph, Rockingham, Rutherford, Sampson, Stanly, Stokes, Transylvania, and Yancey. (1981, c. 763, ss. 6, 14; c. 830; 1983, c. 418; 1985, c. 563, s. 7.2; 1987, c. 196, s. 1; 1989, c. 296; c. 497, s. 2; 1991, c. 395, s. 1; c. 558, s. 1; 1995 (Reg. Sess., 1996), c. 683, s. 1; 1997-88, s. 1; 2009-32, s. 1; 2011-126, s. 2.)

§ 153A-28. Compensation of board of commissioners.

The board of commissioners may fix the compensation and allowances of the chairman and other members of the board by inclusion of the compensation and allowances in and adoption of the budget ordinance. In addition, if the chairman or any other member of the board becomes a full-time county official, pursuant to G.S. 153A-81 or 153A-84, his compensation and allowances may be adjusted at any time during his service as a full-time official, for the duration of that service. (Code, s. 709; Rev., s. 2785; 1907, c. 500; C.S., s. 3918; 1969, c. 180, s. 1; 1971, c. 1125, s. 1; 1973, c. 822, s. 1.)

§ 153A-29. Repealed by Session Laws 1975, c. 514, s. 17.

§§ 153A-30 through 153A-33. Reserved for future codification purposes.

Part 2. Structure of the Board of Commissioners.

§ 153A-34. Structure of boards of commissioners.

Each county is governed by a board of commissioners. The structure and manner of election of the board of commissioners in each county shall remain as it is on February 1, 1974, until changed in accordance with law. (Rev., s. 1311; C.S., s. 1292; 1973, c. 822, s. 1.)

§§ 153A-35 through 153A-38. Reserved for future codification purposes.

Part 3. Organization and Procedures of the Board of Commissioners.

§ 153A-39. Selection of chairman and vice-chairman; powers and duties.

On:

(1)   The first Monday in December of each even-numbered year; and

(2)   Its first regular meeting in December of each odd-numbered year,

the board of commissioners shall choose one of its members as chairman for the ensuing year, unless the chairman is elected as such by the people or otherwise designated by law. The board shall also at that time choose a vice-chairman to act in the absence or disability of the chairman. If the chairman and the vice-chairman are both absent from a meeting of the board, the members present may choose a temporary chairman.

The chairman is the presiding officer of the board of commissioners. Unless excused by rule of the board, the presiding officer has the duty to vote on any question before the board, but he has no right to break a tie vote in which he participated. (Code, s. 706; Rev., s. 1317; C.S., s. 1296; 1945, c. 132; 1951, c. 904, s. 1; 1961, c. 154; 1967, c. 617, s. 1; 1969, c. 349, s. 1; c. 1036; 1973, c. 822, s. 1; 1993, c. 95.)

§ 153A-40. Regular and special meetings.

(a) The board of commissioners shall hold a regular meeting at least once a month, and may hold more frequent regular meetings. The board may by resolution fix the time and place of its regular meetings. If such a resolution is adopted, at least 10 days before the first meeting to which the resolution is to apply, the board shall cause a copy of it to be posted on the courthouse bulletin board and a summary of it to be published. If no such resolution is adopted, the board shall meet at the courthouse on the first Monday of each month, or on the next succeeding business day if the first Monday is a holiday.

If use of the courthouse or other designated regular meeting place is made temporarily impossible, inconvenient, or unwise, the board may change the time or place or both of a regular meeting or of all regular meetings within a specified period of time. The board shall cause notice of the temporary change to be posted at or near the regular meeting place and shall take any other action it considers helpful in informing the public of the temporary change.

The board may adjourn a regular meeting from day to day or to a day certain until the business before the board is completed.

(b) The chairman or a majority of the members of the board may at any time call a special meeting of the board of commissioners by signing a written notice stating the time and place of the meeting and the subjects to be considered. The person or persons calling the meeting shall cause the notice to be delivered to the chairman and each other member of the board or left at the usual dwelling place of each at least 48 hours before the meeting and shall cause a copy of the notice to be posted on the courthouse bulletin board at least 48 hours before the meeting. Only those items of business specified in the notice may be transacted at a special meeting, unless all members are present or those not present have signed a written waiver.

If a special meeting is called to deal with an emergency, the notice requirements of this subsection do not apply. However, the person or persons calling such a special meeting shall take reasonable action to inform the other members and the public of the meeting. Only business connected with the emergency may be discussed at a meeting called pursuant to this paragraph.

In addition to the procedures set out in this subsection, a person or persons calling a special or emergency meeting of the board of commissioners shall comply with the notice requirements of Article 33B of General Statutes Chapter 143.

(c)   The board of commissioners shall hold all its meetings within the county except:

(1)   In connection with a joint meeting of two or more public bodies; provided, however, that such a meeting shall be held within the boundaries of the political subdivision represented by the members of one of the public bodies participating;

(2)   In connection with a retreat, forum, or similar gathering held solely for the purpose of providing members of the board with general information relating to the performance of their public duties; provided, however, that members of the board of commissioners shall not vote upon or otherwise transact public business while in attendance at such a gathering;

(3)   In connection with a meeting between the board of commissioners and its local legislative delegation during a session of the General Assembly; provided, however, that at any such meeting the members of the board of commissioners may not vote upon or otherwise transact public business except with regard to matters directly relating to legislation proposed to or pending before the General Assembly;

(4)   While in attendance at a convention, association meeting or similar gathering; provided, however, that any such meeting may be held solely to discuss or deliberate the board's position concerning convention resolutions,

elections of association officers and similar issues that are not legally binding upon the board of commissioners or its constituents.

All meetings held outside the county shall be deemed "official meetings" within the meaning of G.S. 143-318.10(d). (Code, s. 706; Rev., s. 1317; C.S., s. 1296; 1945, c. 132; 1951, c. 904, s. 1; 1961, c. 154; 1967, c. 617, s. 1; 1969, c. 349, s. 1; c. 1036; 1973, c. 822, s. 1; 1977, 2nd Sess., c. 1191, s. 6; 1985, c. 745.)

§ 153A-41. Procedures.

The board of commissioners may adopt its own rules of procedure, in keeping with the size and nature of the board and in the spirit of generally accepted principles of parliamentary procedure. (Code, s. 706; Rev., s. 1317; C.S., s. 1296; 1945, c. 132; 1951, c. 904, s. 1; 1961, c. 154; 1967, c. 617, s. 1; 1969, c. 349, s. 1; c. 1036; 1973, c. 822, s. 1.)

§ 153A-42. Minutes to be kept; ayes and noes.

The clerk shall keep full and accurate minutes of the proceedings of the board of commissioners, which shall be available for public inspection. The clerk shall record the results of each vote in the minutes; and upon the request of any member of the board, the ayes and noes upon any question shall be taken and recorded. (Code, s. 712; 1905, c. 530; Rev., s. 1325; C.S., s. 1310; 1953, c. 973, s. 3; 1973, c. 822, s. 1.)

§ 153A-43. Quorum.

A majority of the membership of the board of commissioners constitutes a quorum. The number required for a quorum is not affected by vacancies. If a member has withdrawn from a meeting without being excused by majority vote of the remaining members present, he shall be counted as present for the purposes of determining whether a quorum is present. The board may compel the attendance of an absent member by ordering the sheriff to take the member into custody. (Code, s. 706; Rev., s. 1317; C.S., s. 1296; 1945, c. 132; 1951, c.

904, s. 1; 1961, c. 154; 1967, c. 617, s. 1; 1969, c. 349, s. 1; c. 1036; 1973, c. 822, s. 1.)

§ 153A-44. Members excused from voting.

The board may excuse a member from voting, but only upon questions involving the member's own financial interest or official conduct or on matters on which the member is prohibited from voting under G.S. 14-234, 153A-340(g), or 160A-388(e)(2). For purposes of this section, the question of the compensation and allowances of members of the board does not involve a member's own financial interest or official conduct. (Code, s. 706; Rev., s. 1317; C.S., s. 1296; 1945, c. 132; 1951, c. 904, s. 1; 1961, c. 154; 1967, c. 617, s. 1; 1969, c. 349, s. 1; c. 1036; 1973, c. 822, s. 1; 2001-409, s. 8; 2005-426, s. 5.1(b); 2013-126, s. 6.)

§ 153A-45. Adoption of ordinances.

To be adopted at the meeting at which it is first introduced, an ordinance or any action having the effect of an ordinance (except the budget ordinance, any bond order, or any other ordinance on which a public hearing must be held before the ordinance may be adopted) must receive the approval of all the members of the board of commissioners. If the ordinance is approved by a majority of those voting but not by all the members of the board, or if the ordinance is not voted on at that meeting, it shall be considered at the next regular meeting of the board. If it then or at any time thereafter within 100 days of its introduction receives a majority of the votes cast, a quorum being present, the ordinance is adopted. (1963, c. 1060, ss. 1, 1 1/2; 1965, cc. 388, 567, 1083, 1158; 1967, c. 495, s. 2; 1969, c. 36, s. 1; 1971, c. 702, ss. 1-3; 1973, c. 822, s. 1.)

§ 153A-46. Franchises.

No ordinance making a grant, renewal, extension, or amendment of any franchise may be finally adopted until it has been passed at two regular meetings of the board of commissioners. No such grant, renewal, extension, or amendment may be made except by ordinance. (1973, c. 822, s. 1.)

§ 153A-47. Technical ordinances.

Subject to G.S. 143-138(e), a county may in an ordinance adopt by reference a published technical code or a standard or regulation promulgated by a public agency. A technical code or standard or regulation so adopted has the force of law in any area of the county in which the ordinance is applicable. An official copy of a technical code or standard or regulation adopted by reference shall be available for public inspection in the office of the clerk and need not be filed in the ordinance book. (1973, c. 822, s. 1.)

§ 153A-48. Ordinance book.

The clerk shall maintain an ordinance book, separate from the minute book of the board of commissioners. The ordinance book shall be indexed and shall be available for public inspection in the office of the clerk. Except as provided in this section and in G.S. 153A-47, each county ordinance shall be filed and indexed in the ordinance book.

The budget ordinance and any amendments thereto, any bond order, and any other ordinance of limited interest or transitory nature may be omitted from the ordinance book. However, the ordinance book shall contain a section showing the caption of each omitted ordinance and the page in the commissioners' minute book at which the ordinance may be found.

If a county adopts and issues a code of its ordinances, county ordinances need be recorded and indexed in the ordinance book only until they are placed in the codification. (1963, c. 1060, ss. 1, 1 1/2; 1965, cc. 388, 567, 1083, 1158; 1967, c. 495, s. 2; 1969, c. 36, s. 1; 1971, c. 702, ss. 1-3; 1973, c. 822, s. 1.)

§ 153A-49. Code of ordinances.

A county may adopt and issue a code of its ordinances. The code may be reproduced by any method that gives legible and permanent copies, and may be issued as a securely bound book or books with periodic separately bound supplements, or as a loose-leaf book maintained by replacement pages. Supplements or replacement pages should be adopted and issued at least annually, unless there have been no additions to or modifications of the code during the year.

A code may consist of two parts, the "General Ordinances" and the "Technical Ordinances." The technical ordinances may be published as separate books or pamphlets, and may include ordinances regarding the construction of buildings, the installation of plumbing and electric wiring, and the installation of cooling and heating equipment; ordinances regarding the use of public utilities, buildings, or facilities operated by the county; the zoning ordinance; the subdivision control ordinance; the privilege license tax ordinance; and other similar ordinances designated as technical ordinances by the board of commissioners. The board may omit from the code the budget ordinance, any bond orders, and other designated classes of ordinances of limited interest or transitory nature, but the code shall clearly describe the classes of ordinances omitted from it.

The board of commissioners may provide that ordinances (i) establishing or amending the boundaries of county zoning areas or (ii) establishing or amending the boundaries of zoning districts shall be codified by appropriate entries upon official map books to be retained permanently in the office of the clerk or some other county office generally accessible to the public. (1973, c. 822, s. 1.)

§ 153A-50. Pleading and proving county ordinances.

County ordinances shall be pleaded and proved under the rules and procedures of G.S. 160A-79. References to G.S. 160A-77 and G.S. 160A-78 appearing in G.S. 160A-79 are deemed, for purposes of this section, to refer to G.S. 153A-49 and G.S. 153A-48, respectively. (1973, c. 822, s. 1.)

§ 153A-51. Reserved for future codification purposes.

§ 153A-52. Conduct of public hearing.

The board of commissioners may hold public hearings at any place within the county. The board may adopt reasonable rules governing the conduct of public hearings, including but not limited to rules (i) fixing the maximum time allotted to each speaker, (ii) providing for the designation of spokesmen for groups of persons supporting or opposing the same position, (iii) providing for the selection of delegates from groups of persons supporting or opposing the same positions when the number of persons wishing to attend the hearing exceeds the capacity of the hall, and (iv) providing for the maintenance of order and decorum in the conduct of the hearing.

The board may continue a public hearing without further advertisement. If a public hearing is set for a given date and a quorum of the board is not then present, the board shall continue the hearing without further advertisement until its next regular meeting. (1973, c. 822, s. 1.)

§ 153A-52.1. Public comment period during regular meetings.

The board of commissioners shall provide at least one period for public comment per month at a regular meeting of the board. The board may adopt reasonable rules governing the conduct of the public comment period, including, but not limited to, rules (i) fixing the maximum time allotted to each speaker, (ii) providing for the designation of spokesmen for groups of persons supporting or opposing the same positions, (iii) providing for the selection of delegates from groups of persons supporting or opposing the same positions when the number of persons wishing to attend the hearing exceeds the capacity of the hall, and (iv) providing for the maintenance of order and decorum in the conduct of the hearing. The board is not required to provide a public comment period under this section if no regular meeting is held during the month. (2005-170, s. 2.)

§ 153A-53. Ethics.

(a)   The board of commissioners shall adopt a resolution or policy containing a code of ethics, as required by G.S. 160A-86.

(b)   All members of the board of commissioners, whether elected or appointed, shall receive the ethics education required by G.S. 160A-87. (2009-403, s. 4.)

§ 153A-54: Reserved for future codification purposes.

§ 153A-55: Reserved for future codification purposes.

§ 153A-56: Reserved for future codification purposes.

§ 153A-57: Reserved for future codification purposes.

Part 4. Modification in the Structure of the Board of Commissioners.

§ 153A-58. Optional structures.

A county may alter the structure of its board of commissioners by adopting one or any combination of the options prescribed by this section.

(1)	Number of members of the board of commissioners: The board may consist of any number of members not less than three, except as limited by subdivision (2)d of this section.

(2)	Terms of office of members of the board of commissioners:

a.	Members shall be elected for two-year terms of office.

b.	Members shall be elected for four-year terms of office.

c.	Members shall be elected for overlapping four-year terms of office.

d.	The board shall consist of an odd number of members, who are elected for a combination of four-and two-year terms of office, so that a majority of members is elected each two years. This option may be used only if all members of the board are nominated and elected by the voters of the entire county, and only if the chairman of the board is elected by and from the members of the board.

(3)	Mode of election of the board of commissioners:

a.	The qualified voters of the entire county shall nominate all candidates for and elect all members of the board.

For options b, c, and d, the county shall be divided into electoral districts, and board members shall be apportioned to the districts so that the quotients obtained by dividing the population of each district by the number of commissioners apportioned to the district are as nearly equal as practicable.

b. The qualified voters of each district shall nominate candidates and elect members who reside in the district for seats apportioned to that district; and the qualified voters of the entire county shall nominate candidates and elect members apportioned to the county at large, if any.

c. The qualified voters of each district shall nominate candidates who reside in the district for seats apportioned to that district, and the qualified voters of the entire county shall nominate candidates for seats apportioned to the county at large, if any; and the qualified voters of the entire county shall elect all the members of the board.

d. Members shall reside in and represent the districts according to the apportionment plan adopted, but the qualified voters of the entire county shall nominate all candidates for and elect all members of the board.

If any of options b, c, or d is adopted, the board shall divide the county into the requisite number of electoral districts according to the apportionment plan adopted, and shall cause a delineation of the districts so laid out to be drawn up and filed as required by G.S. 153A-20. No more than half the board may be apportioned to the county at large.

(4) Selection of chairman of the board of commissioners:

a. The board shall elect a chairman from among its membership to serve a one-year term, as provided by G.S. 153A-39.

b. The chairmanship shall be a separate office. The qualified voters of the entire county nominate candidates for and elect the chairman for a two-or four-year term. (1927, c. 91, s. 3; 1969, c. 717, s. 1; 1973, c. 822, s. 1.)

§ 153A-59. Implementation when board has members serving a combination of four-and two-year terms.

If the structure of the board of commissioners is altered to establish a board with an odd number of members serving a combination of four-and two-year terms of office, the new structure shall be implemented as follows:

At the first election all members of the board shall be elected. A simple majority of those elected shall be elected for two-year terms, and the remaining members shall be elected for four-year terms. The candidate or candidates receiving the highest number of votes shall be elected for the four-year terms.

At each subsequent general election, a simple majority of the board shall be elected. That candidate who is elected with the least number of votes shall be elected for a two-year term, and the other member or members elected shall be elected for four-year terms. (1927, c. 91, s. 3; 1969, c. 717, s. 1; 1973, c. 822, s. 1.)

§ 153A-60. Initiation of alterations by resolution.

The board of commissioners shall initiate any alteration in the structure of the board by adopting a resolution. The resolution shall:

(1)   Briefly but completely describe the proposed alterations;

(2)   Prescribe the manner of transition from the existing structure to the altered structure;

(3)   Define the electoral districts, if any, and apportion the members among the districts;

(4)   Call a special referendum on the question of adoption of the alterations. The referendum shall be held and conducted by the county board of elections. The referendum may be held only on a date permitted by G.S. 163-287.

Upon its adoption, the resolution shall be published in full. (1927, c. 91, s. 4; 1969, c. 717, s. 1; 1973, c. 822, s. 1; 1977, c. 382; 2013-381, s. 10.23.)

§ 153A-61. Submission of proposition to voters; form of ballot.

A proposition to approve an alteration shall be printed on the ballot in substantially the following form:

"Shall the structure of the board of commissioners be altered? (Describe the effect of the alteration.)

[] YES

[] NO"

The ballot shall be separate from other ballots used at the election.

If a majority of the votes cast on the proposition are in the affirmative, the plan contained in the resolution shall be put into effect as provided in this Part. If a majority of the votes cast are in the negative, the resolution and the plan contained therein are void. (1927, c. 91, s. 4; 1969, c. 717, s. 1; 1973, c. 822, s. 1.)

§ 153A-62. Effective date of any alteration.

Any approved alteration shall be the basis for nominating and electing the members of the board of commissioners at the first succeeding primary and general election for county offices held after approval of the alteration; and the alteration takes effect on the first Monday in December following that general election. (1927, c. 91, s. 4; 1969, c. 717, s. 1; 1973, c. 822, s. 1.)

§ 153A-63. Filing copy of resolution.

A copy of a resolution approved pursuant to this Part shall be filed and indexed in the ordinance book required by G.S. 153A-48. (1927, c. 91, s. 4; 1969, c. 717, s. 1; 1973, c. 822, s. 1.)

§ 153A-64. Filing results of election.

If the proposition is approved under G.S. 153A-61, a certified true copy of the resolution and a copy of the abstract of the election shall be filed with the Secretary of State and with the Legislative Library. (1985 (Reg. Sess., 1986), c. 935, s. 1; 1989, c. 191, s. 1.)

§§ 153A-65 through 153A-75. Reserved for future codification purposes.

Article 5.

Administration.

Part 1. Organization and Reorganization of County Government.

§ 153A-76. Board of commissioners to organize county government.

The board of commissioners may create, change, abolish, and consolidate offices, positions, departments, boards, commissions, and agencies of the county government, may impose ex officio the duties of more than one office on a single officer, may change the composition and manner of selection of boards, commissions, and agencies, and may generally organize and reorganize the county government in order to promote orderly and efficient administration of county affairs, subject to the following limitations:

(1)   The board may not abolish an office, position, department, board, commission, or agency established or required by law.

(2)   The board may not combine offices or confer certain duties on the same officer when this action is specifically forbidden by law.

(3)   The board may not discontinue or assign elsewhere a function or duty assigned by law to a particular office, position, department, board, commission, or agency.

(4)   The board may not change the composition or manner of selection of a local board of education, the board of elections, or the board of alcoholic beverage control.

(5)   The board may not abolish nor consolidate into a human services agency a hospital authority assigned to provide public health services pursuant to Section 12 of S.L. 1997-502 or a public health authority assigned the power, duties, and responsibilities to provide public health services as outlined in G.S. 130A-1.1.

(6)   A board may not consolidate an area mental health, developmental disabilities, and substance abuse services board into a consolidated human

services board. The board may not abolish an area mental health, developmental disabilities, and substance abuse services board, except as provided in Chapter 122C of the General Statutes. This subdivision shall not apply to any board that has exercised the powers and duties of an area mental health, developmental disabilities, and substance abuse services board as of January 1, 2012.

(7) The board may not abolish, assume control over, or consolidate into a human services agency a public hospital as defined in G.S. 159-39(a) pursuant to G.S. 153A-77. (1973, c. 822, s. 1; 2012-126, s. 2.)

§ 153A-77. Authority of boards of commissioners over commissions, boards, agencies, etc.

(a) In the exercise of its jurisdiction over commissions, boards and agencies, the board of county commissioners may assume direct control of any activities theretofore conducted by or through any commission, board or agency by the adoption of a resolution assuming and conferring upon the board of county commissioners all powers, responsibilities and duties of any such commission, board or agency. This section shall apply to the board of health, the social services board, area mental health, developmental disabilities, and substance abuse area board or any other commission, board or agency appointed by the board of county commissioners or acting under and pursuant to authority of the board of county commissioners of said county except as provided in G.S. 153A-76. A board of county commissioners exercising the power and authority under this subsection may, notwithstanding G.S. 130A-25, enforce public health rules adopted by the board through the imposition of civil penalties. If a public health rule adopted by a board of county commissioners imposes a civil penalty, the provisions of G.S. 130A-25 making its violation a misdemeanor shall not be applicable to that public health rule unless the rule states that a violation of the rule is a misdemeanor. The board of county commissioners may exercise the power and authority herein conferred only after a public hearing held by said board pursuant to 30 days' notice of said public hearing given in a newspaper having general circulation in said county.

The board of county commissioners may also appoint advisory boards, committees, councils and agencies composed of qualified and interested county residents to study, interpret and develop community support and cooperation in activities conducted by or under the authority of the board of county commissioners of said county.

A board of county commissioners that has assumed direct control of a local health board after January 1, 2012, and that does not delegate the powers and duties of that board to a consolidated health service board shall appoint an advisory committee consistent with the membership described in G.S. 130A-35.

(b) In the exercise of its jurisdiction over commissions, boards, and agencies, the board of county commissioners of a county having a county manager pursuant to G.S. 153A-81 may:

(1) Consolidate certain provisions of human services in the county under the direct control of a human services director appointed and supervised by the county manager in accordance with subsection (e) of this section;

(2) Create a consolidated human services board having the powers conferred by subsection (c) of this section;

(3) Create a consolidated county human services agency having the authority to carry out the functions of any combination of commissions, boards, or agencies appointed by the board of county commissioners or acting under and pursuant to authority of the board of county commissioners, including the local health department, the county department of social services, or the area mental health, developmental disabilities, and substance abuse services authority; and

(4) Assign other county human services functions to be performed by the consolidated human services agency under the direction of the human services director, with policy-making authority granted to the consolidated human services board as determined by the board of county commissioners.

(c) A consolidated human services board appointed by the board of county commissioners shall serve as the policy-making, rule-making, and administrative board of the consolidated human services agency. The consolidated human services board shall be composed of no more than 25 members. The composition of the board shall reasonably reflect the population makeup of the county and shall include:

(1) Eight persons who are consumers of human services, public advocates, or family members of clients of the consolidated human services agency,

including: one person with mental illness, one person with a developmental disability, one person in recovery from substance abuse, one family member of a person with mental illness, one family member of a person with a developmental disability, one family member of a person with a substance abuse problem, and two consumers of other human services.

(1a)   Notwithstanding subdivision (1) of this subsection, a consolidated human services board not exercising powers and duties of an area mental health, developmental disabilities, and substance abuse services board shall include four persons who are consumers of human services.

(2)   Eight persons who are professionals, each with qualifications in one of these categories: one psychologist, one pharmacist, one engineer, one dentist, one optometrist, one veterinarian, one social worker, and one registered nurse.

(3)   Two physicians licensed to practice medicine in this State, one of whom shall be a psychiatrist.

(4)   One member of the board of county commissioners.

(5)   Other persons, including members of the general public representing various occupations.

The board of county commissioners may elect to appoint a member of the consolidated human services board to fill concurrently more than one category of membership if the member has the qualifications or attributes of more than one category of membership.

All members of the consolidated human services board shall be residents of the county. The members of the board shall serve four-year terms. No member may serve more than two consecutive four-year terms. The county commissioner member shall serve only as long as the member is a county commissioner.

The initial board shall be appointed by the board of county commissioners upon the recommendation of a nominating committee comprised of members of the preconsolidation board of health, social services board, and area mental health, developmental disabilities, and substance abuse services board. In order to establish a uniform staggered term structure for the board, a member may be appointed for less than a four-year term. After the subsequent establishment of the board, its board shall be appointed by the board of county commissioners from nominees presented by the human services board. Vacancies shall be filled for any unexpired portion of a term.

A chairperson shall be elected annually by the members of the consolidated human services board. A majority of the members shall constitute a quorum. A member may be removed from office by the county board of commissioners for (i) commission of a felony or other crime involving moral turpitude; (ii) violation of a State law governing conflict of interest; (iii) violation of a written policy adopted by the county board of commissioners; (iv) habitual failure to attend meetings; (v) conduct that tends to bring the office into disrepute; or (vi) failure to maintain qualifications for appointment required under this subsection. A board member may be removed only after the member has been given written notice of the basis for removal and has had the opportunity to respond.

A member may receive a per diem in an amount established by the county board of commissioners. Reimbursement for subsistence and travel shall be in accordance with a policy set by the county board of commissioners. The board shall meet at least quarterly. The chairperson or three of the members may call a special meeting.

(d)   The consolidated human services board shall have authority to:

(1)   Set fees for departmental services based upon recommendations of the human services director. Fees set under this subdivision are subject to the same restrictions on amount and scope that would apply if the fees were set by a county board of health, a county board of social services, or a mental health, developmental disabilities, and substance abuse area authority.

(2)   Assure compliance with laws related to State and federal programs.

(3)   Recommend creation of local human services programs.

(4)   Adopt local health regulations and participate in enforcement appeals of local regulations.

(5)   Perform regulatory health functions required by State law.

(6)   Act as coordinator or agent of the State to the extent required by State or federal law.

(7)   Plan and recommend a consolidated human services budget.

(8) Conduct audits and reviews of human services programs, including quality assurance activities, as required by State and federal law or as may otherwise be necessary periodically.

(9) Advise local officials through the county manager.

(10) Perform public relations and advocacy functions.

(11) Protect the public health to the extent required by law.

(12) Perform comprehensive mental health services planning if the county is exercising the powers and duties of an area mental health, developmental disabilities, and substance abuse services board under the consolidated human services board.

(13) Develop dispute resolution procedures for human services contractors and clients and public advocates, subject to applicable State and federal dispute resolution procedures for human services programs, when applicable.

Except as otherwise provided, the consolidated human services board shall have the powers and duties conferred by law upon a board of health, a social services board, and an area mental health, developmental disabilities, and substance abuse services board.

Local employees who serve as staff of a consolidated county human services agency are subject to county personnel policies and ordinances only and are not subject to the provisions of the North Carolina Human Resources Act, unless the county board of commissioners elects to subject the local employees to the provisions of that Act. All consolidated county human services agencies shall comply with all applicable federal laws, rules, and regulations requiring the establishment of merit personnel systems.

(e) The human services director of a consolidated county human services agency shall be appointed and dismissed by the county manager with the advice and consent of the consolidated human services board. The human services director shall report directly to the county manager. The human services director shall:

(1) Appoint staff of the consolidated human services agency with the county manager's approval.

(2)   Administer State human services programs.

(3)   Administer human services programs of the local board of county commissioners.

(4)   Act as secretary and staff to the consolidated human services board under the direction of the county manager.

(5)   Plan the budget of the consolidated human services agency.

(6)   Advise the board of county commissioners through the county manager.

(7)   Perform regulatory functions of investigation and enforcement of State and local health regulations, as required by State law.

(8)   Act as an agent of and liaison to the State, to the extent required by law.

(9)   Appoint, with the county manager's approval, an individual that meets the requirements of G.S. 130A-40(a).

Except as otherwise provided by law, the human services director or the director's designee shall have the same powers and duties as a social services director, a local health director, or a director of an area mental health, developmental disabilities, and substance abuse services authority.

(f)   Repealed by Session Laws 2012-126, s. 1, effective June 29, 2012. (1973, c. 454, ss. 1-21/2; 1985, c. 589, s. 56; c. 754, s. 1; 1987, c. 217, ss. 1, 2; 1995 (Reg. Sess., 1996), c. 690, s. 3; 2001-120, s. 1; 2012-126, s. 1; 2013-382, s. 9.1(c).)

§ 153A-77.1. Single portal of entry.

A county may develop for human services a single portal of entry, a consolidated case management system, and a common data base; provided that if the county is part of a district health department or multicounty public health authority or a multicounty area mental health, developmental disabilities, and substance abuse authority, such action must be approved by the district board of health or public health authority board or the area mental health, developmental disabilities, and substance abuse board to affect any matter within the jurisdiction of that board. Nothing in this section shall be construed to abrogate a patient's right to confidentiality as provided by law. (1987, c. 422, s. 1; 1991 (Reg. Sess., 1992), c. 1030, s. 47; 1997-502, s. 5.)

§ 153A-78. Reserved for future codification purposes.

§ 153A-79. Reserved for future codification purposes.

§ 153A-80. Reserved for future codification purposes.

Part 2. Administration in Counties Having Managers.

§ 153A-81. Adoption of county-manager plan; appointment or designation of manager.

The board of commissioners may by resolution adopt or discontinue the county-manager plan. If it adopts the county-manager plan, the board may, in the alternative:

(1) Appoint a county manager to serve at its pleasure. The manager shall be appointed solely on the basis of his executive and administrative qualifications. He need not be a resident of the county or the State at the time of his appointment.

(2) Confer upon the chairman or some other member of the board of commissioners the duties of county manager. If this is done, the chairman or member shall become a full-time county official, and the board may increase his salary pursuant to G.S. 153A-28.

(3) Confer upon any other officer, employee, or agent of the county the duties of county manager.

As used in this Part, the word "manager" includes the chairman or any member of the board of commissioners exercising the duties of manager or any officer, employee, or agent of a county exercising the duties of manager. (1927, c. 91, ss. 5, 8; 1973, c. 822, s. 1.)

§ 153A-82. Powers and duties of manager.

The manager is the chief administrator of county government. He is responsible to the board of commissioners for the administration of all departments of county government under the board's general control and has the following powers and duties:

(1) He shall appoint with the approval of the board of commissioners and suspend or remove all county officers, employees, and agents except those who are elected by the people or whose appointment is otherwise provided for by law. The board may by resolution permit the manager to appoint officers, employees, and agents without first securing the board's approval. The manager shall make his appointments, suspensions, and removals in accordance with any general personnel rules, regulations, policies, or ordinances that the board may adopt. The board may require the manager to report each suspension or removal to the board at the board's first regular meeting following the suspension or removal; and, if the board has permitted the manager to make appointments without board approval, the board may require the manager to report each appointment to the board at the board's first regular meeting following the appointment.

(2) He shall direct and supervise the administration of all county offices, departments, boards, commissions and agencies under the general control of the board of commissioners, subject to the general direction and control of the board.

(3) He shall attend all meetings of the board of commissioners and recommend any measures that he considers expedient.

(4) He shall see that the orders, ordinances, resolutions, and regulations of the board of commissioners are faithfully executed within the county.

(5) He shall prepare and submit the annual budget and capital program to the board of commissioners.

(6) He shall annually submit to the board of commissioners and make available to the public a complete report on the finances and administrative activities of the county as of the end of the fiscal year.

(7) He shall make any other reports that the board of commissioners may require concerning the operations of county offices, departments, boards, commissions, and agencies.

(8) He shall perform any other duties that may be required or authorized by the board of commissioners. (1927, c. 91, ss. 6, 7; 1973, c. 822, s. 1.)

§ 153A-83. Acting county manager.

By letter filed with the clerk, the manager may designate, subject to the approval of the board of commissioners, a qualified person to exercise the powers and perform the duties of manager during the manager's temporary absence or disability. During an absence or disability, the board may revoke the designation at any time and appoint another person to serve until the manager returns or his disability ceases. (1973, c. 822, s. 1.)

§ 153A-84. Interim county manager.

Whenever the position of county manager is vacant, the board of commissioners shall designate a qualified person to exercise the powers and perform the duties of manager until the vacancy is filled. The board may designate the chairman or some other member as interim manager; for the interim the chairman or member shall become a full-time county official, and the board may increase his salary pursuant to G.S. 153A-28. (1973, c. 822, s. 1.)

§§ 153A-85 through 153A-86. Reserved for future codification purposes.

Part 3. Administration in Counties Not Having Managers.

§ 153A-87. Administration in counties not having managers.

In a county that has not adopted or does not operate under the county-manager plan, the board of commissioners shall appoint, suspend, and remove all county officers, employees, and agents except those who are elected by the people or whose appointment is otherwise provided for by law. The board may delegate to the head of any county department the power to appoint, suspend, and remove county officers or employees assigned to his department. (1973, c. 822, s. 1.)

§ 153A-88. Acting department heads.

By letter filed with the clerk, the head of a department may designate, subject to the approval of the board of commissioners, a qualified person to exercise the powers and perform the duties of head of that department during the department head's temporary absence or disability. During an absence or disability, the board may revoke the designation at any time and appoint another person to serve until the department head returns or his disability ceases. (1973, c. 822, s. 1.)

§ 153A-89. Interim department heads.

Whenever the position of head of a department is vacant, the board may designate a qualified person to exercise the powers and perform the duties of head of the department until the vacancy is filled. (1973, c. 822, s. 1.)

§§ 153A-90 through 153A-91. Reserved for future codification purposes.

Part 4. Personnel.

§ 153A-92. Compensation.

(a)   Subject to the limitations set forth in subsection (b) of this section, the board of commissioners shall fix or approve the schedule of pay, expense allowances, and other compensation of all county officers and employees, whether elected or appointed, and may adopt position classification plans.

(b)   In exercising the authority granted by subsection (a) of this section, the board of commissioners is subject to the following limitations:

(1) The board of commissioners may not reduce the salary, allowances, or other compensation paid to an officer elected by the people for the duties of his elective office if the reduction is to take effect during the term of office for which the incumbent officer has been elected, unless the officer agrees to the reduction or unless the Local Government Commission pursuant to Chapter 159, Article 10, orders a reduction.

(2) During the year of a general election, the board of commissioners may reduce the salary, allowances, or other compensation of an officer to be elected at the general election only in accordance with this subdivision. The board of commissioners shall by resolution give notice of intention to make the reduction no later than 14 days before the last day for filing notice of candidacy for the office. The resolution shall set forth the reduced salary, allowances, and other compensation and shall provide that the reduction is to take effect at the time the person elected to the office in the general election takes office. Once adopted, the resolution may not be altered until the person elected to the office in the general election has taken office. The filing fee for the office shall be determined by reference to the reduced salary.

(3) If the board of commissioners reduces the salaries, allowances, or other compensation of employees assigned to an officer elected by the people, and the reduction does not apply alike to all county offices and departments, the elected officer involved must approve the reduction. If the elected officer refuses to approve the reduction, he and the board of commissioners shall meet and attempt to reach agreement. If agreement cannot be reached, either the board or the officer may refer the dispute to arbitration by the senior resident superior court judge of the superior court district or set of districts as defined in G.S. 7A-41.1 in which the county is located. The judge shall make an award within 30 days after the day the matter is referred to him. The award may extend for no more than two fiscal years, including the fiscal year for which it is made.

(4) The board of commissioners shall fix their own salaries, allowances, and other compensation in accordance with G.S. 153A-28.

(5) The board of commissioners shall fix the salaries, allowances and other compensation of county employees subject to the North Carolina Human Resources Act according to the procedures set forth in Chapter 126. The board may make these employees subject to a county position classification plan only as provided in Chapter 126.

(c) In counties with a county manager, the manager is responsible for preparing position classification and pay plans for submission to the board of commissioners and for administering the pay plan and any position classification plan in accordance with general policies and directives adopted by the board. In counties without a county manager, the board of commissioners shall appoint or designate a personnel officer, who shall then be responsible for administering the pay plan and any position classification plan in accordance with general policies and directives adopted by the board.

(d) A county may purchase life insurance or health insurance or both for the benefit of all or any class of county officers and employees as a part of their compensation. A county may provide other fringe benefits for county officers and employees. In providing health insurance to county officers and employees, a county shall not provide abortion coverage greater than that provided by the State Health Plan for Teachers and State Employees under Article 3B of Chapter 135 of the General Statutes. (1927, c. 91, s. 8; 1953, c. 1227, ss. 1-3; 1969, c. 358, s. 1; c. 1017; 1973, c. 822, s. 1; 1987 (Reg. Sess., 1988), c. 1037, s. 122; 2013-366, s. 2(b); 2013-382, s. 9.1(c).)

§ 153A-93. Retirement benefits.

(a) The board of commissioners may provide for enrolling county officers and employees in the Local Governmental Employees' Retirement System, the Law-Enforcement Officers' Benefit and Relief Fund, the Firemen's Pension Fund, or a retirement plan certified to be actuarially sound by a qualified actuary as defined in subsection (c) of this section and may make payments into such a retirement system or plan on behalf of its employees.

(b) No county may make payments into a retirement system or plan established or authorized by a local act unless the system or plan is certified to be actuarially sound by a qualified actuary as defined in subsection (c) of this section.

(c) A qualified actuary means a member of the American Academy of Actuaries or an individual certified as qualified by the Commissioner of Insurance.

(d) A county which is providing health insurance under G.S. 153A-92(d) may provide health insurance for all or any class of former officers and employees of the county. Such health insurance may be paid entirely by the county, partly by the county and former officer or employee, or entirely by the former officer or employee, at the option of the county.

(d1)   On and after October 1, 2009, a county which is providing health insurance under G.S. 153A-92(d) may provide health insurance for all or any class of former officers and employees of the county who have obtained at least 10 years of service with the county prior to separation from the county and who are not receiving benefits under subsection (a) of this section. Such health insurance may be paid entirely by the county, partly by the county and former officer or employee, or entirely by the former officer or employee, at the option of the county.

(d2)   Notwithstanding subsection (d) of this section, any county that has elected to and is covering its active employees only, or its active and retired employees, under the State Health Plan, or elects such coverage under the Plan, may not provide health insurance through the State Health Plan to all or any class of former officers and employees who are not receiving benefits under subsection (a) of this section. The county may, however, provide health insurance to such former officers and employees by any other means authorized by G.S. 153A-92(d). The health insurance premium may be paid entirely by the county, partly by the county and former officer or employee, or entirely by the former officer or employee, at the option of the county.

(e)   The board of commissioners may provide a deferred compensation plan. Where the board of commissioners provides a deferred compensation plan, the investment of funds for the plan shall be exempt from the provisions of G.S. 159-30 and G.S. 159-31. Counties may invest deferred compensation plan funds in life insurance, fixed or variable annuities and retirement income contracts, regulated investment trusts, or other forms of investments approved by the Board of Trustees of the North Carolina Public Employee Deferred Compensation Plan. (1973, c. 822, s. 1; 1981, c. 347, s. 1; 1991, c. 277, s. 1; 2009-564, ss. 1, 2.)

§ 153A-94. Personnel rules; office hours, workdays, and holidays.

(a)   The board of commissioners may adopt or provide for rules and regulations or ordinances concerning but not limited to annual leave, sick leave, special leave with full pay or with partial pay supplementing workers' compensation payments for employees injured in accidents arising out of and in the course of employment, working conditions, service award and incentive award programs, other personnel policies, and any other measures that promote the hiring and retention of capable, diligent, and honest career employees.

(b) The board of commissioners may prescribe the office hours, workdays, and holidays to be observed by the various offices, departments, boards, commissions, and agencies of the county. (1959, c. 251; 1973, c. 822, s. 1; 1991, c. 636, s. 3.)

§ 153A-94.1. (See note on condition precedent) Smallpox vaccination policy.

All counties that employ firefighters, law enforcement officers, paramedics, other first responders, or health department employees shall, not later than 90 days after this section becomes law, enact a policy regarding sick leave and salary continuation for those employees for absence from work due to an adverse medical reaction resulting from the employee receiving in employment vaccination against smallpox incident to the Administration of Smallpox Countermeasures by Health Professionals, section 304 of the Homeland Security Act, Pub. L. No. 107-296 (Nov. 25, 2002) (to be codified at 42 U.S.C. § 233(p)). (2003-169, s. 6.)

§ 153A-94.2. Criminal history record checks of employees permitted.

The board of commissioners may adopt or provide for rules and regulations or ordinances concerning a requirement that any applicant for employment be subject to a criminal history record check of State and National Repositories of Criminal Histories conducted by the Department of Justice in accordance with G.S. 114-19.14. The local or regional public employer may consider the results of these criminal history record checks in its hiring decisions. (2005-358, s. 2.)

§ 153A-95. Personnel board.

The board of commissioners may establish a personnel board with authority, as regards employees in offices, departments, boards, commissions, and agencies under the general control of the board of commissioners, to administer tests designed to determine the merit and fitness of candidates for appointment or promotion, to conduct hearings upon the appeal of employees who have been suspended, demoted, or discharged, to hear employee grievances, or to undertake any other duties relating to personnel administration that the board of commissioners may direct. (1973, c. 822, s. 1.)

§ 153A-96. Participation in the Social Security Act.

The board of commissioners may take any action necessary to allow county officers and employees to participate fully in benefits provided by the Federal Social Security Act. (1973, c. 822, s. 1.)

§ 153A-97. Defense of officers, employees and others.

A county may, pursuant to G.S. 160A-167, provide for the defense of:

(1)   Any county officer or employee, including the county board of elections or any county election official.

(2)   Any member of a volunteer fire department or rescue squad which receives public funds.

(2a)   Any soil and water conservation supervisor, and any local soil and water conservation employee, whether the employee is a county employee or an employee of a soil and water conservation district.

(3)   Any person or professional association who at the request of the board of county commissioners provides medical or dental services to inmates in the custody of the sheriff and is sued pursuant to 42 U.S.C. § 1983 with respect to the services. (1957, c. 436; 1973, c. 822, s. 1; 1977, c. 307, s. 1; 1989, c. 733, s. 2; 2001-300, s. 1.)

§ 153A-98. Privacy of employee personnel records.

(a) Notwithstanding the provisions of G.S. 132-6 or any other general law or local act concerning access to public records, personnel files of employees, former employees, or applicants for employment maintained by a county are subject to inspection and may be disclosed only as provided by this section. For purposes of this section, an employee's personnel file consists of any information in any form gathered by the county with respect to that employee and, by way of illustration but not limitation, relating to his application, selection or nonselection, performance, promotions, demotions, transfers, suspension and other disciplinary actions, evaluation forms, leave, salary, and termination of employment. As used in this section, "employee" includes former employees of the county.

(b) The following information with respect to each county employee is a matter of public record:

(1) Name.

(2) Age.

(3) Date of original employment or appointment to the county service.

(4) The terms of any contract by which the employee is employed whether written or oral, past and current, to the extent that the county has the written contract or a record of the oral contract in its possession.

(5) Current position.

(6) Title.

(7) Current salary.

(8) Date and amount of each increase or decrease in salary with that county.

(9) Date and type of each promotion, demotion, transfer, suspension, separation or other change in position classification with that county.

(10) Date and general description of the reasons for each promotion with that county.

(11) Date and type of each dismissal, suspension, or demotion for disciplinary reasons taken by the county. If the disciplinary action was a dismissal, a copy of the written notice of the final decision of the county setting forth the specific acts or omissions that are the basis of the dismissal.

(12) The office to which the employee is currently assigned.

(b1) For the purposes of this subsection, the term "salary" includes pay, benefits, incentives, bonuses, and deferred and all other forms of compensation paid by the employing entity.

(b2) The board of county commissioners shall determine in what form and by whom this information will be maintained. Any person may have access to this information for the purpose of inspection, examination, and copying, during regular business hours, subject only to such rules and regulations for the safekeeping of public records as the board of commissioners may have adopted. Any person denied access to this information may apply to the appropriate division of the General Court of Justice for an order compelling disclosure, and the court shall have jurisdiction to issue such orders.

(c) All information contained in a county employee's personnel file, other than the information made public by subsection (b) of this section, is confidential and shall be open to inspection only in the following instances:

(1) The employee or his duly authorized agent may examine all portions of his personnel file except (i) letters of reference solicited prior to employment, and (ii) information concerning a medical disability, mental or physical, that a prudent physician would not divulge to his patient.

(2) A licensed physician designated in writing by the employee may examine the employee's medical record.

(3) A county employee having supervisory authority over the employee may examine all material in the employee's personnel file.

(4) By order of a court of competent jurisdiction, any person may examine such portion of an employee's personnel file as may be ordered by the court.

(5) An official of an agency of the State or federal government, or any political subdivision of the State, may inspect any portion of a personnel file

when such inspection is deemed by the official having custody of such records to be inspected to be necessary and essential to the pursuance of a proper function of the inspecting agency, but no information shall be divulged for the purpose of assisting in a criminal prosecution of the employee, or for the purpose of assisting in an investigation of the employee's tax liability. However, the official having custody of such records may release the name, address, and telephone number from a personnel file for the purpose of assisting in a criminal investigation.

(6) An employee may sign a written release, to be placed with his personnel file, that permits the person with custody of the file to provide, either in person, by telephone, or by mail, information specified in the release to prospective employers, educational institutions, or other persons specified in the release.

(7) The county manager, with concurrence of the board of county commissioners, or, in counties not having a manager, the board of county commissioners may inform any person of the employment or nonemployment, promotion, demotion, suspension or other disciplinary action, reinstatement, transfer, or termination of a county employee and the reasons for that personnel action. Before releasing the information, the manager or board shall determine in writing that the release is essential to maintaining public confidence in the administration of county services or to maintaining the level and quality of county services. This written determination shall be retained in the office of the manager or the county clerk, is a record available for public inspection and shall become part of the employee's personnel file.

(c1) Even if considered part of an employee's personnel file, the following information need not be disclosed to an employee nor to any other person:

(1) Testing or examination material used solely to determine individual qualifications for appointment, employment, or promotion in the county's service, when disclosure would compromise the objectivity or the fairness of the testing or examination process.

(2) Investigative reports or memoranda and other information concerning the investigation of possible criminal actions of an employee, until the investigation is completed and no criminal action taken, or until the criminal action is concluded.

(3) Information that might identify an undercover law enforcement officer or a law enforcement informer.

(4) Notes, preliminary drafts and internal communications concerning an employee. In the event such materials are used for any official personnel decision, then the employee or his duly authorized agent shall have a right to inspect such materials.

(c2) The board of county commissioners may permit access, subject to limitations they may impose, to selected personnel files by a professional representative of a training, research, or academic institution if that person certifies that he will not release information identifying the employees whose files are opened and that the information will be used solely for statistical, research, or teaching purposes. This certification shall be retained by the county as long as each personnel file so examined is retained.

(c3) Notwithstanding any provision of this section to the contrary, the Retirement Systems Division of the Department of State Treasurer may disclose the name and mailing address of former local governmental employees to domiciled, nonprofit organizations representing 2,000 or more active or retired State government, local government, or public school employees.

(d) The board of commissioners of a county that maintains personnel files containing information other than the information mentioned in subsection (b) of this section shall establish procedures whereby an employee who objects to material in his file on grounds that it is inaccurate or misleading may seek to have the material removed from the file or may place in the file a statement relating to the material.

(e) A public official or employee who knowingly, willfully, and with malice permits any person to have access to information contained in a personnel file, except as is permitted by this section, is guilty of a Class 3 misdemeanor and upon conviction shall only be fined an amount not more than five hundred dollars ($500.00).

(f) Any person, not specifically authorized by this section to have access to a personnel file designated as confidential, who shall knowingly and willfully examine in its official filing place, remove or copy any portion of a confidential personnel file shall be guilty of a Class 3 misdemeanor and upon conviction shall only be fined in the discretion of the court but not in excess of five hundred dollars ($500.00). (1975, c. 701, s. 1; 1981, c. 926, ss. 1, 5-8; 1993, c. 539, ss. 1059, 1060; 1994, Ex. Sess., c. 24, s. 14(c); 2007-508, s. 6; 2008-194, s. 11(d); 2010-169, s. 18(e).)

§ 153A-99. County employee political activity.

(a)   Purpose. The purpose of this section is to ensure that county employees are not subjected to political or partisan coercion while performing their job duties, to ensure that employees are not restricted from political activities while off duty, and to ensure that public funds are not used for political or partisan activities.

It is not the purpose of this section to allow infringement upon the rights of employees to engage in free speech and free association. Every county employee has a civic responsibility to support good government by every available means and in every appropriate manner. Employees shall not be restricted from affiliating with civic organizations of a partisan or political nature, nor shall employees, while off duty, be restricted from attending political meetings, or advocating and supporting the principles or policies of civic or political organizations, or supporting partisan or nonpartisan candidates of their choice in accordance with the Constitution and laws of the State and the Constitution and laws of the United States of America.

(b)   Definitions. For the purposes of this section:

(1)   "County employee" or "employee" means any person employed by a county or any department or program thereof that is supported, in whole or in part, by county funds;

(2)   "On duty" means that time period when an employee is engaged in the duties of his or her employment; and

(3)   "Workplace" means any place where an employee engages in his or her job duties.

(c)   No employee while on duty or in the workplace may:

(1)   Use his or her official authority or influence for the purpose of interfering with or affecting the result of an election or nomination for political office; or

(2)   Coerce, solicit, or compel contributions for political or partisan purposes by another employee.

(d)   No employee may be required as a duty or condition of employment, promotion, or tenure of office to contribute funds for political or partisan purposes.

(e)   No employee may use county funds, supplies, or equipment for partisan purposes, or for political purposes except where such political uses are otherwise permitted by law.

(f)   To the extent that this section conflicts with the provisions of any local act, local ordinance, resolution, or policy, this section prevails to the extent of the conflict. (1991, c. 619, s. 1; 1993, c. 298, s. 1.)

§ 153A-99.1. County verification of employee work authorization.

(a)   Counties Must Use E-Verify. - Each county shall register and participate in E-Verify to verify the work authorization of new employees hired to work in the United States.

(b)   E-Verify Defined. - As used in this section, the term "E-Verify" means the federal E-Verify program operated by the United States Department of Homeland Security and other federal agencies, or any successor or equivalent program used to verify the work authorization of newly hired employees pursuant to federal law.

(c)   Nondiscrimination. - This section shall be enforced without regard to race, religion, gender, ethnicity, or national origin. (2011-263, s. 4.)

§ 153A-100. Reserved for future codification purposes.

Part 5. Board of Commissioners and Other Officers, Boards, Departments, and Agencies of the County.

§ 153A-101. Board of commissioners to direct fiscal policy of the county.

The board of commissioners has and shall exercise the responsibility of developing and directing the fiscal policy of the county government under the provisions and procedures of the Local Government Budget and Fiscal Control Act. (1777, c. 129, s. 4, P.R.; R.C., c. 28, s. 16; Code, s. 753; Rev., s. 1379; C.S., s. 1325; 1927, c. 91, s. 11; 1953, c. 973, s. 2; 1973, c. 822, s. 1.)

§ 153A-102. Commissioners to fix fees.

The board of commissioners may fix the fees and commissions charged by county officers and employees for performing services or duties permitted or required by law. The board may not, however, fix fees in the General Court of Justice or modify the fees of the register of deeds prescribed by G.S. 161-10 or the fees of the board of elections prescribed by G.S. 163-107. (1953, c. 1227, ss. 1-3; 1969, c. 358, s. 1; c. 1017; 1973, c. 822, s. 1.)

§ 153A-102.1. Notice of new fees and fee increases; public comment period.

(a) A county shall provide notice to interested parties of the imposition of or increase in fees or charges applicable solely to the construction of development subject to the provisions of Part 2 of Article 18 of this Chapter at least seven days prior to the first meeting where the imposition of or increase in the fees or charges is on the agenda for consideration. The county shall employ at least two of the following means of communication in order to provide the notice required by this section:

(1) Notice of the meeting in a prominent location on a Web site managed or maintained by the county.

(2) Notice of the meeting in a prominent physical location, including, but not limited to, any government building, library, or courthouse within the county.

(3) Notice of the meeting by electronic mail to a list of interested parties that is created by the county for the purpose of notification as required by this section.

(4) Notice of the meeting by facsimile to a list of interested parties that is created by the county for the purpose of notification as required by this section.

(a1)   If a county manages or maintains a Web site, it may provide the notice required pursuant to G.S. 160A-4.1, 130A-64.1, or 162A-9 on its Web site at the request of a city, sanitary district, or water and sewer authority that does not manage or maintain a Web site of its own. Any county that elects to provide such notice shall post the notice to its Web site within seven days of the request made by the city, sanitary district, or water and sewer authority.

(b)   During the consideration of the imposition of or increase in fees or charges as provided in subsection (a) of this section, the governing body of the county shall permit a period of public comment.

(c)   This section shall not apply if the imposition of or increase in fees or charges is contained in a budget filed in accordance with the requirements of G.S. 159-12. (2009-436, s. 1; 2010-180, s. 11(a).)

§ 153A-103. Number of employees in offices of sheriff and register of deeds.

Subject to the limitations set forth below, the board of commissioners may fix the number of salaried employees in the offices of the sheriff and the register of deeds. In exercising the authority granted by this section, the board of commissioners is subject to the following limitations:

(1)   Each sheriff and register of deeds elected by the people has the exclusive right to hire, discharge, and supervise the employees in his office. However, the board of commissioners must approve the appointment by such an officer of a relative by blood or marriage of nearer kinship than first cousin or of a person who has been convicted of a crime involving moral turpitude.

(2)   Each sheriff and register of deeds elected by the people is entitled to at least two deputies who shall be reasonably compensated by the county, provided that the register of deeds justifies to the Board of County Commissioners the necessity of the second deputy. Each deputy so appointed shall serve at the pleasure of the appointing officer.

Notwithstanding the foregoing provisions of this section, approval of the board of commissioners is not required for the reappointment or continued employment of a near relative of a sheriff or register of deeds who was not related to the appointing officer at the time of initial appointment. (1953, c. 1227, ss. 1, 2; 1969, c. 358, s. 1; 1973, c. 822, s. 1; 1977, c. 36; 1979, c. 551; 1987, c. 362.)

§ 153A-104. Reports from officers, employees, and agents of the county.

The board of commissioners may require any officer, employee, or agent of the county to make to the board, either directly or through the county manager, periodic or special reports concerning any matter connected with the officer's, employee's or agent's duties. The board may require that such a report be made under oath. If a person fails or refuses to obey a reasonable order to make a report, issued pursuant to this section, the board may apply to the appropriate division of the General Court of Justice for an order requiring that its order be obeyed. The court has jurisdiction to issue these orders. (1868, c. 20, s. 8; Code, s. 707; Rev., s. 1318; C.S., s. 1297; 1973, c. 822, s. 1.)

§§ 153A-105 through 153A-110. Reserved for future codification purposes.

Part 6. Clerk to the Board of Commissioners.

§ 153A-111. Appointment; powers and duties.

The board of commissioners shall appoint or designate a clerk to the board. The board may designate the register of deeds or any other county officer or employee as clerk. The clerk shall perform any duties that may be required by law or the board of commissioners. The clerk shall serve as such at the pleasure of the board. (Const., art. 7, s. 2; Code, s. 710; 1895, c. 135, s. 4; Rev., s. 1324; C.S., s. 1309; 1955, c. 247, s. 1; 1963, c. 372; 1969, c. 207; 1973, c. 822, s. 1.)

§§ 153A-112 through 153A-113. Reserved for future codification purposes.

Part 7. County Attorney.

§ 153A-114. Appointment; duties.

The board of commissioners shall appoint a county attorney to serve at its pleasure and to be its legal adviser. (1973, c. 822, s. 1.)

§§ 153A-115 through 153A-120. Reserved for future codification purposes.

Article 6.

Delegation and Exercise of the General Police Power.

§ 153A-121. General ordinance-making power.

(a)   A county may by ordinance define, regulate, prohibit, or abate acts, omissions, or conditions detrimental to the health, safety, or welfare of its citizens and the peace and dignity of the county; and may define and abate nuisances.

(b)   This section does not authorize a county to regulate or control vehicular or pedestrian traffic on a street or highway under the control of the Board of Transportation, nor to regulate or control any right-of-way or right-of-passage belonging to a public utility, electric or telephone membership corporation, or public agency of the State. In addition, no county ordinance may regulate or control a highway right-of-way in a manner inconsistent with State law or an ordinance of the Board of Transportation.

(c)   This section does not impair the authority of local boards of health to adopt rules and regulations to protect and promote public health. (1963, c. 1060, ss. 1, 1 1/2; 1965, cc. 388, 567, 1083, 1158; 1967, c. 495, s. 2; 1969, c. 36, s. 1; 1971, c. 702, ss. 1-3; 1973, c. 507, s. 5; c. 822, s. 1.)

§ 153A-122. Territorial jurisdiction of county ordinances.

Except as otherwise provided in this Article, the board of commissioners may make any ordinance adopted pursuant to this Article applicable to any part of the county not within a city. In addition, the governing board of a city may by resolution permit a county ordinance adopted pursuant to this Article to be applicable within the city. The city may by resolution withdraw its permission to such an ordinance. If it does so, the city shall give written notice to the county of its withdrawal of permission; 30 days after the day the county receives this notice the county ordinance ceases to be applicable within the city. (1963, c. 1060, ss. 1, 1 1/2; 1965, cc. 388, 567, 1083, 1158; 1967, c. 495, s. 2; 1969, c. 36, s. 1; 1971, c. 702, ss. 1-3; 1973, c. 822, s. 1.)

§ 153A-123. Enforcement of ordinances.

(a) A county may provide for fines and penalties for violation of its ordinances and may secure injunctions and abatement orders to further insure compliance with its ordinances, as provided by this section.

(b) Unless the board of commissioners has provided otherwise, violation of a county ordinance is a misdemeanor or infraction as provided by G.S. 14-4. An ordinance may provide by express statement that the maximum fine, term of imprisonment, or infraction penalty to be imposed for a violation is some amount of money or number of days less than the maximum imposed by G.S. 14-4.

(c) An ordinance may provide that violation subjects the offender to a civil penalty to be recovered by the county in a civil action in the nature of debt if the offender does not pay the penalty within a prescribed period of time after he has been cited for violation of the ordinance.

(c1) An ordinance may provide for the recovery of a civil penalty by the county for violation of the fire prevention code of the State Building Code as authorized under G.S. 143-139.

(d) An ordinance may provide that it may be enforced by an appropriate equitable remedy issuing from a court of competent jurisdiction. In such a case, the General Court of Justice has jurisdiction to issue any order that may be appropriate, and it is not a defense to the county's application for equitable relief that there is an adequate remedy at law.

(e) An ordinance that makes unlawful a condition existing upon or use made of real property may provide that it may be enforced by injunction and order of abatement, and the General Court of Justice has jurisdiction to issue such an order. When a violation of such an ordinance occurs, the county may apply to the appropriate division of the General Court of Justice for a mandatory or prohibitory injunction and order of abatement commanding the defendant to correct the unlawful condition upon or cease the unlawful use of the property. The action shall be governed in all respects by the laws and rules governing civil proceedings, including the Rules of Civil Procedure in general and Rule 65 in particular.

In addition to an injunction, the court may enter an order of abatement as a part of the judgment in the cause. An order of abatement may direct that buildings or other structures on the property be closed, demolished, or removed; that fixtures, furniture, or other movable property be removed from buildings on the property; that grass and weeds be cut; that improvements or repairs be made; or that any other action be taken that is necessary to bring the property into compliance with the ordinance. If the defendant fails or refuses to comply with an injunction or with an order of abatement within the time allowed by the court, he may be cited for contempt and the county may execute the order of abatement. If the county executes the order, it has a lien on the property, in the nature of a mechanic's and materialman's lien, for the costs of executing the order. The defendant may secure cancellation of an order of abatement by paying all costs of the proceedings and posting a bond for compliance with the order. The bond shall be given with sureties approved by the clerk of superior court in an amount approved by the judge before whom the matter was heard and shall be conditioned on the defendant's full compliance with the terms of the order of abatement within the time fixed by the judge. Cancellation of an order of abatement does not suspend or cancel an injunction issued in conjunction with the order.

(f)   Subject to the express terms of the ordinance, a county ordinance may be enforced by any one or more of the remedies authorized by this section.

(g)   A county ordinance may provide, when appropriate, that each day's continuing violation is a separate and distinct offense.

(h)   Notwithstanding any authority under this Article or any local act of the General Assembly, no ordinance regulating trees may be enforced on land owned or operated by a public airport authority. (1973, c. 822, s. 1; 1985, c. 764, s. 34; 1985 (Reg. Sess., 1986), c. 852, s. 17; 1993, c. 329, s. 5; 2013-331, s. 1.)

§ 153A-124. Enumeration not exclusive.

The enumeration in this Article or other portions of this Chapter of specific powers to define, regulate, prohibit, or abate acts, omissions, or conditions is not exclusive, nor is it a limit on the general authority to adopt ordinances conferred on counties by G.S. 153A-121. (1973, c. 822, s. 1.)

§ 153A-125. Regulation of solicitation campaigns, flea markets and itinerant merchants.

A county may by ordinance regulate, restrict, or prohibit the solicitation of contributions from the public for charitable or eleemosynary purposes, and also the business activities of itinerant merchants, salesmen, promoters, drummers, peddlers, flea market operators and flea market vendors and hawkers. These ordinances may include, but are not limited to, requirements that an application be made and a permit issued, that an investigation be made, that activities be reasonably limited as to time and place, that proper credentials and proof of financial stability be submitted, that not more than a stated percentage of contributions to solicitation campaigns be retained for administrative expenses, and that an adequate bond be posted to protect the public from fraud. A county may charge a fee for a permit issued pursuant to such an ordinance. (1967, c. 80, ss. 1-2 1/2; 1973, c. 822, s. 1; 1987, c. 708, s. 7.)

§ 153A-126. Regulation of begging.

A county may by ordinance prohibit or regulate begging or otherwise canvassing the public for contributions for the private benefit of the solicitor or any other person. (1973, c. 822, s. 1.)

§ 153A-127. Abuse of animals.

A county may by ordinance define and prohibit the abuse of animals. (1973, c. 822, s. 1.)

§ 153A-128. Regulation of explosive, corrosive, inflammable, or radioactive substances.

A county may by ordinance regulate, restrict, or prohibit the sale, possession, storage, use or conveyance of any explosive, corrosive, inflammable, or radioactive substance or of any weapon or instrumentality of mass death and destruction. (1973, c. 822, s. 1.)

§ 153A-129. Firearms.

A county may by ordinance regulate, restrict, or prohibit the discharge of firearms at any time or place except when used to take birds or animals pursuant to Chapter 113, Subchapter IV, when used in defense of person or property, or when used pursuant to lawful directions of law-enforcement officers. A county may also regulate the display of firearms on the public roads, sidewalks, alleys, or other public property. This section does not limit a county's authority to take action under Article 1A of Chapter 166A of the General Statutes. (1973, c. 822, s. 1; 2006-264, s. 16; 2012-12, s. 2(yy).)

§ 153A-130. Pellet guns.

A county may by ordinance regulate, restrict, or prohibit the sale, possession, or use of pellet guns or any other mechanism or device designed or used to project a missile by compressed air or mechanical action with less than deadly force. (1973, c. 822, s. 1.)

§ 153A-131. Possession or harboring of dangerous animals.

A county may by ordinance regulate, restrict, or prohibit the possession or harboring of animals which are dangerous to persons or property. No such ordinance shall have the effect of permitting any activity or condition with respect to a wild animal which is prohibited or more severely restricted by regulations of the Wildlife Resources Commission. (1973, c. 822, s. 1; 1977, c. 407, s. 1.)

§ 153A-132. Removal and disposal of abandoned and junked motor vehicles.

(a) Grant of Power. - A county may by ordinance prohibit the abandonment of motor vehicles on public grounds and private property within the county's ordinance-making jurisdiction and on county-owned property wherever located. The county may enforce the ordinance by removing and disposing of abandoned or junked motor vehicles according to the procedures prescribed in this section.

(b)   Definitions. - "Motor vehicle" includes any machine designed or intended to travel over land or water by self-propulsion or while attached to self-propelled vehicle.

(1)   An "abandoned motor vehicle" is one that:

a.   Is left on public grounds or county-owned property in violation of a law or ordinance prohibiting parking; or

b.   Is left for longer than 24 hours on property owned or operated by the county; or

c.   Is left for longer than two hours on private property without the consent of the owner, occupant, or lessee of the property; or

d.   Is left for longer than seven days on public grounds.

(2)   A "junked motor vehicle" is an abandoned motor vehicle that also:

a.   Is partially dismantled or wrecked; or

b.   Cannot be self-propelled or moved in the manner in which it originally was intended to move; or

c.   Is more than five years old and appears to be worth less than one hundred dollars ($100.00); or

d.   Does not display a current license plate.

(c)   Removal of Vehicles. - A county may remove to a storage garage or area an abandoned or junked motor vehicle found to be in violation of an ordinance adopted pursuant to this section. A vehicle may not be removed from private property, however, without the written request of the owner, lessee, or occupant of the premises unless the board of commissioners or a duly authorized county official or employee has declared the vehicle to be a health or safety hazard. Appropriate county officers and employees have a right, upon presentation of proper credentials, to enter on any premises within the county ordinance-making jurisdiction at any reasonable hour in order to determine if any vehicles are health or safety hazards. The county may require a person requesting the removal from private property of an abandoned or junked motor vehicle to indemnify the county against any loss, expense, or liability incurred because of the vehicle's removal, storage, or sale.

When an abandoned or junked motor vehicle is removed, the county shall give notice to the owner as required by G.S. 20-219.11(a) and (b).

(d) Hearing Procedure. - Regardless of whether a county does its own removal and disposal of motor vehicles or contracts with another person to do so, the county shall provide a hearing procedure for the owner. For purposes of this subsection, the definitions in G.S. 20-219.9 apply.

(1) If the county operates in such a way that the person who tows the vehicle is responsible for collecting towing fees, all provisions of Article 7A, Chapter 20, apply.

(2) If the county operates in such a way that it is responsible for collecting towing fees, it shall:

a. Provide by contract or ordinance for a schedule of reasonable towing fees,

b. Provide a procedure for a prompt fair hearing to contest the towing,

c. Provide for an appeal to district court from that hearing,

d. Authorize release of the vehicle at any time after towing by the posting of a bond or paying of the fees due, and

e. Provide a sale procedure similar to that provided in G.S. 44A-4, 44A-5, and 44A-6, except that no hearing in addition to the probable cause hearing is required. If no one purchases the vehicle at the sale and if the value of the vehicle is less than the amount of the lien, the county may destroy it.

(e) and (f) Repealed by Session Laws 1983, c. 420, s. 10.

(g) No Liability. - No person nor any county may be held to answer in a civil or criminal action to any owner or other person legally entitled to the possession of an abandoned, junked, lost, or stolen motor vehicle for disposing of the vehicle as provided in this section.

(h) Exceptions. - This section does not apply to any vehicle in an enclosed building, to any vehicle on the premises of a business enterprise being operated in a lawful place and manner if the vehicle is necessary to the operation of the enterprise, or to any vehicle in an appropriate storage place or depository maintained in a lawful place and manner by the county. (1971, c. 489; 1973, c. 822, s. 1; 1975, c. 716, s. 5; 1983, c. 420, ss. 8-10; 1997-456, s. 27.)

§ 153A-132.1. To provide for the removal and disposal of trash, garbage, etc.

The board of county commissioners of any county is hereby authorized to enact ordinances governing the removal, method or manner of disposal, depositing or dumping of any trash, debris, garbage, litter, discarded cans or receptacles or any waste matter whatsoever within the rural areas of the county and outside and beyond the corporate limits of any municipality of said county. An ordinance adopted pursuant hereto may make it unlawful to place, discard, dispose, leave or dump any trash, debris, garbage, litter, discarded cans or receptacles or any waste matter whatsoever upon a street or highway located within that county or upon property owned or operated by the county unless such trash, debris, garbage, litter, discarded cans or receptacles or any waste matter is placed in a designated location or container for removal by a specific garbage or trash service collector.

Boards of county commissioners may also provide by ordinance enacted pursuant to this section, that the placing, discarding, disposing, leaving or dumping of the articles forbidden by this section shall, for each day or portion thereof the articles or matter are left, constitute a separate offense, and that a person in violation of the ordinance may be punished by a fine not exceeding fifty dollars ($50.00) or imprisoned not exceeding 30 days, or both, for each offense. (1973, c. 952.)

§ 153A-132.2. Regulation, restraint and prohibition of abandonment of junked motor vehicles.

(a) A county may by ordinance regulate, restrain or prohibit the abandonment of junked motor vehicles on public grounds and on private property within the county's ordinance-making jurisdiction upon a finding that such regulation, restraint or prohibition is necessary and desirable to promote or enhance community, neighborhood or area appearance, and may enforce any such ordinance by removing and disposing of junked motor vehicles subject to the ordinance according to the procedures prescribed in this section. The authority granted by this section shall be supplemental to any other authority conferred upon counties. Nothing in this section shall be construed to authorize a county to require the removal or disposal of a motor vehicle kept or stored at a bona fide "automobile graveyard" or "junkyard" as defined in G.S. 136-143.

For purposes of this section, the term "junked motor vehicle" means a vehicle that does not display a current license plate and that:

(1)   Is partially dismantled or wrecked; or

(2)   Cannot be self-propelled or moved in the manner in which it originally was intended to move; or

(3)   Is more than five years old and appears to be worth less than one hundred dollars ($100.00).

(a1) Any junked motor vehicle found to be in violation of an ordinance adopted pursuant to this section may be removed to a storage garage or area, but no such vehicle shall be removed from private property without the written request of the owner, lessee, or occupant of the premises unless the board of commissioners or a duly authorized county official or employee finds in writing that the aesthetic benefits of removing the vehicle outweigh the burdens imposed on the private property owner. Such finding shall be based on a balancing of the monetary loss of the apparent owner against the corresponding gain to the public by promoting or enhancing community, neighborhood or area appearance. The following, among other relevant factors, may be considered:

(1)   Protection of property values;

(2)   Promotion of tourism and other economic development opportunities;

(3)   Indirect protection of public health and safety;

(4)   Preservation of the character and integrity of the community; and

(5)   Promotion of the comfort, happiness, and emotional stability of area residents.

(a2) The county may require any person requesting the removal of a junked or abandoned motor vehicle from private property to indemnify the county against any loss, expense, or liability incurred because of the removal, storage, or sale thereof. When an abandoned or junked motor vehicle is removed, the county shall give notice to the owner as required by G.S. 20-219.11(a) and (b).

(a3) Hearing Procedure. - Regardless of whether a county does its own removal and disposal of motor vehicles or contracts with another person to do so, the county shall provide a prior hearing procedure for the owner. For purposes of this subsection, the definitions in G.S. 20-219.9 apply.

(1) If the county operates in such a way that the person who tows the vehicle is responsible for collecting towing fees, all provisions of Article 7A, Chapter 20, apply.

(2) If the county operates in such a way that it is responsible for collecting towing fees, it shall:

a. Provide by contract or ordinance for a schedule of reasonable towing fees,

b. Provide a procedure for a prompt fair hearing to contest the towing,

c. Provide for an appeal to district court from that hearing,

d. Authorize release of the vehicle at any time after towing by the posting of a bond or paying of the fees due, and

e. Provide a sale procedure similar to that provided in G.S. 44A-4, 44A-5, and 44A-6, except that no hearing in addition to the probable cause hearing is required. If no one purchases the vehicle at the sale and if the value of the vehicle is less than the amount of the lien, the city may destroy it.

(a4) Any person who removes a vehicle pursuant to this section shall not be held liable for damages for the removal of the vehicle to the owner, lienholder or other person legally entitled to the possession of the vehicle removed; however, any person who intentionally or negligently damages a vehicle in the removal of such vehicle, or intentionally or negligently inflicts injury upon any person in the removal of such vehicle, may be held liable for damages.

(b) Any ordinance adopted pursuant to this section shall include a prohibition against removing or disposing of any motor vehicle that is used on a regular basis for business or personal use. (1983, c. 841, s. 1; 1985, c. 737, s. 1; 1987, c. 42, s. 1, c. 451, s. 1; 1987 (Reg. Sess., 1988), c. 902, s. 1; 1989, c. 743, s. 1.)

§ 153A-133. Noise regulation.

A county may by ordinance regulate, restrict, or prohibit the production or emission of noises or amplified speech, music, or other sounds that tend to annoy, disturb, or frighten its citizens. (1973, c. 822, s. 1.)

§ 153A-134. Regulating and licensing businesses, trades, etc.

(a)   A county may by ordinance, subject to the general law of the State, regulate and license occupations, businesses, trades, professions, and forms of amusement or entertainment and prohibit those that may be inimical to the public health, welfare, safety, order, or convenience. In licensing trades, occupations, and professions, the county may, consistent with the general law of the State, require applicants for licenses to be examined and charge a reasonable fee therefor. This section does not authorize a county to examine or license a person holding a license issued by an occupational licensing board of this State as to the profession or trade that he has been licensed to practice or pursue by the State.

(b)   This section does not impair the county's power to levy privilege license taxes on occupations, businesses, trades, professions, and other activities pursuant to G.S. 153A-152.

(c)   Nothing in this section shall authorize a county to regulate and license digital dispatching services for prearranged transportation services for hire. (1868, c. 20, s. 8; Code, s. 707; Rev., s. 1318; C.S., s. 1297; 1973, c. 822, s. 1; 2013-413, s. 12.1(c).)

§ 153A-135. Regulation of places of amusement.

A county may by ordinance regulate places of amusement and entertainment, and may regulate, restrict, or prohibit the operation of pool and billiard halls, dance halls, carnivals, circuses, or itinerant shows or exhibitions of any kind. Places of amusement and entertainment include coffeehouses, cocktail lounges, nightclubs, beer halls, and similar establishments, but any regulation of such places shall be consistent with any permit or license issued by the North Carolina Alcoholic Beverage Control Commission. (1963, c. 1060, ss. 1, 1 1/2; 1965, cc. 388, 567, 1083, 1158; 1967, c. 495, s. 2; 1969, c. 36, s. 1; 1971, c. 702, ss. 1-3; 1973, c. 822, s. 1; 1981, c. 412, ss. 4, 5.)

§ 153A-136. Regulation of solid wastes.

(a)   A county may by ordinance regulate the storage, collection, transportation, use, disposal, and other disposition of solid wastes. Such an ordinance may:

(1)   Regulate the activities of persons, firms, and corporations, both public and private.

(2)   Require each person wishing to commercially collect or dispose of solid wastes to secure a license from the county and prohibit any person from commercially collecting or disposing of solid wastes without a license. A fee may be charged for a license.

(3)   Grant a franchise to one or more persons for the exclusive right to commercially collect or dispose of solid wastes within all or a defined portion of the county and prohibit any other person from commercially collecting or disposing of solid wastes in that area. The board of commissioners may set the terms of any franchise, except that no franchise may be granted for a period exceeding 30 years, nor may any franchise by its terms impair the authority of the board of commissioners to regulate fees as authorized by this section.

(4)   Regulate the fees, if any, that may be charged by licensed or franchised persons for collecting or disposing of solid wastes.

(5)   Require the source separation of materials prior to collection of solid waste for disposal.

(6) Require participation in a recycling program by requiring separation of designated materials by the owner or occupant of the property prior to disposal. An owner of recovered materials as defined by G.S. 130A-290(a)(24) retains ownership of the recovered materials until the owner conveys, sells, donates, or otherwise transfers the recovered materials to a person, firm, company, corporation, or unit of local government. A county may not require an owner to convey, sell, donate, or otherwise transfer recovered materials to the county or its designee. If an owner places recovered materials in receptacles or delivers recovered materials to specific locations, receptacles, and facilities that are owned or operated by the county or its designee, then ownership of these materials is transferred to the county or its designee.

(6a) Regulate the illegal disposal of solid waste, including littering on public and private property, provide for enforcement by civil penalties as well as other remedies, and provide that such regulations may be enforced by county employees specially appointed as environmental enforcement officers.

(7) Include any other proper matter.

(b) Any ordinance adopted pursuant to this section shall be consistent with and supplementary to any rules adopted by the Commission for Public Health or the Department of Environment and Natural Resources.

(c) The board of commissioners of a county shall consider alternative sites and socioeconomic and demographic data and shall hold a public hearing prior to selecting or approving a site for a new sanitary landfill that receives residential solid waste that is located within one mile of an existing sanitary landfill within the State. The distance between an existing and a proposed site shall be determined by measurement between the closest points on the outer boundary of each site. The definitions set out in G.S. 130A-290 apply to this subsection. As used in this subsection:

(1) "Approving a site" refers to prior approval of a site under G.S. 130A-294(a)(4).

(2) "Existing sanitary landfill" means a sanitary landfill that is in operation or that has been in operation within the five-year period immediately prior to the date on which an application for a permit is submitted.

(3) "New sanitary landfill" means a sanitary landfill that includes areas not within the legal description of an existing sanitary landfill as set out in the permit for the existing sanitary landfill.

(4) "Socioeconomic and demographic data" means the most recent socioeconomic and demographic data compiled by the United States Bureau of the Census and any additional socioeconomic and demographic data submitted at the public hearing.

(d) As used in this section, "solid waste" means nonhazardous solid waste, that is, solid waste as defined in G.S. 130A-290 but not including hazardous waste.

(e) A county that has planning jurisdiction over any portion of the site of a sanitary landfill may employ a local government landfill liaison. No person who is responsible for any aspect of the management or operation of the landfill may serve as a local government landfill liaison. A local government landfill liaison shall have a right to enter public or private lands on which the landfill facility is located at reasonable times to inspect the landfill operation in order to:

(1) Ensure that the facility meets all local requirements.

(2) Identify and notify the Department of suspected violations of applicable federal or State laws, regulations, or rules.

(3) Identify and notify the Department of potentially hazardous conditions at the facility.

(f) Entry pursuant to subsection (e) of this section shall not constitute a trespass or taking of property. (1955, c. 1050; 1957, cc. 120, 376; 1961, c. 40; c. 514, s. 1; cc. 711, 803; c. 806, s. 1; 1965, c. 452; 1967, cc. 34, 90; c. 183, s. 1; cc. 304, 339; c. 495, s. 4; 1969, cc. 79, 155, 176; c. 234, s. 1; c. 452; c. 1003, s. 4; 1973, c. 476, s. 128; c. 822, s. 1; 1989 (Reg. Sess., 1990), c. 1009, s. 1; 1991 (Reg. Sess., 1992), c. 1013, s. 1; 1993, c. 165, s. 1; 1997-443, s. 11A.123; 2001-512, s. 5; 2007-182, s. 2; 2007-550, s. 11(a).)

§ 153A-137: Repealed by Session Laws 2006-151, s. 10, effective January 1, 2007.

§ 153A-138. Registration of mobile homes, house trailers, etc.

A county may by ordinance provide for the annual registration of mobile homes, house trailers and similar vehicular equipment designed for use as living or business quarters and for the display of a sticker or other device thereon as evidence of such registration. No fee shall be charged for such registration. (1975, c. 693.)

§ 153A-139. Regulation of traffic at parking areas and driveways.

The governing body of any county may, by ordinance, regulate the stopping, standing, or parking of vehicles in specified areas of any parking areas or driveways of a hospital, shopping center, apartment house, condominium complex, or commercial office complex or any other privately owned public vehicular area, or prohibit such stopping, standing, or parking during any specified hours, provided the owner or person in general charge of the operation and control of that area requests in writing that such an ordinance be adopted. The owner of a vehicle parked in violation of an ordinance adopted pursuant to this subsection shall be deemed to have appointed any appropriate law-enforcement officer as his agent for the purpose of arranging for the transportation and safe storage of such vehicle. (1979, c. 745, s. 1.)

§ 153A-140. Abatement of public health nuisances.

A county shall have authority, subject to the provisions of Article 57 of Chapter 106 of the General Statutes, to remove, abate, or remedy everything that is dangerous or prejudicial to the public health or safety. Pursuant to this section, a board of commissioners may order the removal of a swimming pool and its appurtenances upon a finding that the swimming pool or its appurtenances is dangerous or prejudicial to public health or safety. The expense of the action shall be paid by the person in default, and, if not paid, shall be a lien upon the land or premises where the nuisance arose, and shall be collected as unpaid taxes. The authority granted by this section may only be exercised upon adequate notice, the right to a hearing, and the right to appeal to the General Court of Justice. Nothing in this section shall be deemed to restrict or repeal the authority of any municipality to abate or remedy health nuisances pursuant to G.S. 160A-174, 160A-193, or any other general or local law. This section shall not affect bona fide farms, but any use of farm property for nonfarm purposes is subject to this section. (1981 (Reg. Sess., 1982), c. 1314, s. 1; 2002-116, s. 2.)

§ 153A-140.1. Stream-clearing programs.

(a)   A county shall have the authority to remove natural and man-made obstructions in stream channels and in the floodway of streams that may impede the passage of water during rain events.

(b)   The actions of a county to clear obstructions from a stream shall not create or increase the responsibility of the county for the clearing or maintenance of the stream, or for flooding of the stream. In addition, actions by a county to clear obstructions from a stream shall not create in the county any ownership in the stream, obligation to control the stream, or affect any otherwise existing private property right, responsibility, or entitlement regarding the stream. These provisions shall not relieve a county for negligence that might be found under otherwise applicable law.

(c)   Nothing in this section shall be construed to affect existing rights of the State to control or regulate streams or activities within streams. In implementing a stream-clearing program, the county shall comply with all requirements in State or federal statutes and rules. (2005-441, s. 1.)

§ 153A-140.2. Annual notice to chronic violators of public nuisance ordinance.

A county may notify a chronic violator of the county's public nuisance ordinance that, if the violator's property is found to be in violation of the ordinance, the county shall, without further notice in the calendar year in which notice is given, take action to remedy the violation, and the expense of the action shall become a lien upon the property and shall be collected as unpaid taxes. The notice shall be sent by certified mail. A chronic violator is a person who owns property whereupon, in the previous calendar year, the county gave notice of violation at least three times under any provision of the public nuisance ordinance. (2009-287, s. 2.)

§ 153A-141: Repealed by Session Laws 1995, c. 501. s. 3.

§ 153A-142. Curfews.

A county may by an appropriate ordinance impose a curfew on persons of any age less than 18. (1997-189, s. 2.)

§ 153A-143. Regulation of outdoor advertising.

(a)   As used in this section, the term "off-premises outdoor advertising" includes off-premises outdoor advertising visible from the main-traveled way of any road.

(b)   A county may require the removal of an off-premises outdoor advertising sign that is nonconforming under a local ordinance and may regulate the use of off-premises outdoor advertising within the jurisdiction of the county in accordance with the applicable provisions of this Chapter.

(c)   A county shall give written notice of its intent to require removal of off-premises outdoor advertising by sending a letter by certified mail to the last known address of the owner of the outdoor advertising and the owner of the property on which the outdoor advertising is located.

(d)   No county may enact or amend an ordinance of general applicability to require the removal of any nonconforming, lawfully erected off-premises outdoor advertising sign without the payment of monetary compensation to the owners of the off-premises outdoor advertising, except as provided below. The payment of monetary compensation is not required if:

(1)   The county and the owner of the nonconforming off-premises outdoor advertising enter into a relocation agreement pursuant to subsection (g) of this section.

(2)   The county and the owner of the nonconforming off-premises outdoor advertising enter into an agreement pursuant to subsection (k) of this section.

(3)   The off-premises outdoor advertising is determined to be a public nuisance or detrimental to the health or safety of the populace.

(4) The removal is required for establishing, extending, enlarging, or improving any of the public enterprises listed in G.S. 153A-274, and the county allows the off-premises outdoor advertising to be relocated to a comparable location.

(5) The off-premises outdoor advertising is subject to removal pursuant to statutes, ordinances or regulations generally applicable to the demolition or removal of damaged structures.

(e) Monetary compensation is the fair market value of the off-premises outdoor advertising in place immediately prior to its removal and without consideration of the effect of the ordinance or any diminution in value caused by the ordinance requiring its removal. Monetary compensation shall be determined based on:

(1) The factors listed in G.S. 105-317.1(a); and

(2) The listed property tax value of the property and any documents regarding value submitted to the taxing authority.

(f) If the parties are unable to reach an agreement on monetary compensation to be paid by the county to the owner of the nonconforming off-premises outdoor advertising sign for its removal, and the county elects to proceed with the removal, the county may bring an action in superior court for a determination of the monetary compensation to be paid. In determining monetary compensation, the court shall consider the factors set forth in subsection (e) of this section. Upon payment of monetary compensation for the sign, the county shall own the sign.

(g) In lieu of paying monetary compensation, a county may enter into an agreement with the owner of a nonconforming off-premises outdoor advertising sign to relocate and reconstruct the sign. The agreement shall include the following:

(1) Provision for relocation of the sign to a site reasonably comparable to or better than the existing location. In determining whether a location is comparable or better, the following factors shall be taken into consideration:

a. The size and format of the sign.

b. The characteristics of the proposed relocation site, including visibility, traffic count, area demographics, zoning, and any uncompensated differential in the sign owner's cost to lease the replacement site.

c. The timing of the relocation.

(2) Provision for payment by the county of the reasonable costs of relocating and reconstructing the sign including:

a. The actual cost of removing the sign.

b. The actual cost of any necessary repairs to the real property for damages caused in the removal of the sign.

c. The actual cost of installing the sign at the new location.

d. An amount of money equivalent to the income received from the lease of the sign for a period of up to 30 days if income is lost during the relocation of the sign.

(h) For the purposes of relocating and reconstructing a nonconforming off-premises outdoor advertising sign pursuant to subsection (g) of this section, a county, consistent with the welfare and safety of the community as a whole, may adopt a resolution or adopt or modify its ordinances to provide for the issuance of a permit or other approval, including conditions as appropriate, or to provide for dimensional, spacing, setback, or use variances as it deems appropriate.

(i) If a county has offered to enter into an agreement to relocate a nonconforming off-premises outdoor advertising sign pursuant to subsection (g) of this section, and within 120 days after the initial notice by the county the parties have not been able to agree that the site or sites offered by the county for relocation of the sign are reasonably comparable or better than the existing site, the parties shall enter into binding arbitration to resolve their disagreements. Unless a different method of arbitration is agreed upon by the parties, the arbitration shall be conducted by a panel of three arbitrators. Each party shall select one arbitrator and the two arbitrators chosen by the parties shall select the third member of the panel. The American Arbitration Association rules shall apply to the arbitration unless the parties agree otherwise.

(j) If the arbitration results in a determination that the site or sites offered by the county for relocation of the nonconforming sign are not reasonably comparable to or better than the existing site, and the county elects to proceed with the removal of the sign, the parties shall determine the monetary compensation under subsection (e) of this section to be paid to the owner of the sign. If the parties are unable to reach an agreement regarding monetary compensation within 30 days of the receipt of the arbitrators' determination, and the county elects to proceed with the removal of the sign, then the county may bring an action in superior court for a determination of the monetary compensation to be paid by the county to the owner for the removal of the sign. In determining monetary compensation, the court shall consider the factors set forth in subsection (e) of this section. Upon payment of monetary compensation for the sign, the county shall own the sign.

(k)   Notwithstanding the provisions of this section, a county and an off-premises outdoor advertising sign owner may enter into a voluntary agreement allowing for the removal of the sign after a set period of time in lieu of monetary compensation. A county may adopt an ordinance or resolution providing for a relocation, reconstruction, or removal agreement.

(l)   A county has up to three years from the effective date of an ordinance enacted under this section to pay monetary compensation to the owner of the off-premises outdoor advertising provided the affected property remains in place until the compensation is paid.

(m)   This section does not apply to any ordinance in effect on the effective date of this section. A county may repeal or amend an ordinance in effect on the effective date of this section so long as an amendment to the existing ordinance does not reduce the period of amortization in effect on the effective date of this section.

(n)   The provisions of this section shall not be used to interpret, construe, alter, or otherwise modify the exercise of the power of eminent domain by an entity pursuant to Chapter 40A or Chapter 136 of the General Statutes.

(o)   Nothing in this section shall limit a county's authority to use amortization as a means of phasing out nonconforming uses other than off-premises outdoor advertising. (2004-152, s. 1.)

§ 153A-144. Limitations on regulating solar collectors.

(a) Except as provided in subsection (c) of this section, no county ordinance shall prohibit, or have the effect of prohibiting, the installation of a solar collector that gathers solar radiation as a substitute for traditional energy for water heating, active space heating and cooling, passive heating, or generating electricity for a residential property. No person shall be denied permission by a county to install a solar collector that gathers solar radiation as a substitute for traditional energy for water heating, active space heating and cooling, passive heating, or generating electricity for a residential property. As used in this section, the term "residential property" means property where the predominant use is for residential purposes.

(b) This section does not prohibit an ordinance regulating the location or screening of solar collectors as described in subsection (a) of this section, provided the ordinance does not have the effect of preventing the reasonable use of a solar collector for a residential property.

(c) This section does not prohibit an ordinance that would prohibit the location of solar collectors as described in subsection (a) of this section that are visible by a person on the ground:

(1) On the facade of a structure that faces areas open to common or public access;

(2) On a roof surface that slopes downward toward the same areas open to common or public access that the facade of the structure faces; or

(3) Within the area set off by a line running across the facade of the structure extending to the property boundaries on either side of the facade, and those areas of common or public access faced by the structure.

(d) In any civil action arising under this section, the court may award costs and reasonable attorneys' fees to the prevailing party. (2007-279, s. 2; 2009-553, s. 2.)

§ 153A-145. Limitations on regulating cisterns and rain barrels.

No county ordinance may prohibit or have the effect of prohibiting the installation and maintenance of cisterns and rain barrel collection systems used to collect water for irrigation purposes. A county may regulate the installation and maintenance of those cisterns and rain barrel collection systems for the purpose of protecting the public health and safety and for the purpose of preventing them from becoming a public nuisance. (2011-394, s. 12(d).)

§ 153A-145.1. Transportation impact mitigation ordinances prohibited.

No county may enact or enforce an ordinance, rule, or regulation that requires an employer to assume financial, legal, or other responsibility for the mitigation of the impact of his or her employees' commute or transportation to or from the employer's workplace, which may result in the employer being subject to a fine, fee, or other monetary, legal, or negative consequences. (2013-413, s. 10.1(b).)

§ 153A-145.2. Limitations on regulating soft drink sizes.

No county ordinance may prohibit the sale of soft drinks above a particular size. This section does not prohibit any ordinance regulating the sanitation or other operational aspect of a device for the dispensing of soft drinks. For purposes of this section, "soft drink" shall have the meaning set forth in G.S. 105-164.3. (2013-309, s. 3.)

Article 7.

Taxation.

§ 153A-146. (Effective until July 1, 2015 - see notes) General power to impose taxes.

A county may impose taxes only as specifically authorized by act of the General Assembly. Except when the statute authorizing a tax provides for penalties and interest, the power to impose a tax includes the power to impose reasonable penalties for failure to declare tax liability, if required, and to impose penalties or interest for failure to pay taxes lawfully due within the time prescribed by law or ordinance. In determining the liability of any taxpayer for a tax, a county may not employ an agent who is compensated in whole or in part by the county for services rendered on a contingent basis or any other basis related to the amount of tax, interest, or penalty assessed against or collected from the taxpayer. The power to impose a tax also includes the power to provide for its administration in a manner not inconsistent with the statute authorizing the tax. (1868, c. 20, s. 8; Code, s. 707; Rev., s. 1318; C.S., s. 1297; 1973, c. 822, s. 1; 2012-152, s. 4; 2012-194, s. 61.5(b).)

§ 153A-146. (Effective July 1, 2015 - see notes) General power to impose taxes.

A county may impose taxes only as specifically authorized by act of the General Assembly. Except when the statute authorizing a tax provides for penalties and interest, the power to impose a tax includes the power to impose reasonable penalties for failure to declare tax liability, if required, and to impose penalties or interest for failure to pay taxes lawfully due within the time prescribed by law or ordinance. The power to impose a tax also includes the power to provide for its administration in a manner not inconsistent with the statute authorizing the tax. (1868, c. 20, s. 8; Code, s. 707; Rev., s. 1318; C.S., s. 1297; 1973, c. 822, s. 1; 2012-152, s. 4; 2012-194, s. 61.5(b).)

§ 153A-147. Remedies for collecting taxes other than property taxes.

In addition to any other remedies provided by law, a county may collect any county tax by use of the remedies of levy and sale and attachment and garnishment, under the rules and according to the procedures prescribed by the Machinery Act (Chapter 105, Subchapter II) for the enforcement of tax liability against personal property. However, these remedies become available only on the due date of the tax and not before that time. (1973, c. 822, s. 1.)

§ 153A-148. Continuing taxes.

Except for taxes levied on property under the Machinery Act (Chapter 105, Subchapter II), a county may impose any authorized tax by a permanent ordinance that shall stand from year to year until amended or repealed, and it is not necessary to reimpose the tax in each annual budget ordinance. (1973, c. 822, s. 1.)

§ 153A-148.1. Disclosure of certain information prohibited.

(a) Disclosure Prohibited. - Notwithstanding Chapter 132 of the General Statutes or any other law regarding access to public records, local tax records that contain information about a taxpayer's income or receipts are not public records. A current or former officer, employee, or agent of a county who in the course of service to or employment by the county has access to information about the amount of a taxpayer's income or receipts may not disclose the information to any other person unless the disclosure is made for one of the following purposes:

(1) To comply with a court order or a law.

(2) Review by the Attorney General or a representative of the Attorney General.

(3) To sort, process, or deliver tax information on behalf of the county, as necessary to administer a tax.

(4) To exchange information with a regional public transportation authority or a regional transportation authority created pursuant to Article 26 or Article 27 of Chapter 160A of the General Statutes, when the information is needed to fulfill a duty imposed on the authority or on the county.

(5) To exchange information with the Department of Revenue, when the information is needed to fulfill a duty imposed on the Department or on the county.

(6) To include on a property tax receipt the amount of property taxes due and the amount of property taxes deferred on a residence classified under G.S. 105-277.1B, the property tax homestead circuit breaker.

(b) Punishment. - A person who violates this section is guilty of a Class 1 misdemeanor. If the person committing the violation is an officer or employee, that person shall be dismissed from public office or public employment and may not hold any public office or public employment in this State for five years after the violation. (1993, c. 485, s. 33; 1994, Ex. Sess., c. 14, s. 66; 1998-139, s. 2; 2008-35, s. 1.4.)

§ 153A-149. Property taxes; authorized purposes; rate limitation.

(a)   Pursuant to Article V, Sec. 2(5) of the Constitution of North Carolina, the General Assembly confers upon each county in this State the power to levy, within the limitations set out in this section, taxes on property having a situs within the county under the rules and according to the procedures prescribed in the Machinery Act (Chapter 105, Subchapter II).

(b)   Each county may levy property taxes without restriction as to rate or amount for the following purposes:

(1)   Courts. - To provide adequate facilities for and the county's share of the cost of operating the General Court of Justice in the county.

(2)   Debt Service. - To pay the principal of and interest on all general obligation bonds and notes of the county.

(3)   Deficits. - To supply an unforeseen deficiency in the revenue (other than revenues of public enterprises), when revenues actually collected or received fall below revenue estimates made in good faith and in accordance with the Local Government Budget and Fiscal Control Act.

(4)   Elections. - To provide for all federal, State, district and county elections.

(5)   Jails. - To provide for the operation of a jail and other local confinement facilities.

(6)   Joint Undertakings. - To cooperate with any other county, city, or political subdivision in providing any of the functions, services, or activities listed in this subsection.

(7)   Schools. - To provide for the county's share of the cost of kindergarten, elementary, secondary, and post-secondary public education.

(8)   Social Services. - To provide for public assistance required by Chapters 108A and 111 of the General Statutes.

(c)   Each county may levy property taxes for one or more of the purposes listed in this subsection up to a combined rate of one dollar and fifty cents ($1.50) on the one hundred dollars ($100.00) appraised value of property subject to taxation. Authorized purposes subject to the rate limitation are:

(1) To provide for the general administration of the county through the board of county commissioners, the office of the county manager, the office of the county budget officer, the office of the county finance officer, the office of the county assessor, the office of the county tax collector, the county purchasing agent, and the county attorney, and for all other general administrative costs not allocated to a particular board, commission, office, agency, or activity of the county.

(2) Agricultural Extension. - To provide for the county's share of the cost of maintaining and administering programs and services offered to agriculture by or through the Agricultural Extension Service or other agencies.

(3) Air Pollution. - To maintain and administer air pollution control programs.

(4) Airports. - To establish and maintain airports and related aeronautical facilities.

(5) Ambulance Service. - To provide ambulance services, rescue squads, and other emergency medical services.

(6) Animal Protection and Control. - To provide animal protection and control programs.

(6a) Arts Programs and Museums. - To provide for arts programs and museums as authorized in G.S. 160A-488.

(6b) Auditoriums, coliseums, and convention and civic centers. - To provide public auditoriums, coliseums, and convention and civic centers.

(7) Beach Erosion and Natural Disasters. - To provide for shoreline protection, beach erosion control, and flood and hurricane protection.

(8) Cemeteries. - To provide for cemeteries.

(9) Civil Preparedness. - To provide for civil preparedness programs.

(10) Debts and Judgments. - To pay and discharge any valid debt of the county or any judgment lodged against it, other than debts and judgments evidenced by or based on bonds and notes.

(10a)   Defense of Employees and Officers. - To provide for the defense of, and payment of civil judgments against, employees and officers or former employees and officers, as authorized by this Chapter.

(10b)   (Effective until June 30, 2014) Economic Development. - To provide for economic development as authorized by G.S. 158-7.1 and G.S. 158-12.

(10b)   (Effective June 30, 2014) Economic Development. - To provide for economic development as authorized by G.S. 158-7.1.

(10c)   Energy Financing. - To provide financing for renewable energy and energy efficiency in accordance with a program established under G.S. 153A-455.

(11)   Fire Protection. - To provide fire protection services and fire prevention programs.

(12)   Forest Protection. - To provide forest management and protection programs.

(13)   Health. - To provide for the county's share of maintaining and administering services offered by or through the local health department.

(14)   Historic Preservation. - To undertake historic preservation programs and projects.

(15)   Hospitals. - To establish, support and maintain public hospitals and clinics, and other related health programs and facilities, or to aid any private, nonprofit hospital, clinic, related facility, or other health program or facility.

(15a)   Housing Rehabilitation. - To provide for housing rehabilitation programs authorized by G.S. 153A-376, including personnel costs related to the planning and administration of these programs. This subdivision applies only to counties with a population of 400,000 or more, according to the most recent decennial federal census.

(15b)   Housing. - To undertake housing programs for low- and moderate-income persons as provided in G.S. 153A-378.

(16)   Human Relations. - To undertake human relations programs.

(16a) Industrial Development. - To provide for industrial development as authorized by G.S. 158-7.1.

(17) Joint Undertakings. - To cooperate with any other county, city, or political subdivision in providing any of the functions, services, or activities listed in this subsection.

(18) Law Enforcement. - To provide for the operation of the office of the sheriff of the county and for any other county law-enforcement agency not under the sheriff's jurisdiction.

(19) Libraries. - To establish and maintain public libraries.

(20) Mapping. - To provide for mapping the lands of the county.

(21) Medical Examiner. - To provide for the county medical examiner or coroner.

(22) Mental Health. - To provide for the county's share of the cost of maintaining and administering services offered by or through the area mental health, developmental disabilities, and substance abuse authority.

(23) Open Space. - To acquire open space land and easements in accordance with Article 19, Part 4, Chapter 160A of the General Statutes.

(24) Parking. - To provide off-street lots and garages for the parking and storage of motor vehicles.

(25) Parks and Recreation. - To establish, support and maintain public parks and programs of supervised recreation.

(26) Planning. - To provide for a program of planning and regulation of development in accordance with Article 18 of this Chapter and Article 19, Parts 3A and 6, of Chapter 160A of the General Statutes.

(26a) Ports and Harbors. - To participate in programs with the North Carolina Ports Authority and provide for harbor masters.

(27) Public Transportation. - To provide public transportation by rail, motor vehicle, or another means of conveyance other than a ferry, including any facility or equipment needed to provide the public transportation. This

subdivision does not authorize a county to provide public roads in the county in violation of G.S. 136-51.

(27a) Railway Corridor Preservation. - To acquire property for railroad corridor preservation as authorized by G.S. 160A-498.

(28) Register of Deeds. - To provide for the operation of the office of the register of deeds of the county.

(28a) Roads. - To provide for the maintenance of county roads as authorized by G.S. 153A-301(d).

(29) Sewage. - To provide sewage collection and treatment services as defined in G.S. 153A-274(2).

(30) Social Services. - To provide for the public welfare through the maintenance and administration of public assistance programs not required by Chapters 108A and 111 of the General Statutes, and by establishing and maintaining a county home.

(31) Solid Waste. - To provide solid waste collection and disposal services, and to acquire and operate landfills.

(31a) Stormwater. - To provide structural and natural stormwater and drainage systems of all types.

(32) Surveyor. - To provide for a county surveyor.

(33) Veterans' Service Officer. - To provide for the county's share of the cost of services offered by or through the county veterans' service officer.

(34) Water. - To provide water supply and distribution systems.

(35) Watershed Improvement. - To undertake watershed improvement projects.

(36) Water Resources. - To participate in federal water resources development projects.

(37) Armories. - To supplement available State or federal funds to be used for the construction (including the acquisition of land), enlargement or repair of armory facilities for the North Carolina National Guard.

(d) With an approving vote of the people, any county may levy property taxes for any purpose for which the county is authorized by law to appropriate money. Any property tax levy approved by a vote of the people shall not be counted for purposes of the rate limitation imposed in subsection (c).

The county commissioners may call a referendum on approval of a property tax levy. The referendum may be held at the same time as any other referendum or election, but may not be otherwise held within the period of time beginning 30 days before and ending 10 days after any other referendum or election to be held in the county and already validly called or scheduled by law at the time the tax referendum is called. The referendum shall be conducted by the county board of elections. The clerk to the board of commissioners shall publish a notice of the referendum at least twice. The first publication shall be not less than 14 days and the second publication not less than seven days before the last day on which voters may register for the referendum. The notice shall state the date of the referendum, the purpose for which it is being held, and a statement as to the last day for registration for the referendum under the election laws then in effect.

The proposition submitted to the voters shall be substantially in one of the following forms:

(1) Shall ____ County be authorized to levy annually a property tax at a rate not in excess of ____ cents on the one hundred dollars ($100.00) value of property subject to taxation for the purpose of ____?

(2) Shall ____ County be authorized to levy annually a property tax at a rate not in excess of that which will produce $____ for the purpose of ____?

(3) Shall ____ County be authorized to levy annually a property tax without restriction as to rate or amount for the purpose of ____?

If a majority of those participating in the referendum approve the proposition, the board of commissioners may proceed to levy annually a property tax within the limitations (if any) described in the proposition.

The board of elections shall canvass the referendum and certify the results to the board of commissioners. The board of commissioners shall then certify and declare the result of the referendum and shall publish a statement of the result once, with the following statement appended: "Any action or proceeding challenging the regularity or validity of this tax referendum must be begun within 30 days after (date of publication)." The statement of results shall be filed in the clerk's office and inserted in the minutes of the board.

Any action or proceeding in any court challenging the regularity or validity of a tax referendum must be begun within 30 days after the publication of the results of the referendum. After the expiration of this period of limitation, no right of action or defense based upon the invalidity of or any irregularity in the referendum shall be asserted, nor shall the validity of the referendum be open to question in any court upon any ground whatever, except in an action or proceeding begun within the period of limitation prescribed herein.

Except for supplemental school taxes and except for tax referendums on functions not included in subsection (c) of this section, any referendum held before July 1, 1973, on the levy of property taxes is not valid for the purposes of this subsection. Counties in which such referendums have been held may support programs formerly supported by voted property taxes within the general rate limitation set out in subsection (c) at any appropriate level and are not subject to the former voted rate limitation.

(e)   With an approving vote of the people, any county may increase the property tax rate limitation imposed in subsection (c) and may call a referendum for that purpose. The referendum may be held at the same time as any other referendum or election, but may not be otherwise held within the period of time beginning 30 days before and ending 30 days after any other referendum or election. The referendum shall be conducted by the county board of elections.

The proposition submitted to the voters shall be substantially in the following form: "Shall the property tax rate limitation applicable to ____ County be increased from ____ on the one hundred dollars ($100.00) value of property subject to taxation to ____ on the one hundred dollars ($100.00) value of property subject to taxation?"

If a majority of those participating in the referendum approve the proposition, the rate limitation imposed in subsection (c) shall be increased for the county.

(f) With respect to any of the categories listed in subsections (b) and (c) of this section, the county may provide the necessary personnel, land, buildings, equipment, supplies, and financial support from property tax revenues for the program, function, or service.

(g) This section does not authorize any county to undertake any program, function, joint undertaking, or service not otherwise authorized by law. It is intended only to authorize the levy of property taxes within the limitations set out herein to finance programs, functions, or services authorized by other portions of the General Statutes or by local acts. (1973, c. 803, s. 1; c. 822, s. 2; c. 963; c. 1446, s. 25; 1975, c. 734, s. 17; 1977, c. 148, s. 5; c. 834, s. 3; 1979, c. 619, s. 4; 1981, c. 66, s. 2; c. 562, s. 11; c. 692, s. 1; 1983, c. 511, ss. 1, 2; 1985, c. 589, s. 57; 1987, c. 45, s. 2; c. 697, s. 2; 1989, c. 600, s. 5; c. 625, s. 25; c. 643, s. 1; 1989 (Reg. Sess., 1990), c. 1005, ss. 3-5; 1991 (Reg. Sess., 1992), c. 764, s. 1; c. 896, s. 1; 1993, c. 378, s. 2; 1997-502, s. 6; 1999-366, s. 3; 2002-159, s. 50(a); 2002-172, s. 2.4(a); 2003-416, s. 2; 2009-281, s. 1; 2010-167, s. 4(b); 2013-360, s. 15.28(f).)

Vision Books Order Form

Fax Orders:	1-980-299-5965
Phone Orders:	1-704-898-0770
E-mail Orders:	www.visionbooks.org
Mail Orders:	Vision Books, LLC P.O. Box 42406 Charlotte, NC 28215

Shipp To:
Name_____
Address_____
City_____State_____Zip_____
Phone_____Fax_____
Email_____@_____

Bill To: We can bill a third party on your behalf.
Name_____
Address_____
City_____State_____Zip_____
Phone____(_____)_____Fax_____
Email_____@_____

Pamphlet Number ($15.00 Each)	Qty	Total Cost
_____	_____	_____
_____	_____	_____
_____	_____	_____
_____	_____	_____
_____	_____	_____
_____	_____	_____
_____	_____	_____
Full Volume Set 1-92	92 Pamphlets	1,380.00

Free Shipping Shipping & Handling on Full Volume Orders
Add $1.00 Shipping & Handling Per Pamphlet $_____

Total Cost $_____

Thank you for your support. Management!

DID YOU ENJOY THIS BOOK?

Vision Books, LLC would like to hear from you! If you or someone you know has been fasely imprisoned, we would like to hear your story. If the 'North Carolina Criminal Law and Procedure' has had an effect in your life or if you have suggestions, we would like to hear from you. Send your letters to:

Vision Books, LLC
Attn: Staff Writers
P.O. Box 42406
Charlotte, NC 28215
Email: staff@visionbooks.org

Order Additional Copies:

Fax Orders:	1-980-299-9565
Phone Orders:	1-704-898-0770
E-mail Orders:	www.visionbooks.org
Mail Orders:	Vision Books, LLC P.O. Box 42406 Charlotte, NC 28215

www.ingramcontent.com/pod-product-compliance
Lightning Source LLC
Chambersburg PA
CBHW051629170526
45167CB00001B/124